Connecting
Across Differences
2ND EDITION

Finding Common Ground With
Anyone, Anywhere, Anytime

Jane Marantz Connor, Ph.D.
and Dian Killian, Ph.D.

PuddleDancer
P R E S S

2240 Encinitas Blvd., Ste. D-911, Encinitas, CA 92024
email@PuddleDancer.com • www.PuddleDancer.com

For additional information:
Center for Nonviolent Communication
5600 San Francisco Rd., NE, Suite A, Albuquerque, NM 87109
Ph: 505-244-4041 • Fax: 505-247-0414 • Email: cnvc@cnvc.org • Website: www.cnvc.org

Connecting Across Differences
Finding Common Ground With Anyone, Anywhere, Anytime
2ND Edition

© 2012 PuddleDancer Press
A PuddleDancer Press Book

First Edition © 2005 Jane Marantz Connor and Dian Killian
None of the situations described in this book pertain to actual people or circumstances, and any similarity is coincidental.

PuddleDancer Press, Permissions Dept.
2240 Encinitas Blvd., Ste. D-911, Encinitas, CA 92024
Tel: 1-760-652-5754 Fax: 1-760-274-6400
www.NonviolentCommunication.com Email@PuddleDancer.com

Ordering Information: Please contact Independent Publishers Group, Tel: 312-337-0747; Fax: 312-337-5985; Email: frontdesk@ipgbook.com or visit www.IPGbook.com for other contact information and details about ordering online

Author: Jane Marantz Connor, Ph.D. and Dian Killian, Ph.D.
Editor: Sheridan McCarthy
Index: Phyllis Linn
Cover and Interior Design: Lightbourne, Inc.
Cover Photograph: www.iStockPhoto.com

Manufactured in the United States of America

1st Printing, April 2012

10 9 8 7 6 5 4 3 2

ISBN: 978-1-892005-24-3

Library of Congress Cataloging-in-Publication Data

Connor, Jane Marantz.
  Connecting across differences : finding common ground with anyone, anywhere, anytime / Jane Marantz Connor and Dian Killian. -- 2nd ed.
     p. cm.
  Includes bibliographical references and index.
  ISBN 978-1-892005-24-3 (trade paper : alk. paper)
  1. Interpersonal communication. 2. Interpersonal relations. 3. Interpersonal conflict.
  4. Nonviolence. I. Killian, Dian. II. Title.
  BF637.C45C676 2011
  153.6--dc23
                         2011031833

What People Are Saying About
Connecting Across Differences, 2ND Edition

"*Connecting Across Differences* has changed how I approach my work and life. Using empathy to connect with my feelings and needs and with the feelings and needs of the people around me has made me happier and more effective. Jane and Dian, thank you for guiding me on this journey."

—ROBERT MCGUIRE, Executive Director, Merck, Inc.

"Dian Killian is a remarkable woman with a great message that brings wisdom to the field of nonviolence."

—HOWARD GLASSER, Author, *Transforming the Difficult Child: The Nurtured Heart Approach*

"*Connecting Across Differences* capacitates learners with essential personal and interpersonal skills and knowledge needed to nurture and build a culture of peace. Killian and Connor's thoughtfully constructed guidebook opens doors to the possibility for authentic dialogue between self and others and illuminates multiple paths to living with integrity. This book should be on the shelf of every peacemaker."

—TONY JENKIS, Director of Education, National Peace Academy

"Having taught Nonviolent Communication for many years, it seems to me that this book covers every question that I have had myself or been asked about how to learn and integrate this simple yet challenging reframe of communication with self and others. I am grateful to Dian and Jane for this contribution to the field of applied nonviolence."

—KIT MILLER, Director, M.K. Gandhi Institute For Nonviolence

What People Have Said About
Connecting Across Differences, 1st Edition

"*Connecting Across Differences* describes how to communicate in a way that leads to greater understanding and more positive relationships. Ultimately, it provides not just practical methods; it espouses a philosophy of personal responsibility and respect for others and ourselves. The wisdom of this book is a great guide in living with full awareness and compassion."

—DANIEL PHARR, Ph.D., Chief Psychologist,
Bronx Psychiatric Center

"Fabulous book for developing better relationships! If you want to build awareness, find peace, and make a difference, this practical book helps you communicate with love and compassion and shift from old ways of judging self and others toward connecting more deeply."

—MARTHA LASLEY, Author, *Courageous Visions: How to Unleash Passionate Energy in Your Life and Organizations*

"*Connecting Across Differences* addresses real life concerns with candor, clarity, and compassion. The authors use a variety of engaging dialogues, exercises, and examples to show how the powerful process of Nonviolent Communication can enrich personal relationships. It is engaging reading for people of all ages who long for more connection and understanding in the world."

—SURA HART, Coauthor, *Respectful Parents, Respectful Kids, The Compassionate Classroom,* and *The No-Fault Classroom*

"I've utilized *Connecting Across Differences* in both my education and my clinical work as a social worker. As a student, I found the book enlightening and revolutionary in its application of compassion and real world communication skills. As a professional, it has allowed me to be a leader and social advocate and has maximized my ability to hold others with compassion during emotionally difficult times. This is an incredible tool for anyone attempting to live a more compassionate and satisfying life in any context."

—PETER PRZERADZKI, Case Manager and Psychotherapist

"NVC has been an invaluable tool for connecting with those around me—my clients, family, and friends. NVC has helped me to move beyond doing what is expected and customary to formulating goals and making choices that enrich me and truly meet my needs."

—ROXANE MANNING, Ph.D., Clinical Psychologist, Raleigh-Durham

"In my twenty-six years as a professor of communication, I have found that students rarely like textbooks. *Connecting Across Differences* marks a major exception. Students love how this book is written—in a compelling and clear way—and how the examples deal with their everyday lives. Connor and Killian teach how we can communicate and connect, live and love in empathic and compassionate ways that meet our needs and the needs of others. In this time of war, both students and I feel thrilled to learn that alternatives exist to our traditional patterns of linear thinking, judging, criticizing, comparing and contrasting."

—LOIS EINHORN, Professor of Rhetoric and Composition

"As both a mother and mature student, my communication skills have improved with *Connecting Across Differences*. I find that my relationships, especially with my children, are dramatically changing for the better. Most of all, I have gained insight into how I communicate with myself. I am now learning self-empathy and how to heal some deep-rooted wounds."

—MAGGIE CLEMENTS, Binghamton University Student

"I taught Nonviolent Communication to a class of peace and social activists using Jane and Dian's book. The students found it inspiring and invaluable in their learning experience. I love the clarity, organization, and universality of their approach to NVC."

—CHRISTINE KING, CNVC Certified Trainer

"*Connecting Across Differences,* through numerous illustrations and examples, raises awareness about the covert, passive violence that M.K. Gandhi described as being more insidious than physical violence. Nonviolent Communication and this book offer an antidote."

—CYNTHIA MOE, Georgia Network for Nonviolent Communication

"This book gives a step-by-step guide for getting closer to our inner world and achieving a better understanding of oneself and others. I especially like the exercises, the sequence of chapters, and how easy to read and understand the language is."

—MERIKE KAHJA, Empathy Trainer, Talinn, Estonia

"A captivating book where we are shown tools to increase our understanding of one another and ourselves . . . and the compassion we so desperately want."

—MICHELLE RUSSO, Binghamton University Student

"Empathy isn't limited to certain subjects—it works for situations being gay, straight, with school problems, roommate issues, and even comes in handy when dealing with teachers. I think you should have great results with this book because the examples are real life problems—and solutions."

—JONATHAN CRIMES, Multicultural Psychology Student

"Basic concepts covered in Marshall Rosenberg's *Nonviolent Communication: A Language of Life* are given a much broader discussion in *Connecting Across Differences*, including more exercises to test my understanding of the practice of communicating nonviolently. This is not another communications-theories book. I found it to be a practical guide to improving interpersonal communications and mediating conflict in my life—at work and at home; with loved ones, colleagues, and even with strangers. I highly recommend this book for those interested in improving the quality of their life through greater connection and more meaningful interaction with the people in their lives."

—ANONYMOUS, Amazon.com

"I've studied Marshall Rosenberg's *Nonviolent Communication: A Language of Life* for three years, and have gotten huge benefits out of it. So why another book on NVC? This book is a wonderful complement to Rosenberg's book. With clear and detailed explanations, extensive exercises, cartoons and photos, tables and charts, it helps make NVC even more alive and doable. This guidebook is like taking a workshop in compassionate communication."

—ANONYMOUS, Amazon.com

*To those everywhere with passion and vision
who are willing to take the leap of
imagining and creating change.*

An enemy is one whose story we have not heard.

—GENE KNUDSEN-HOFFMAN

CONTENTS

List of Illustrations and Tables   xiii

Introduction: Living With Awareness and Choice   1

1   Another Way to See the World   11

2   Getting to the Root of Life   41

3   Really Listening   71

4   Creating Shared Reality via Observations   111

5   Fostering Trust and Collaboration:
The Power of Requests   129

6   Empathy in the Fast Lane: Self-Empathy
and Choice   175

7   Stepping Into the Fire: Enjoying and
Responding to Anger   219

8   When Communication Isn't Possible:
The Protective Use of Force   253

9   Thanks, But No Thanks   269

10   Integrating NVC in Your Life—and on the Streets   303

Afterword: Creating a Nonviolent World   341

Gratitude   345

Appendix 1: Beyond Good and Evil: Creating a Nonviolent
World—An Interview With Marshall Rosenberg   349

Appendix 2: List of Feelings and Needs   367

Notes   369

Bibliography   370

Resources for Learning Nonviolent Communication   371

Index   379

The Four-Part Nonviolent Communication Process   391

About Nonviolent Communication   392

About PuddleDancer Press   393

About the Center for Nonviolent Communication   394

Trade Books From PuddleDancer Press   395

Trade Booklets From PuddleDancer Press   400

About the Authors   402

ILLUSTRATIONS AND TABLES

ILLUSTRATIONS

Practicing Self-Empathy—The Force of Empathy   105

ONFR—External World; Internal World   130

ONFR and Support Steps   161

A Model of Compassionate Communication   168–70

Anger Floor Map   238

TABLES

Sentences in which the word "feel" is used to
express thoughts   33–34

Separating the Bee From the Sting:
Sentence Frames for Empathy Guesses   83

Some Words That Imply Judgment   114

The NVC Model: First 3 Steps   123

Different Uses of Reflection   138–39

Different Uses of Connection Requests   141

The NVC Model—4 Steps   165

Four Steps of Self-Empathy   177

Four Types of Response (Empathic and Nonempathic)   202

Four Types of Compassionate Responses   204

Our Anger Is Caused by Our Thinking   221

Street Expression of Feelings   324

Street Expression of Needs   325

INTRODUCTION

Living With Awareness and Choice

You just don't understand me. You never listen, do you?

*How could I make such a stupid mistake again?
It seems like I never learn.*

I just don't know what to do. There are too many choices.

He's just a jerk. All he cares about is himself.

When you read these statements, how do you feel? Put yourself in the speakers' shoes. What do you notice in your body? Do you feel tense or tight? Do you feel anxious, sad, angry, or confused? If you do, it's not surprising. While each statement addresses a different issue, they all involve some kind of judgment. Each indicates a level of miscommunication, disconnection, or blame. And no one enjoys being judged—even by themselves. Also, none of these statements addresses the root cause of what's contributing to the tension and misunderstanding that are taking place, so there is no clear path toward resolving the discomfort involved.

Now read the following statements, which address the same issues in the same order as those above. Here, each fully expresses what the speaker is thinking and feeling.

I'm so frustrated. That's not what I recall saying, and I really value accuracy.

This is the second time this year I've forgotten to pay my Visa bill. I hate getting those late charges, and I really want to attend to my personal matters with care.

Seeing that there are twenty-two different courses that meet the writing requirement, I feel totally overwhelmed. I need to know which to take.

I'm furious. My housemate just spent twenty-five minutes in the shower, and now there's no hot water left. I'd really like some consideration and awareness!

When you read the second set of statements, you may feel a very different kind of response. Do you feel more relaxed, connected, and at ease? Do you notice greater appreciation and understanding—especially when you read what each speaker is wanting (accuracy, care, clarity, and consideration)? Do you find yourself more open to what the speaker desires, and would you be more willing to engage with them?

Now each speaker is taking responsibility for their own experience. Rather than engaging in judgment (which often provides little information), the speaker clearly describes what is bothering them, what they are feeling, and what they're wanting.

These two sets of statements illustrate the practices we'll be exploring in this book: how to move past judgment, and how to name our own experiences in a way that enhances people's ability to listen and care about what is important for each party, including ourselves. These are the practices of Nonviolent Communication™ (NVC), also called Compassionate Communication.* As we

---

* Some people also like to call NVC authentic or collaborative communication. The name Nonviolent Communication is a translation from the Sanskrit word *ahimsa*, used by Gandhi, which literally means "love in action" or "the force unleashed when the desire to harm is eradicated." The source of these definitions is http://www.mettacenter.org/definitions/ahimsa, where you can find further context for these concepts.

introduce you to these practices, we will also offer a view of the world and of human relations that contributes to interpersonal and intergroup harmony in profound ways. The communication tools presented here and the worldview underlying them support and enhance each other. Together they foster an empathic mind-set and consciousness, and support a compassionate way of seeing and being in the world.

Different—Together

In taking the NVC approach, we examine the commonalities among people. As living organisms, we all have numerous physical needs, including for food, air, water, and rest. We need clothing and shelter for comfort and protection from the elements. We need confidence that we can be safe from illness and other physical harm. And we have needs for warmth, touch, and intimacy, as well as tenderness, care, and sexual expression.

Beyond physical needs, there are numerous other qualities and values that we humans like to experience and express. These include honesty, authenticity, and integrity; community and connection; and spaciousness, autonomy, and choice. Most of us value, at least in some situations, efficiency, effectiveness, movement, and ease. There are many other needs that, when met, contribute to our well-being, such as needs for order, beauty, and meaning. There are dozens of other qualities, such as mutuality, companionship, and consideration, that could be considered primal and basic human needs.

In your own life, what do you value and try to live by, especially in relating to others? Perhaps you value kindness, care, consideration, and autonomy, and the freedom to decide how you want to live. Perhaps you also value self-expression, empowerment, and responsibility. You may also care about dignity, understanding, honesty, and trust. There are probably dozens of other values that you care about. If you reflect on it, going through life without ever experiencing these qualities as fulfilled would be very hard—like crossing a parched desert. These qualities help us to live life fully and be fully alive.

Now stop and think for a moment. Think about your family, friends, colleagues, and people you simply pass on the street. Is there anyone among them who would not enjoy experiencing the qualities we've mentioned? Is there anyone in the world who would not enjoy food and drink, warmth and shelter, consideration, care, support, ease, and respect? All of these are appreciated and desired by humans everywhere, regardless of where they live or what culture they are a part of. While people address these basic, universal needs in diverse ways and experience them at different times and in different circumstances, there is little doubt that we all share them. This is a theme we explore throughout this book.

Needs—Understanding and Acting on Them

So we are agreed: we all have needs. That's the simple part. Applying this knowledge and using it to create a more compassionate world is more complex. How do we meet our needs in ways that we enjoy, in ways that are consistent with our values and with how we want to live? How can we be confident that everyone's needs—including our own—can be addressed? And then there is this riddle to solve: if we have so much in common, how is it that we so often experience difference, misunderstanding, and conflict?

These are the questions we take up in this book, and we do so by exploring two basic principles. The first is that when we have disagreements or experience disconnection from others, it is because we are disagreeing over *strategies* to meet needs, over what we want to *do* in a given situation. If we are to reconnect with others and resolve the conflict, the needs driving the strategies must first be discovered. The key to doing this is to truly hear and understand one another on the level of shared values, while holding everyone's needs with care. Once this is accomplished—and this is what the practices in this book are designed to achieve—we are free to discover new strategies that will be far more satisfying, enriching, and unifying. In fact, once all parties have an experience of being heard and knowing that their needs matter, strategies usually organically evolve that are win-wins for all involved.

The second principle is that connecting with and contributing to the well-being of others are instinctive human behaviors that are intrinsically rewarding. If we believe this second principle—that contributing to others is satisfying in itself—finding ways to meet everyone's needs becomes much easier to do. Win-win solutions become the ultimate prize.

The Contribution Test

Do you doubt the second principle? If so, we invite you to try it out in the laboratory of your own life. Take a moment now and think about when you last contributed to another's well-being. Perhaps you gave directions to someone who was lost, helped a child with a task, did something kind for your pet, or ran an errand for a friend. Perhaps you listened with care to a person who wanted your companionship. Or maybe you told a joke, adding some humor, fun, and creativity to the day. Perhaps you expressed gratitude, love, or appreciation to another person.

Now think about how you felt when you contributed to another in this way. As you recall the event, what sensations do you notice in your body? How do you feel? You may feel warm and openhearted, with an expansiveness in your throat, chest, or limbs. You may feel happy, calm, satisfied, or at ease. You may enjoy a sense of fullness, peace, and completion. There is a very important insight to be gained from this exercise: these are the feelings we typically experience *when our needs are being met.* And this is one way we know that contributing to others is one of the most basic and compelling of human needs: we feel happy when we do so. We all have a desire to contribute to life, to enrich and enhance it for the benefit of all.

Now imagine that all the people you know are enjoying the sensations you just experienced. What would the world look like and how might our daily lives be transformed if people everywhere increased their experience of meeting human needs? What if it were a given that everyone's needs mattered? How would communication and decision making change? What would be the prevailing response to difference and misunderstanding? How might our jobs be structured differently? Our neighborhoods, communities, and schools?

Given the number of people whose needs are not being met in the world today and, further, who believe their needs don't matter, how do we imagine this new world, what it would look like, and how it would function? How is it possible to assure that everyone's needs are held with consideration and care?

Creating Abundance Through Nonviolent Communication

The Nonviolent Communication model offers a blueprint—one that has been tested and proven internationally for decades—for creating such abundance, in our own lives and the world around us.

The approach was developed by Marshall Rosenberg, Ph.D., who was fascinated by a basic question: what is it that contributes to human beings enjoying moments of profound connection and compassion for one another at some times and, at other times, experiencing a lack of compassion, even antipathy and contempt? At a young age, Marshall observed both firsthand. He witnessed race riots in Detroit in the 1940s, in which people were killed, and acts of immense compassion, including the care his uncle joyfully gave his elderly mother.

Desiring to understand compassion and how to foster it, he studied psychology, learning from the humanistic psychologist Carl Rogers, among others. Then, after completing his studies, he put his insights to work in a wide array of settings—many of them fraught with conflict and violence, both physical and institutional. As he worked with gangs and prisoners, corporations and other organizations, he created and honed the model that is now being used to increase understanding and cooperation and to resolve conflict among diverse groups of people around the world.

You will find that Nonviolent Communication has limitless applications. As well as fostering self-awareness and connection with others, NVC skills can contribute to decision making, mediation, and needs assessment. NVC works in facilitating meetings in which everyone feels included and involved. The practices you will learn in this book—the fruit of Marshall Rosenberg's countless journeys to the very heart of conflict—have the power to transform your experience. They can help you live in your own skin and find mutuality with others—in the home, at school and work, and in your most intimate relationships.

Sounds Great. How Hard Is It to Learn?

The principles of NVC are not hard to understand. As you will see, the model involves four basic steps that can be expressed in shorthand as "OFNR": making clear *observations*, identifying *feelings* in relation to what you're observing, identifying *needs* in relation to what you're feeling, and making a *request* that might contribute to meeting your needs. Learning this new way of communicating, however, requires a willingness to step outside your comfort zone and be a beginner. At first, it involves a certain amount of risk taking, learning about yourself, and trusting that the "real you" (with all your feelings and needs) has something worthwhile to contribute and communicate to others.

To learn NVC, it is essential that you practice. Learning a communication skill is not like learning history or math. It's not just about principles or theory; it needs to be *lived* every day. Only by applying NVC to your life will you see how it works, and from there you will gain confidence. Because practice is so essential, you will find many exercises in this book to support your practice. All of them are designed to be done more than once. When you revisit them, just think of a different situation that you would like to improve or better understand.

You may also wish to keep a journal while reading this book and learning to practice Nonviolent Communication. In it, you can take notes, record your own insights and reflections, and respond to exercises that ask you to observe and comment on your interactions. You can work on choices you're making or behavior you're interested in understanding and perhaps changing. You can also rewrite and rework situations from the past where you didn't communicate with the connection, awareness, or effectiveness you would have liked.

When you travel to another country, knowing even a few words of its language is helpful. Similarly, even though it takes time to integrate NVC into the fabric of your life, you will benefit as soon as you start. Simply learning to identify feelings and needs, the topics of the first two chapters, is powerful. Over time, as your confidence grows, you will find that you are able to respond effectively to the most challenging people and situations.

A Note About This Book and Language, Choice, and Inclusion

Because we want to include both genders, and for ease and simplicity, in this book, we do not use "he" to refer to an individual person. Consistent with trends in English toward gender neutrality, we use the third person plural, "they."

Also, while there are two authors of this book, when one of us speaks about our own experience, we use the first person singular pronoun, "I." If you are curious about which author is speaking, Jane Marantz Connor lives near Washington, D.C., and includes stories in this book describing how NVC informs her interactions with her daughter and ex-husband, and at the university where she used to teach. Dian Killian lives in Brooklyn, New York, and gives examples of practicing NVC while riding her bicycle, from her teaching NVC and mediating with couples, and when dialoguing with her mother.

Another note on language usage: You may notice that we will frequently say, "I'm wanting," not "I want," or "You're feeling" instead of "You feel." This is because our feelings and needs are not static; they are always occurring in this specific moment. If we say, for example, "Do you feel happy?" this could suggest that you feel happy all the time. We know this is literally not the case, and by using the continuous tense, "Are you feeling happy?" we highlight this fact. This is a common practice among those who practice NVC; as you will see, the classic model follows this convention.

Your Journey Begins

Now it is time to begin your journey toward bringing greater understanding, compassion, and fulfillment into your life and the lives of those around you. The ten chapters that follow will give you a thorough orientation to the principles and practices of Nonviolent Communication that will guide you on this journey.

In chapter 1, we introduce you to a new way of looking at the world and begin to explore the full range of human feeling. Chapter 2 gets to the root of life: the needs that are our constant companions. In chapter 3, we introduce you to the power of empathy, which integrates the awareness of feelings and needs. Chapter 4 explores the differences between judgment and observation and the importance of seeing and describing, clearly and objectively, our experiences and the experiences of others.

Chapter 5 discusses the power of making requests that will best serve the cause of ensuring that needs are met. In chapter 6, a very important tool, self-empathy, is discussed. In chapter 7, we explore the fiery emotion of anger. Chapter 8 describes the protective use of force in situations where dialogue is not possible. In chapter 9, we learn to express compliments and gratitude without judgment. Finally, in chapter 10, we explore how to integrate NVC in your everyday life, including a colloquial (nonclassical) practice of the model.

It is our intention and wish that this book will inspire you to embrace and foster the qualities you most want to see in your life, and that through learning the techniques of NVC, you will enjoy ever-deepening connection: with yourself, your colleagues and friends, your loved ones, your community, and the world.

1

Another Way to See the World

Feeling and longing are the motive forces behind
all human endeavor and human creations.
—ALBERT EINSTEIN

Sticks and stones can break my bones
but names can never hurt me.
—CHILDREN'S RHYME

When people first hear the term "Nonviolent Communication," they may be surprised and confused. We are accustomed to thinking about violence as physical force, and it can be puzzling to think of communication—mere words—as aggressive. In fact, communication is usually seen as an *alternative* to violence. Negotiations are attempted before acts of war in order to avoid physical conflict. Police (ideally) will say, "Stop! Drop your gun!" before firing when they see an armed person committing a crime. If a parent sees her child hitting a playmate or grabbing a toy away—an act of physical force—the child might be reminded to "use your words." As the children's rhyme goes, "Sticks and stones can break my bones but names can never hurt me."

Yet we all know that words can generate much hurt and pain. While the hurt may not be physical, our thoughts and words inform the kinds of actions we take. If we have critical thoughts or images of another group or person, it becomes far more likely that physical force or a destructive act will ensue.

If you reflect on physical violence and what leads to it, you may, in each case, first blame a physical act or stimulus—"He hit me first!" or "He cut me off on the road!" But if you reflect further, you will find that before a person strikes physically, even in perceived retaliation, words or thoughts precede the act: "How dare you!" "What a jerk!" "I'll teach you a lesson." Violent actions follow from talking to ourselves in this kind of way.

Violence can be most broadly defined as a breakdown in human connection and understanding. When such fissures occur, opportunities for physical violence become more likely. In contrast, if we love and care for someone, the last thing we want is for them to suffer or experience harm. While we may not be able to love and care for everyone else with equal energy and attention, learning *how* to connect compassionately with others can contribute to resolving conflicts when they arise and to fostering greater understanding where connection already exists. It is this kind of "Nonviolent" or "Compassionate" Communication that we address in this book.

Beyond Boxed-Up Thinking

Out beyond ideas of wrongdoing and rightdoing, there is a field. I will meet you there.

—RUMI

Much of our daily interactions with our fellow human beings is empathic because that is our core nature. Empathy is the very means by which we create social life and advance civilization.

—JEREMY RIFKIN

Communicating compassionately involves changing our thinking. It involves challenging a primary assumption that has informed our culture for thousands of years: that it is useful to classify people and things as "right" or "wrong." According to this kind of thinking, some people are good, some bad; some smart, others stupid; some caring, others insensitive. This yo-yo, right-wrong thinking can be found at every level of our society. Comic book heroes fight arch villains; in TV and films, the police are out to get "the bad guys"; President George W. Bush, when launching the Iraq war, referred repeatedly to an "axis of evil." A popular bumper sticker reads, "Mean People Suck!" This assumes that some people are mean, others are nice, and, implicitly, mean people are mean all the time. Meanness is the very definition of who they are. If this is so, why bother with them? Mean people, according to this kind of thinking, should be avoided—or even controlled or punished.

Who's right? Who's wrong? Who deserves sympathy, understanding, and support? And who should be excluded, judged, punished, fired, executed, or (in the case of countries) attacked? When I was in college, I spent hours discussing questions like this with my peers. We talked about relationships, family, and politics. We wanted to understand the world and the choices people were making. Even today, I can find such questions compelling. I want to understand the cause of a given situation and know who is responsible. I want to be informed and aware, have a sense of safety and security in the world, and be confident about there being accountability, restoration, hope, and change. I know I'm not alone in this. The popularity of "confessional" talk shows and courtroom programs such as *Judge Judy* attests to a continuing interest in right-wrong thinking as a means of solving problems and understanding the world, ourselves, and those around us.

> *Reality is much more complex than any judgment of right and wrong encourages you to believe. When you really understand the ethical, spiritual, social, economic, and psychological forces that shape individuals, you will see that people's choices are not based on a desire to hurt. Instead, they are in accord with what they know and what worldviews are available to them. Most are doing the best they can, given what information they've received and what problems they are facing.*
>
> —MICHAEL LERNER

This kind of thinking has a long tradition (at least in the West) and lies at the core of our dominant cultural norms and beliefs. According to the Old Testament, it accounts for the very start of human history: Adam and Eve were cast out of paradise (punished) for their *wrong*doing. According to Walter Wink, this Myth of Redemptive Violence, as he calls it, dates back even earlier to a Babylonian creation story from around 1250 BCE,[1] upon which all later myths involving punitive violence are based. This myth still informs much of our culture today, impacting almost every institution, belief, and practice in our society; it is seen as natural, obvious, and the "truth." As Wink points out, ". . . [A] story told often enough, and confirmed often enough in daily life, ceases to be a tale and is accepted as reality itself."[2]

So if right-wrong thinking is so popular and prevalent and has been around for thousands of years, why change it? Clearly, it meets some needs. It can offer us a sense of safety, meaning, fairness, and order. It can seem effective in making choices and distinguishing values. And it's familiar, so it can feel comfortable and easy—even intrinsic to human nature.

Yet right-wrong thinking diminishes human connection. It separates us from one another and ourselves. It draws a line in the sand: You are either with us, or against us. Innocent or guilty. Deserving of reward or punishment. Saved or damned. It negates the complexity of life and full human experience. It implies a static view of human beings and their behavior. According to such thinking, "bad" people will always do "bad" things and "good" or "just" people must stop or control

I hate having to choose sides. Last year, a couple I was friendly with got divorced and there were hard feelings between them. It seemed like each one wanted me to support them in blaming the other for the break-up, that it was all the other person's fault. I wanted to remain friends with both of them, but at the time, I couldn't figure out how to do that and wound up losing one friend. I really would like to do things differently.

—PAULA

them. This view confuses a person's *behavior*—the particular acts a person chooses to take—with who the person *is*. And if someone is intrinsically evil, what hope is there for learning, connection, compassion, or change? It is this kind of thinking that leads to conflict and violence, in all its forms.

Empirical research paints a very different picture, showing that human behavior is fluid and primarily determined by what we *think* about the situation we find ourselves in. Given our circumstances and our cultural conditioning, we are all capable of doing "bad" things. The proportion of college students, for example, who admit to behavior that could be classified as a felony is consistently more than 90 percent (for example, damaging other's property, giving illegal substances to those under the age of eighteen, or entering a premises and taking an item that belongs to another). When asked if they would commit various illegal acts if they were 100 percent guaranteed that they wouldn't get caught, the proportion of students who said they would steal, cheat, or physically hurt someone who has hurt them in some way is very high. In effect, if you want to get someone to cheat, make the stakes high enough and the chances of getting caught low enough.

As the writer Jorge Luis Borges has observed, we human beings live by justification alone—even if only to bring a glass of water to our lips. What Borges means is that we all have reasons for doing what we do. Our given circumstances and our needs—not who we intrinsically *are*—determine the course of action we take. It's safe to say, for example, that most human beings would abhor eating human flesh. Yet when stranded by an accident and given the choice of starving or eating the bodies of dead companions, you might choose to eat. There are well-documented cases, involving climbing and airplane accidents, of people making this choice. If you reflect on an action you took that you now regret, you can probably find some need or important value that motivated that action—even if you're not fully happy with the choice or its impact.

Research also documents that while right-wrong thinking is the norm in our society today, early humans lived very differently, based on compassion and connection. Riane Eisler, in *The Chalice and the Blade: Our History and Our Future*, explores recent evidence that paints a very different picture of pre-human history from the popular cliché of a caveman with a wooden club. Historical, anthropological, and archaeological data suggest that "just as some of the most primitive existing societies, like those of the BaMbuti and !Kung, are not characterized by warlike caveman dragging women around by the hair, it now appears that the Paleolithic was a remarkably peaceful time." Indeed, popular notions of early human society as aggressive and violent can be seen more as an extension of our current way of viewing the world than an accurate representation of how early humans actually lived:

> The old view was that the earliest human kinship (and later economic) relations developed from men hunting and killing. The new view is that the foundations for social organization came from mothers and children sharing. The old view was of prehistory as the story of "man the hunter-warrior." The new view is of both women and men using our unique human faculties to support and enhance life.[3]

Biological and cognitive research confirms this view: all mammals, and especially humans (with our more developed neocortex), are "particularly hard-wired for empathy . . . the empathic predisposition is embedded in our biology." Newborn infants, for example, are "able to identify the cries of other newborns and will cry in return" and toddlers "will often wince in discomfort at the sight of another child's suffering and come over to him to share a toy, or cuddle, or bring them over to their own mother for assistance."[4]

The limitation of right-wrong thinking is that it diminishes our natural capacity for empathy and compassion for ourselves and others. It takes us out of the moment, distracting us from specific needs and circumstances and obscuring the choices we can make that are fully aligned with our values. It also curtails the possibilities for the kind of world we can collectively envision and create. In this book, we explore how a different kind of analysis, focused on feelings and needs, can enrich our understanding of human behavior and foster greater compassion and connection—for human beings and all life on the planet. It is this kind of orientation, based on empathy and compassion, that can transform how we relate to others and ourselves and bring us closer to recreating what Eisler calls a "partnership-based" culture, transforming "our world from strife to peaceful co-existence . . . [with] conflict productive rather than destructive."[5]

EXERCISE 1: Force and Feeling

A. Take a moment to reflect on an act of physical force or violence that you have considered, fantasized about, or acted upon. This could involve simply slamming your books on a table, breaking an object, or physically hurting someone. What was the stimulus for the action you took or wanted to take? What were you feeling and thinking at the time? What is the link between your thoughts and the action, real or imagined?

B. Make a list of social institutions' beliefs and practices, including, for example, how schools and learning are structured, the criminal justice system, policing, religious beliefs, health care, etc. How does right-wrong thinking inform their beliefs and practices? For example, in schools, it is common practice to give grades, which can be seen as a form of reward.

C. Consider recent and historical events, such as wars or highly publicized court cases. How do you see right-wrong thinking in the language (justification) and actions that took place? How was one side presented as the "enemy," or morally wrong, or less than the other?

The "F" Word: At the Heart of Empathy

How do we find a way to communicate that is free of judgment and blame while expressing and sharing with others our experience of their words and actions and what we see in the world? A core element in empathic connection is the awareness of our own and others' feelings. The very definition of empathy is the capacity to "understand and enter into another's feelings,"[6] with the root of the word, *pathos*, coming from the Greek word for "feeling." Empathic connection means to "feel with someone," extending ourselves toward understanding another's view and walking—even if only for a moment—in their shoes.

While our ability to experience feelings gives us crucial social skills, unless we've done some form of training in this area (such as Emotional Intelligence), most of us are unaccustomed to paying attention to our feelings. We're out of practice. How many times a day, for example, does someone ask you, "How are you?" When you see a neighbor, co-worker, or friend, this question most likely comes up. If you're like most people, you probably answer in passing: "Fine," "OK," "Great," "Not bad." Yet like Morse code or shorthand for what we are actually experiencing, none of these responses are feelings, and none of them gives us much information. Perhaps the only time we answer this question fully and accurately is when asked by a doctor, counselor, or loved one. Even when talking to those we are most intimate with, we may also avoid expressing what we're fully experiencing and feeling. In our culture, we're not accustomed to talking about our emotions. We're taught to be "polite": to not say "too much" or assume others are interested in us or our concerns. We learn to be guarded and unrevealing. We associate feelings with weakness and vulnerability rather than strength, inner grounding, awareness, and resourcefulness.

In part, this is because in the West, since at least the Age of Reason and the development of empirical science, feelings have been cast as subjective and untrustworthy. We are told instead to "use our heads" and not get emotional. The philosopher René Descartes summed up our very existence in our ability to think: "I think, therefore I am." And we're told that if we believe something, especially if it is subjective like an opinion or a feeling, we need to "prove it." Logical thought, like a mathematics equation, can indeed be written out and tested step by step. Yet how do we "test" human emotion and feeling? From the scientific point of view and our rational way of looking at the world, feelings have little value.

For many men especially, feelings are a largely unknown and dangerous territory. Growing up, boys are told to "Take it like a man" and that "Only sissies cry." Men are not supposed to have feelings, especially sadness, fear, or vulnerability. Perhaps the only feeling men are allowed or even expected to express is anger. One NVC trainer from Texas, Ike Lasater, says that for years the only feelings he was ever aware of experiencing were *good, bad,* and *angry.* Whenever someone asked him how he was feeling about something, his response was either "good" or "bad." "Good" and "bad" could refer to many different experiences; in fact, they are not feelings at all—they're adjectives marking approval or disapproval.

While it is more socially acceptable for women to show their feelings, their expression still is not valued. Historically, women have been discriminated against for the very qualities they are expected to exhibit. "Hysteria," "wild, uncontrolled excitement or feeling," comes from the Greek for uterus, *hystera,* expressing the notion that women are prone to becoming hysterical. Cast as overly emotional, irrational, and unstable— "the weaker sex"—women were told for centuries that they were unfit for many occupations, including driving, voting, and working as doctors, soldiers, or scientists. Women, of course, have now proven themselves in all these areas. Statistically, for example, women drivers have lower accident rates than men. Yet as epitomized by the "Iron Lady," the first female prime minister of Great Britain, Margaret Thatcher, women who want to be successful are still often expected to exhibit toughness, "clearheadedness," and indifference.

This way of thinking about feelings is especially true in Anglo American culture. In French, the word for feeling, "sentiment," is not pejorative. Expressing feeling is socially acceptable and even desired. In English, the same root of "sentiment" turns up in "sentimental": fake, overwrought, superficial, and cliché. We hear "Don't be too sensitive" and are told to not "overreact." Rather than being "sensitive" (aware of our feelings—and what we are experiencing), we're supposed to be thick-skinned, with a stiff upper lip. The historical heroes we emulate are pilgrims, pioneers, and cowboys—all "strong, silent" types who were resilient and tough. Our modern pop heroes are equally strong and unfeeling. Athletic stars and those on "survivor" programs are admired for their endurance and putting "mind over matter." Urban "gangsta" culture is about "coolness" and disaffection.

In our fast-food culture, we're proactive and product orientated. We want effectiveness and immediate results. If something is "wrong," especially if it's unpleasant, stressful, or painful, we want a solution—*now*. Like changing a TV channel or popping a painkiller, we either try to "fix" feelings—telling others and ourselves what to feel—or not: "Just get over it." "Just suck it up." "Get a grip." In doing so, we fail to fully understand what we're feeling and why.

I always figured it was a good idea to ignore my emotions. I believed that our feelings are irrational and could lead me to do things I would regret.

—ARTHUR

If things go badly for you, my dad, who was in the Army, taught me you just have to "suck it up."

—JESSICA

The last time I cried was when I was six years old.

—ROBERTA

If I am feeling bad, I just try to talk myself out of it, to not let it show.

—HAROLD

True to Life—and in Our Limbs

Trust your feelings, Luke . . .

—OBI WAN KENOBI

We dismiss our feelings, thinking they're irrational and unreal. Yet in fact they are closely linked to our very physical bodies. When our bodies need something, they tell us. If we're hungry, tired, hot, or cold, we experience physical sensations. Our bodies might tighten, our hairs stand on end, or our stomachs grumble or churn. As happens when we have physical needs, our bodies let us know when we're feeling emotions such as anger, happiness, sadness, or contentment. If we're angry, we may feel tension or heat. If sad, we may feel tightness or heaviness. If happy or content, we might feel lightness, openness, and expansiveness. Each of us experiences our emotions differently, via different sensations, yet there's no doubt that our emotions (feelings) have a direct relationship to our physical sensations. When we experience an emotion, there is, in fact, a chemical response in every cell of our organism. The fact that we use the same verb in English ("feel") for physical sensations and for emotional states (feeling "happy," "scared," "sad," "itchy," "hot," or physically cold) suggests the close relationship between these two types of experiences.

We are so accustomed to using our heads and disregarding our feelings and sensations that, in some ways, we are cut off from the rest of our bodies. We may not be fully aware of what our physical needs are, never mind our emotions. I know I lived this way for much of my life. At best, I ignored my feelings or sought to control or suppress them. I didn't understand them and found them to be a distraction and even a nuisance. As someone with a Ph.D., I valued rational thought over all else. For years, my way of relating to my body and my feelings was similar to what I now call my "mascot" during those years of my life (pictured on the following page):

I lived much of my life in my head and lacked, I now see, self-connection. Feelings were troublesome, irksome, and confusing. What triggered them? Sometimes it was clear, other times not. And what led my feelings to suddenly change, like clouds casting shadows over what had moments earlier been a bright, sunny day? I often had no understanding of this. I found

All Head and No Body—What Happens When We Ignore Our Feelings

some feelings painful (such as sadness or fear), and I thought I could relieve myself of them by practicing "mind over matter": "Why are you feeling so nervous? You know everything is going to be all right. Be more optimistic!" Bullying my feelings in this way— trying to talk myself out of what I was experiencing—never really worked. I was seeking understanding, relief, and skill in managing what I was experiencing. Trying to force my feelings to obey my will only increased my suffering and confusion—and my level of disconnection from myself.

I know from talking with many others about how they relate to their feelings and observe sensations in their bodies that I am not alone in this "denial." Many people, if asked how they feel about something, will give an assessment or opinion instead: information from their heads, not their hearts or bodies. At trainings I lead, when I ask participants to notice what they are feeling or what's going on in their bodies, they often draw a blank. Most of us, unless we have had training or coaching in this area or do some form of bodywork (such as yoga or massage), simply are unaccustomed to paying attention to—and valuing—what's going on inside of us as physical and emotional beings.

Yet our sensations and feelings serve as important indicators of what's going on for us. Because we can feel heat, we are able to pull back from a hot stove before getting burned. Because we feel thirst and hunger, we know when we need to nourish and hydrate our bodies. Emotional states such as happiness and fear provide us with equally crucial information. Our feelings tell us something about what we're experiencing in our environment and what we're enjoying (wanting more of) or needing (wanting to modify or change). In the next chapter, we will look more closely at how our feelings relate to our needs.

For the moment, I'd like you to consider the value of feelings. Intimately related to our senses, feelings are part of being fully alive, "sentient" beings aware of our environment and our experience in the world. As can be seen in the etymology of "emotion," our feelings move us. They can lead us to action; they foster self-awareness. When we pay attention only to our thoughts and dismiss our feelings, we're playing with only half a deck. And why play with half a deck, especially when the other half has some of the most valuable cards with which to play the game of life?

Marshall Rosenberg, who developed the NVC model, has traveled to hundreds of countries around the world in his effort so share peacemaking skills with others. He has commented that in every country he has visited, the initial greeting is the same: How are you? It would seem that for us as human beings, this is crucial information—knowing how we and others are feeling—as well as a basic way of creating human connection and trust.

EXERCISE 2: Emoto-Meters

Our bodies are like "emoto-meters," highly tuned and sophisticated gauges that can help us ground ourselves in the present moment and be aware of what we're feeling and needing. By tracking how our feelings relate to physical sensations, we can gain greater awareness and fluency in naming them.

    A. Take a few minutes and brainstorm a list of words that describe physical sensations in your body. Be as specific as possible. For example, sensations may include tingly, itchy, numb, pressure, pulsating, or hot. (These sensations can occur in varied places in your body—in your feet, chest, fingers, or head, for example—and with varying intensities. Some also overlap with feelings. "Warm," for example, can describe both an emotional response/state *and* a physical experience.) See if you can come up with at least twenty sensation words. Once you've brainstormed your own list, you may wish to refer to the list in the appendix (see page 367).

B. Observe your bodily sensations at this moment. What do you notice? What feelings (emotions) are connected to these sensations? For example, I am feeling happy (emotion); my body feels relaxed, with a light, open sense in my chest area (sensation). Or, I am feeling tired; I notice my eyes are sore and heavy. In noticing your feelings, you may find it helpful to refer to the list of feeling words on page 367.

C. When learning to identify our sensations and feelings, it can be helpful to start with "strong" responses where the signals we're receiving from our bodies are the loudest. Consider, for example, fear, depression, anger, surprise, joy, shock, peace, or excitement. What sensations do you notice in particular parts of your body—in your chest, head, hands, or limbs? When you imagine the last time you experienced each of these feelings, what is their intensity? Make a chart in your journal. Here's an example:

Feeling	Sensation	Location/Intensity
Fear	tingling	hands/mild
	restriction, tension,	
	breathless	chest/intense

To add specificity and fun to this exercise, you may wish to draw a rough sketch of a human body and then place sensation words on this sketch to match what you're noticing in your body. For example, if you're feeling "tingly" on the back of your head and scalp, place the word "tingly" on the head area of the body picture. This exercise helps build sensory awareness and self-connection.

EXERCISE 3: The Rush of Feeling

Why do people like to see particular types of films? Clearly, a movie is a form of entertainment that can meet various needs, including fun, learning, relaxation, and companionship. Each film genre can elicit particular feelings, such as apprehension, anxiety, and fear (horror flicks) or tenderness, warmth, and hope (romances). Amusement park rides can also elicit certain physical and emotional responses: roller coasters and other daredevil rides are advertised as "thrilling"; the "tunnel of love" invokes feelings similar to those sparked by a romantic film. Sports can also generate strong emotions. Part of the appeal in playing or watching a game is the apprehension, excitement, disappointment, joy and/or relief we experience as "our" team misses, scores, wins, or loses.

Why do we enjoy activities that elicit emotional responses? Why do we like feeling anxious, thrilled, or ecstatic? Feelings are our lifeblood. When they are aroused—our hearts beating, blood pressure increasing, stomachs dropping, skin crawling—we are aware of being fully alive. When we can experience these intense, vibrant emotions in "controlled" environments (where there is little or no risk of injury or harm, such as when facing a scary monster in a film rather than being mugged on the street), we have both aliveness and control, with a sense of choice and security.

Make a list of some of your favorite activities. This can include hobbies, sports, entertainment, or other pastimes you enjoy, even taking a walk or meeting with friends. What feelings come up for you when you think about the last time you engaged in these activities? What sensations do you notice in your body? Make a chart including the following categories; we have started you off with an example.

Activity:	Feeling(s):	Sensations:
Cycling	happy, joyful, exhilarated	light, open, relaxed, energized

Playing With a Full Deck: Developing Fluency in a Full Range of Feelings

There are hundreds of words in the English language for various feelings. Like colors in a paint box, there is a huge array, with a range of intensity and shades. Most of us, it's safe to say, only use about 10 percent of the vocabulary available. Out of all the available colors, we paint in only white and gray.

Happiness, for example, can range from feeling pleased and content to jubilant and ecstatic. Sadness can descend into brokenheartedness and grief or lighten into feeling blue or simply "down."

At first you may find it challenging to identify what you're feeling and distinguish between different shades. I know that when I first started learning NVC, I often had no idea what I was feeling, and I remember thinking at one point, *I'll never learn to know what I'm feeling—or at least take less than ten minutes to figure it out!* Yet with practice, we can all develop this fluency.

Reading over the list of feelings on page 367, do you see any that are familiar to you? Which feelings belong in a similar group or "family"? After identifying a group, you may wish to organize them in intensity and degree. You may also want to jot down feelings that come up for you on a regular basis or keep a list of feeling words with you that you can refer to. You may also wish to ask, "Which feeling words would I be most comfortable with and likeliest to use at home? With friends? At work or school?" The next time you answer "good" or "bad" in response to "How are you?" you may wish to stop and ask yourself, "What am I *really* feeling at this moment?"

EXERCISE 4: The Movement of Emotions

Have you noticed how quickly feelings can change for young children? At one moment, a child may be smiling and laughing, and the next moment they burst into tears. There's no evidence that children experience more feelings than adults; regardless of age, we probably all encounter similar ranges. The difference may be that children tend to be more in touch with what they're feeling, more inclined to express it, and less experienced in hiding it.

As adults, our feelings can also shift in intensity and degree— from apprehension to fear or terror, from satisfaction to happiness or elation. Our feelings change in response to what we're experiencing in the moment, and how we interpret that experience. We may feel perfectly excited, happy, and satisfied as we head off in the sunshine to enjoy a day at the beach. Then, after being stuck in traffic for an hour and then cut off by a big SUV, we may feel completely different—frustrated, hot, and annoyed! Feelings are not frivolous or irrational; they are indicators of how we are responding to stimuli in the moment. That feelings change easily and quickly is simply a sign of how quickly circumstances, and our thoughts about them, can change; being aware of our feelings can help us respond effectively to what is happening in the here and now.

Think back over the day, or even the last three hours. What feelings have come and gone during that time? See if you can link those feelings to your thoughts about specific stimuli in your environment. Try keeping a "feeling and sensation journal" one day, or even half a day, this week. Note the time of the day, what you are feeling, any sensations you notice, and where you feel them. You may also wish to notice whether you can identify a stimulus (something in the environment and/or your experience that may have triggered the response you have). Below is an example:

Time	Sensation(s)	Feeling(s)	Thought/Stimulus
7 p.m.	clenching in chest	anxious	taxes due in two days— not started them!

The Complexity of Feelings

In addition to noticing a range of feelings and the way they change throughout the day, you have probably also noticed how often you can feel more than one emotion at a time—and sometimes very different emotions. Have you ever felt both hopeful and excited (full of anticipation) and, at the same time, nervous or scared? (I'd probably feel this way if I were going alpine skiing for the first time!) When someone I love who had been ill and suffering passed away, I felt sadness, peace, and relief: sad to lose his everyday presence in my life and also peaceful and happy that he was now free of physical pain. If you reflect on this and the complexity of life and human experience, you can probably find many, many examples like this in your own life. Often this is the case for even everyday events; getting out of the bed in the morning, I can feel both tired and full of anticipation for events I have planned for the day.

Just as we can experience a mix of feelings at any given moment, it's common for one feeling to have others "behind" or underneath it. For example, if you are feeling hurt, this could include a mixture of feeling sad, disappointed and, perhaps, even scared. If you are feeling jealous, this could include heavyheartedness, fear, and sadness. Excitement can sometimes have hope imbedded in it.

EXERCISE 5: Stimulation and Response

   A. Read over the following statements. For each statement, notice what sensations you experience in your body and what you are feeling. Be sure to notice the complexity of your feelings: whether you are both excited and concerned, for example.
   1. You've been asked to an interview for your dream job.
   2. While shopping, you run into a friend you haven't seen for months.

3. You find a $50 bill on the street.

4. You walk fifteen minutes to the subway and realize that you've left your wallet (with your money and your subway card) at the house.

B. Pick a feeling from the feelings list (see page 367) and remember the last time you experienced it. Were there other feelings mixed in with this primary one?

C. What we see, hear, touch, taste, remember, imagine, or think about can all stimulate feelings in us. Often these responses are conditioned by associations with prior experiences or expectations based on prior experiences, even if these experiences are not fully conscious or currently present in our minds. While we may think our "trigger" is what's happening in the moment—what we're seeing or hearing—in fact *our thoughts* about the experience trigger our feelings and the physical sensations (responses) in our bodies.

Part One

Look at one of the photos on the following pages (pages 30–31).

1. How do you feel when looking at the picture? What sensations do you notice in your body? Again, you may wish to refer to the lists of sensations and feeling words.

2. Now take a moment to consider what thoughts or associations are going through your mind about the picture. Is there a connection between your thoughts and associations and how you are feeling when looking at the picture? Is what you see in the picture triggering what you are feeling—or are your thoughts about what you see the trigger?

Example: Looking at the picture of the children standing together and smiling in the village, I notice I feel open and relaxed in my chest and happy and expectant. I am thinking about how much I love to travel and how I would love to take a trip to Africa. Seeing the children's smiles, I also feel wistful, since I would love more fun and play in my life and it looks like they are having fun together. Seeing the building behind them, I'm also feeling some sadness, thinking about how so many people in the world survive on such limited means.

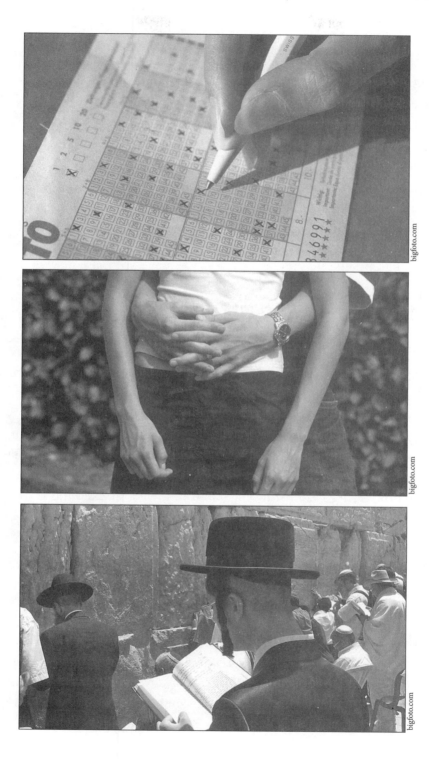

Part Two

Look in a daily newspaper and choose several photos you find of interest. Again, identify what you're seeing in the photo, how you're feeling as you look at this image, and any thoughts and associations you may have.

Part Three

Go to an art museum and/or look at some art in a book. Choose a work of art that you find moving. How do you feel looking at this piece? What do you specifically see that's stimulating your feelings? What associations do you have with what you see?

Disentangling Thoughts and Feelings

It can be hard at first to identify what we're feeling. It's also easy to confuse feelings with thoughts. As we've already explored, the verb "feel" has different uses. We can talk about how we feel in relation to both physical sensations and emotions. We can also use "feel" to talk about thoughts, opinions, and judgments. When we say, for example, "I feel that capital punishment is wrong," what we're really expressing is what we *think* or *believe* about capital punishment— not how we are *feeling* thinking about it. If we unpacked the feelings in this statement, we might find that the speaker is feeling angry, sad, or scared.

Often there are passionate feelings behind our opinions; we're simply not naming them. Using the verb "feel" with an opinion can be an effort to express that passion. For example, "I feel like this always happens!" could express the speaker's frustration and exhaustion and his interpretation that this particular action or event has happened before. "That's racist!" could express fear and anger in addition to naming how a person sees certain words, depictions, or actions. Regardless, when we hear the combination of "feel + like," it is certain that what we are hearing is an opinion, evaluation, or judgment. To support understanding and connection, we can choose to listen at such moments for what the person *is* feeling.

Sometimes we say "I feel . . ." when we want to give an opinion with a somewhat softer or gentler edge (as a way to acknowledge or emphasize that what we're saying is subjective). For example, "I feel she does want to help." In this context, we could just as easily say, "I personally believe (or think) she does really want to help" rather than "I feel." Regardless, when using the word "feel" in this context, it can be helpful to remember that what follows is different from what we mean by "feel" in NVC. When using the word to offer a thought or opinion, we are invited to go back into our heads (the realm of analysis and evaluation) rather than into our bodies or emotions.

How do we recognize when the verb "feel" is followed by a thought rather than a feeling? The easiest way is to see if the word "feel" is followed by the words "like," "that," "that if," or "as if," either explicitly or implied. If these words can be inserted after the word "feel," we are talking about thoughts and opinions—not feelings. For example, "She feels (that) because he left her, he has no heart"; "Tom feels (that) it should be done by noon"; "I feel (that) if it's packed this way, it will be safer." We can also look for subjects, such as "I," "you," "he," "she," "they," "it," or other words that follow a predicate in English. We can also check to see that the word following the verb "feeling" does, in fact, refer to the experience of a feeling or sensation: "hot," "aggravated," "joyful," "excited," and the like. The following table summarizes how the word "feel'" is used to express thoughts.

Sentences in which the word "feel" is used to express thoughts
I feel you look better in blue = I personally believe you look better in blue
(Pronouns—e.g., I, you, it—after "feel" indicate a thought)

I feel I am worthless = I'm convinced that I am worthless
(Pronouns—e.g. I, you, it—after "feel" indicate a thought)
I feel John is sad = I believe that John is sad
(Nouns—e.g. John—after "feel" indicate a thought)
I feel *like* I'm a loser = I think I'm a loser
(*Like* indicates a thought)
I feel *as if* you hate me = I'm sure you hate me
(*As if* indicates a thought)
I feel fat = I think I'm fat
(*Fat* is an evaluation, not an emotion)

EXERCISE 6: Real Feeling

Complete the following sentences with a judgment or opinion.
Then go back and "unpack" the feelings you are experiencing when
thinking about this issue.

   Example: "I feel because he didn't call that I'm not important to
him." Feelings: sad, disappointed, lonely

Opinion: _____

Feeling(s): _____

A. I feel as if . . . _____

B. I feel if . . . _____

C. I feel when you . . . _____

D. I feel that . . . _____

E. I feel because . . . _____

Wolves in Sheep's Clothing

We also confuse feelings in another way. Just as the word "feel" can be used with a thought, we frequently use words that appear to be feelings but are in fact feelings mixed with thoughts, evaluations, or judgments. These words occur in the same place feeling words occur, and we commonly interpret them as feelings. Yet upon closer examination, we can see that there is a thought or judgment mixed in with them. Feeling "misunderstood," for example, refers to a person or concept that has not been accurately understood. Where is the feeling here? We don't know for sure: probably the speaker giving this evaluation is feeling frustrated, disappointed, or hurt. All we know for sure is that they think there has been a misunderstanding. Here's another example: "I feel ignored." What is the feeling here? We don't know for sure. What we do know is that the speaker is not receiving the attention or recognition they'd like. This is an evaluation.

How can we distinguish? Feelings concern what is going on *inside* ourselves (what am *I* feeling?) or what is going on for another person *inside* that person (what are *you* feeling?). Feelings are internal experiences. As such, we can't argue or disagree with them. If you are sad, hurt, peaceful, or excited—whatever your feeling is—it is your feeling. In contrast, if you say "You misunderstood me" or even (in the passive) "I feel misunderstood," the other person could easily disagree: "I didn't misunderstand you! You were the one not listening to me!" On the most basic grammatical level, feeling words in English do not take an object. We don't say "You sad me." You can say, however, "You misunderstood me" (an evaluation, not a feeling). Saying "I feel misunderstood" is a short (passive tense) form of the same evaluation. Implicit is the belief that someone did something *to* you. Feelings, in contrast, are what we are experiencing inside ourselves.

Let's look at an example. When we say, "I feel abandoned," there is, in part, a feeling at play. We probably are feeling sad and lonely. Yet "abandoned" includes much more than a feeling: the thought wrapped up with it is a judgment of what someone (or a circumstance) has done *to* us. Thus "I feel abandoned" could be more directly expressed as "I'm so lonely, and it's your fault because you left me." Or it could mean, "I feel scared and uncertain that no one is ever going to care for me." In effect, the word "abandoned" is a shorthand way of blaming a person or situation for what we are feeling inside. It is a mixture of an internal experience (a feeling) with something we are imagining, thinking, or seeing (perception of the world).

There are many judgment-feeling words that mix feeling information with judgments or interpretations. Some of them include:

Abused	Interrupted	Provoked
Attacked	Intimidated	Put down
Betrayed	Left out	Rejected
Cheated	Loved	Screwed
Cherished	Manipulated	Threatened
Defeated	Misunderstood	Unappreciated
Devalued	Neglected	Unheard
Discriminated	Nurtured	Unwanted
against	Overworked	Used
Forced	Patronized	
Harassed	Pressured	

With each of these words, you can uncover both a feeling and a judgment. "Unappreciated," for example, could mean sad and disappointed, combined with "You did this by not expressing your gratitude." "Overworked" could mean disgruntled and annoyed, plus "You asked that I work late every night this week." An easy way to identify these "judgment-feeling" words is to ask yourself, "Did someone do something *to* me in this situation?" "Have they *made* me feel this way?" "Whose fault is it?" If you're placing responsibility for your feelings (and circumstances) outside yourself, you may very likely be using a feeling mixed with judgment.

Since judgment-feelings involve blame (what someone did to you), they easily lead to breakdowns in communication. At the very moment we want to be understood, by using judgment-feelings, our words can trigger defensiveness and denial. This response is not surprising: no one likes to be judged. If we want mutual understanding, we will succeed more frequently if our statements of feelings reflect only our feelings and not our judgments.

Using judgment-based words can also obscure that fact that we have autonomy, personal power, and choice. Even though we often say, "That makes me feel . . . ," no one's behavior can make us feel anything. By clearly stating a feeling without criticism or blame, we are taking full responsibility for our response. In doing so, we can experience greater awareness, empowerment, and choice—and connection with and understanding of others.

Exercise 7: Like Oil and Water

Go back to the list of words that mix feelings with judgments (see page 36). Choose five of these words and translate what the feeling and judgment might be. Harassed, for example, could be translated as "angry and stressed" with "you're pressuring me."

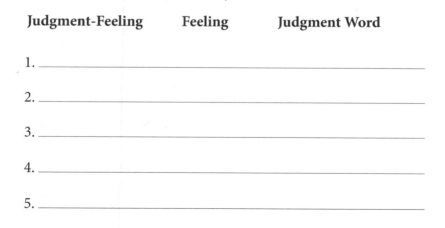

Judgment-Feeling	Feeling	Judgment Word
1.		
2.		
3.		
4.		
5.		

EXERCISE 8: Claiming Our Feelings

To gain more awareness of judgments you may have, what can stimulate feelings, and how these feelings are experienced in your body, you may wish to keep a feelings log for one or two days this week. Check in with yourself ten to fifteen times during the day, or every hour or two. Write down what you notice you're feeling. Then check: does a "judgment-feeling" word come to mind for you? If so, what stimulus (thought, judgment, or evaluation) is imbedded in it: who or what are you holding responsible for your experience? You may also wish to note whether you're telling yourself, "This *made* me feel X . . ." and then translate this to "When I see or hear X, I feel . . . (feeling word).

Moving On

In this chapter, we considered how moving beyond right-wrong thinking can contribute to greater connection with ourselves and others. To overcome this kind of thinking, it helps to connect with what we're feeling emotionally and what our bodies are telling us, since both support awareness—on an intimate level—of our actual, lived experience. In the next chapter, we will examine how feelings can connect us to our needs and how by focusing on needs rather than judgments or evaluations, we can find solutions that are more effective, satisfying, and consistent with our broader beliefs.

INTEGRATION: Questions and Exercises to Further Explore Chapter 1

Decide for each of the following whether you think it is a feeling (mark "F") or a thought (mark "T"). If you mark "T," write a

statement that you think might express what the speaker *is* feeling.
My opinion about each statement follows the exercise.

    A. _____ "I feel he doesn't care about me."

    B. _____ "I'm happy you're coming with me."

    C. _____ "I feel very nervous when you do that."

    D. _____ "When he leaves without me, I feel forgotten."

    E. _____ "You're ridiculous."

    F. _____ "I'm satisfied with my grades."

    G. _____ "I feel like kissing you."

    H. _____ "I feel manipulated."

    I. _____ "I feel good about how I played at the game."

    J. _____ "I feel fat."

My responses for this exercise:

A. If you marked "T," I agree. "He doesn't care about me," expresses, in my view, what the speaker *thinks* the other person is feeling rather than how the speaker *is* feeling. Examples of expressing a feeling might be "I'm lonely" or "I'm feeling sad and want your company."

B. If you marked "F," I agree a feeling was expressed.

C. I agree if you marked "F."

D. If you marked "T," I agree. I consider "forgotten" a judgment-mixed-with-feeling, expressing what the speaker thinks the other person is doing *to* him or her. An expression of a feeling might be "I feel sad."

E. If you marked "T," I agree. I believe "ridiculous" expresses what the speaker is thinking about the other person, rather than how the speaker is feeling. An expression of a feeling might be "I'm annoyed."

F. If you marked "F," I agree that a feeling is being expressed.

G. If you marked "T," I agree. I believe "like kissing you" expresses what the speaker imagines doing, rather than how the speaker is feeling. An expression of a feeling might be "I'm feeling attracted to you."

H. If you marked "T," I agree. "Manipulated" expresses what the speaker thinks the other person has done and a judgment of the other person's intention. An expression of a feeling might be "I feel suspicious."

I. If you marked "T," I agree. "Good" is often used to talk about feelings; in fact it simply expresses approval—that you're happy with how you're feeling. A feeling in this case might be "satisfied, content, excited."

J. If you marked "T," I agree. "Fat" expresses how the speaker thinks about him or herself, rather than how the speaker is feeling. Examples of an expression of a feeling might be "I feel uncomfortable weighing what I do" or "Thinking about my weight, I feel anxious."

2

Getting to the Root of Life

Needs: The Primal Force of Life

As we explored in chapter 1, we can start being fully present to ourselves and others by attending to our feelings—our physical sensations and our emotions. In doing so we notice what we're experiencing internally, in the here and now, in relation to our thoughts and the world around us. Yet awareness of our feelings (and what is stimulating them) is only the first step. Like a red flag, our feelings alert us to the primal experience of life, our needs. Being aware of what we're feeling, we can know whether our needs are being met or not. We can most enrich our lives by focusing on needs—others' and our own—and seeing how everyone's needs matter and can be held with care.

If you think about it, all human beings share the same basic needs. We need physical well-being: air, food, touch, and water. We also have nonmaterial or psychological and spiritual needs, such as for honesty, connection, autonomy, and meaning. Our physical bodies need air and shelter to survive. We also need dignity, choice, purpose, community, and creativity—to name just a few nonmaterial needs—to survive and thrive, as individuals and as a species. For a list of these "universal" needs, see page 368.

We can certainly differ in our likes and preferences, and we can employ innumerable strategies to meet our needs. Yet among various people and cultures, we can observe the same needs underlying different behaviors. Consider the need for food, for example. While many Americans enjoy eating seafood, many South Africans view it as inedible and disgusting. Americans of European descent may have no interest in eating chicken feet and find them repulsive, while in Chinese and other Asian cultures, chicken feet are seen as a delicacy. Similarly, people in all cultures value respect, yet the way respect is experienced and communicated varies. In some cultures, respect is indicated by making eye contact, leaving space between people, or being silent. In others, respect is expressed by lowering or averting one's eyes, allowing less space, or speaking up. Regardless of how they are expressed, the needs for nourishment and respect, along with other universal needs, are valued and acted upon all around the world.

Food, sex, and sleep—and not necessarily in that order!

—ANONYMOUS STUDENT

Universal needs are general, not specific, and can be fulfilled in different ways by employing different strategies. When you're feeling thirsty, for example, you can meet your need for hydration by drinking water, milk, or some other beverage, or eating a juicy piece of fruit. If you choose water, you could buy a bottle, pour some from a tap, or find a water fountain. How we choose to meet our needs can depend on a large number of variables—what other needs are "up" at the moment, what is familiar and socially acceptable to us, and the ease or "do-ability" of how to meet that particular need at that moment. For example, I generally avoid buying bottled water for environmental and health reasons. Yet if I'm very thirsty and the choice is between soda or bottled water, I will usually take the bottled water. All of us in each moment are navigating our needs in this way: discerning what strategies will best meet our various needs.

Regardless of how we act on them, all needs are vital. One need is not inherently more crucial or valuable than another. Nourishment and sleep are vital to physical survival, yet it would be hard to privilege sleep over food; we need both to survive. It could seem that physical needs are more vital than nonmaterial needs. Yet human behavior suggests otherwise. We all have been willing at times to forgo sleep to complete a project, study for a test, talk with a friend, or attend a party. In doing so, we are seeking to meet needs for effectiveness and competence in our performance or, in the case of a party, wanting play, fun, relaxation, and connection with others. The physical need for food is compelling, yet at times, humans choose to abstain from eating out of a desire to meet nonmaterial needs. In many cultures, for example, people voluntarily fast as part of a ritual, contributing to needs for meaning, community, purpose, communion, self-development, or belonging to the larger group. In some cases, people have gone on hunger strikes when wanting autonomy, dignity, choice, and respect. In the 1980s, for example, Bobby Sands, an Irish Republican, wanted recognition from the British government as a political prisoner. This recognition was so important to him that he was willing to fast until his death. Others who shared the same need also made this choice, following his example.

Sometimes it is hard to see the universality of needs because our strategies to meet them can be so different, even seeming at odds at times. The universality of needs can also be hard to see because different needs are more "up" at different times; we may associate a particular need being met so often with one particular strategy that we confuse the need with the strategy. We all need movement, rest, food, and water. At one moment, we may be thirsty and, at another moment, hungry or tired. In a particular situation, we might want care and consideration; another person in the same circumstance may desire spaciousness, play, and ease. Yet while each person may have different needs stimulated, we can all appreciate and understand the basic, universal needs that humans have. "Play" or "spaciousness" might not be needs that are "up" for us in the moment; at the same time, we can understand and appreciate them as valuable and life enriching.

As life serving, all needs can be seen as "positive" and desirable. The need for food, for example, is a "positive" energy; it motivates us to find and consume nutrients to sustain us. Similarly, all cultures value celebrations to mark events of importance to the individual and the community. These life passages, such as birth, death, and marriage, relate to primal human needs for life, hope, community, and connection (among others). If you look at the needs list on page 368, you will probably find inherent value in all the words included there. All people around the world, for example, want to experience a sense of purpose in life, and to enjoy integrity, love, peace, safety, and fun. Needs motivate and energize behavior; they also sustain and enrich the quality of our lives.

All living organisms, including humans, are in a continual process of responding to their needs. Plants and trees soak up water and grow in the direction of the sun to meet their needs for nourishment and energy. With sufficient water and light, a plant will survive. With care—weeding, fertilizing, and pruning so needs for energy and food are efficiently met—a plant will thrive. Humans are the same. If our physical and nonmaterial needs are fully met, we will experience "fulfilled" feelings such as happiness, satisfaction, and peace: much like a plant receiving optimum water and light, we are at "peak" fulfillment and aliveness. When our needs go unmet, we experience "unfulfilled" feelings, such as anxiety, fear, impatience, or anger.

Seeing all needs as positive, life enriching, and equally valuable is crucial to seeing how all our needs—and those of others—can be navigated and held with care. Further, by distinguishing needs from strategies and focusing first on the needs in play (rather than moving immediately to strategies), we can create connection and shared understanding. By focusing on needs, we also increase the odds that all needs "on the table" will be addressed and that the strategy we choose will work for everyone. You may dislike classical music and I may dislike heavy metal; we both can understand, though, the value of music in our lives and the needs met by listening to it, such as aesthetic pleasure, expression, community, relaxation, or aliveness. We can also probably appreciate that we all have a need for choice regarding which music we listen to and play.

To contrast this point, if we value one need over another, we are, in effect, making a moral judgment that one need is better or more important than another. This kind of judgment (an attachment to a particular strategy) can lead to conflict, misunderstanding, and disconnection. Fundamentally, we all want others to hear our needs, and we want to trust that our needs matter to them. Similarly, inside our own skin, we want to know that all our needs matter. If we meet some needs at the expense of others and/or think that some needs are "better," "right," or "wrong," this can create disconnection and conflict, both externally and internally. By holding all needs as valuable, we take the first step in exploring how they can all be addressed in any given situation. This is the first step toward finding "win-win" solutions, including for ourselves and the choices we make in life.

This kind of awareness of shared needs can lead to very different outcomes from those where such awareness is lacking. In one high school, for example, where students of European American, African American, and Latino backgrounds each had different preferences in dance music, the organizing group for the school prom decided to play music from all three preferred styles. They recognized that all the students wanted respect for their musical preferences and wanted to know that their needs mattered. At other schools, in contrast, where organizers lacked this understanding, the songs played were determined by majority vote. The students whose preferences were in the minority missed out on hearing the music they liked best. There was also loss, in my opinion, around collaboration, community, mutual learning, and celebration of differences.

EXERCISE 1: Connecting the Energy of Feelings to Life-Enriching Needs

A. Read over the list of universal needs (see page 368). How would it be to go through life without all these needs being met, at least at some time in your life?

B. Looking at the needs list, pick a need that stands out to you. In what various ways has that need been met in your life?

C. Choose one need from the list. How do different people in your life and/or different cultures that you are familiar with go about meeting that need? For example, both my brother and I have a need for physical exercise: he likes to play tennis and racquetball; I like to ride my bike and swim. In some cultures, respect and reverence are communicated via keeping your head covered; in other cultures, the same needs are communicated by removing your hat.

D. Looking at the needs list, is there a need you'd like to meet more regularly in your life? What are some ways in which this need might be met? For example, needs for rest and fun could be met by seeing a movie, talking with friends, listening to music, gardening, cooking, traveling, or attending a concert. A need for self-care could be met by deciding to go to bed earlier several days this week to get more sleep, or making some changes in what you eat.

E. Think of a specific time when you recently experienced one of the fulfilled feelings shown at the top of the feelings list on page 367.

    1. What were you feeling?

    2. What specific thing happened that stimulated that feeling?

    3. What need(s) (see the list on page 368) did you experience as fulfilled in relation to that feeling?

Form and Essence: Strategies and Needs

As has been discussed, all needs are life serving and "positive." We may not all agree, however, about which *strategies* are life serving. A particular strategy might meet some of my needs and leave others unmet. It may meet some needs for me, and leave them unmet for another person or group. For some people, eating at a fast-food restaurant might meet needs for pleasure, ease, fun, and choice, as well as nourishment. For others, choosing to eat local, organic food might meet needs for health, self-care, care for the environment, sustainability, and integrity. We could disagree and argue for hours about which strategy to take—do we eat at McDonald's or at a vegan, raw food restaurant? Do we eat fast food some days and health food other days? Yet regardless of where you like to eat and when, you can probably understand and appreciate the needs at play even if you choose to meet those needs differently from someone else.

EXERCISE 2: Connecting the Dots—Strategies and Needs

  A. Think about five choices or actions (strategies) you have taken in the last week. What needs were you seeking to meet? Were those needs successfully met?
  B. Think of a situation where you experienced conflict with another. Was there a particular strategy or assessment that each of you were attached to? If so, what were the underlying needs at play?

Think about a decision you are currently trying to make. Make a list of what needs would be met by each available choice (strategy). What would it look like to hold all your own needs with care?

Getting Clear About What We Need

In our culture, it is common to confuse strategies with needs. This confusion is easy to understand. Without employing strategies to meet our needs, we can be left feeling unsatisfied, frustrated, disappointed, or incomplete. Depending on the need and our urgency around meeting it, we may also experience anxiety, anger, or fear. Needs for physical safety, for example, can easily trigger these "intense" feelings. And because we associate *how* we meet the need (the strategy) with the need itself, it can be difficult to distinguish between the two. Yet it is needs—not strategies—that are the primal energy and force of life. Strategies are simply the diverse ways in which we attempt to experience and address our needs. Clearly distinguishing between the two can help us in understanding our needs, enjoying more choice and connection, and be more effective in the choices we make.

It's also easy to mix strategies and needs because we commonly use the word "need" when talking about strategies. We say, for example, "I need a new bike . . . a bigger apartment . . . a faster car . . . a better job . . . a long vacation!" You can substitute countless objects in this equation—such as a new jacket, a book, or a CD. You can also use the verb "need" when referring to outcomes and behaviors (another form of strategy): "I need to eat less"; "I need to find a new job"; "I need better grades."

When I first started thinking about needs, I felt stumped. I just wasn't used to thinking of myself as having needs. I had no problem using the verb "need" in statements like "I need a coffee," "I need to sleep," "I need to study." I thought I "needed" those things. Then I realized that the universal needs underlying "I need coffee" could be a number of different things, depending on the situation. Sometimes when I want a coffee, what I'm really wanting is to take a break and get outside for a few minutes. I was mixing up needs with strategies. In doing so, I was not always attending to what the real needs are themselves.

—SARAH

Yet none of these items are needs as we think of them in Nonviolent Communication. They are particular ways of attempting to meet needs. Beneath each object or objective, you can find the true, universal needs at play—such as wanting aliveness, fun, and learning (a new book), or warmth and beauty (a jacket). Needs, by definition, are intrinsic and intangible. As values or qualities, they are formless and can manifest (and be experienced) in infinite ways.

Strategies, in contrast, are specific, tangible, concrete; they exist in the "outside" world. You can pick up and hold a coat or CD; a new job is something you do or go to. You cannot take, hold, or buy love, understanding, compassion, autonomy, choice, or any other qualities on the needs list. They are not "things" or actions; they are qualities or energies that can manifest in numerous ways.

Your desire for a particular strategy may be so intense that it can seem like an urgent necessity. How often have we heard, "I *have* to get X!" or "If I don't get X, I'll die!" Yet the intensity we feel for a particular outcome arises, in fact, from the energy of the needs we are experiencing or wanting to experience, not the strategy itself.

Have you ever intensely wanted something, convinced that it would give you some quality (such as simplicity or ease), only to be disappointed when you got it because it didn't meet those needs after all? Maybe, in fact, this particular strategy complicated your life! Perhaps life would be easier if we could buy "simplicity" or "companionship" off the shelf or take it in a pill. Meeting needs in life, though, is of course often more challenging. With so many different strategies, life has richness, diversity, and choice. The beauty of needs being intrinsic (qualities we experience internally) and intangible is that we can meet them in so many different ways.

Sometimes we meet our needs in relation to one particular activity or strategy and confuse the need with the strategy; the strategy can seem absolute, or a kind of "truth." Yet the real "truths" are the intrinsic value of needs and our desire to meet them so we can make life more satisfying and enriching. Mahatma Gandhi

When I talk with my friends, I don't talk about feelings and needs. I notice now though that when I really listen carefully and try to figure out what needs they might be having, I have a hugely different and richer understanding of them.

—GARY

noted, "That which meets the most human needs is what comes closest to truth."

We Live What We Learn

Another reason it can be challenging to distinguish needs from strategies is that most of us are unaccustomed to thinking about universal needs. We don't learn about them at home, from our friends, in the media, or at school. In our culture, we're most accustomed to talking about strategies, rather than the needs in play that are motivating them.

Listening to the way many parents speak to their children suggests to me that most messages to children involve strategies. They are about strategies the children are engaging in ("Stop hitting your brother!") or that parents want them to engage in ("Time now to brush your teeth and go to bed!"). They also include strategies as punishment. For example, "Sue, finish your supper right now or no dessert." Other than when I've watched those who practice NVC with their children, I doubt I've ever heard a request made along with the needs offered behind the strategy. For example, "I'm concerned about you getting rest so you can enjoy school tomorrow; given that, I'd like you to head to bed in ten minutes." What we learn in our early years at home becomes a deep part of how we see and experience the world. Given how most of us are raised, it's understandable that we'd be inclined to confuse needs with strategies.

If you turn on the radio or open the newspaper, all you hear about is strategies: strategies already adopted (events that have taken place), potential strategies (decision being considered or debated), and opinions and assessments about strategies and those seen as responsible for them. You also find analysis of what impacts events or the choices made—and this analysis is another form of evaluation. Sometimes there is an oblique reference to a need: for example, "Today the president, wanting to boost consumer confidence, decided to lower taxes and prime interest rates." "Confidence" can be seen as a primal human need; in this case, though, other needs are also probably at play, such as economic security and ease of sustainability. Consumer confidence is a strategy to meet these other needs.

At one point, the study of needs was included in psychology courses, primarily through the work of Abraham Maslow, who wrote during the 1950s. Yet in contemporary American psychology, the concept of needs and how they motivate human behavior is not well represented. In six popular introductory psychology textbooks I examined, each averaging more than six hundred pages and published during the last ten years, the number of pages on the topic of needs ranged from zero to one. The number of pages, in contrast, devoted to cognition and thinking averaged twenty-five pages. At Binghamton University, the motivational psychology course, which included the study of needs, was removed from graduate and undergraduate curricula in 1990. Given how little focus has been given to human needs, it's no wonder we have little awareness or fluency in discussing them.

The Business of Mixing Needs With Strategies

This lack of focus on needs is not true of all disciplines, however. Roaming through a local bookstore recently, I found one discipline where the number of books devoted to the study of human needs occupied a full bookshelf seven feet tall! Can you guess which field of study took up so much needs-based shelf space? Business! The label for the set of shelves was "Business Motivation" and the section included books on how to appeal to human needs in how you market, hire, fire, advertise, manage, or seek to influence people. All these needs, however, were clearly linked to strategies—to manage workers and sell products.

How does business mix strategies and needs? Think about it: the primary job of advertising agencies is to convince us that buying a particular product will meet a whole array of needs. In effect, what they're selling is a strategy. Is there really a connection between the product (the particular strategy advertised) and the needs it claims to meet? You might think, for example, that the most important thing to know in choosing which soft drink to buy is how it tastes and how likely you are to enjoy it. Yet many companies advertise soft drinks featuring words and images that have nothing to do with taste. They depict people in the company of others, talking, laughing, playing sports, kissing, and/or relaxing on the beach. These images suggest an association between the product and primal, universal needs such as fun, rest, ease, intimacy, connection, spaciousness, and belonging. We associate positive feelings—happiness, contentment, ease, and satisfaction—with these needs, and we associate them with the product being advertised.

By implication, many ads suggest that only if you buy *their* product will you see your needs met. If you drink product X or wash your hair with product Z, you will be popular, respected, "cool," sexually appealing, and part of the "in" crowd. All by drinking the "right" brand of soda! Of course, we know rationally this is impossible. How can a soda meet needs for community, belonging, respect, sexual expression, and appreciation—and fun, stimulation, play, and excitement? There are plenty of people who don't drink soda who enjoy meeting these needs. And there are plenty of people sitting alone drinking Coke in front of a TV each night.

Many of the needs being "sold" to us can be met in other ways and are not specific to a particular product, or any product for that matter. A Mercedes-Benz, for example, as a mode of transportation, could be seen as a strategy to meet the need for ease of movement. If this were the only need a Mercedes-Benz met, what would motivate a person to spend $100,000 on it when a $25,000 Honda could also meet this need? If you want to sell a Mercedes, you need to convince people that it will meet other needs beside simple transportation. A Mercedes could be a strategy for comfort and beauty (aesthetic pleasure), or for connection or belonging (to a particular group that drives such a car, or to those who value styling and speed in transportation). This car could also be used to experience and express energy, power, and self-identity.

There are ways other than buying a Mercedes to meet these needs, of course. And in the end, the car may be ineffective in meeting all the needs you'd like it to. I once read a story about a man who responded to his midlife crises by mortgaging his house to buy a sports car. He wanted to feel the excitement, spontaneity, and vitality of his youth again. He ended up working so much overtime to pay for the car that he felt more tired and stressed—more "middle-aged"—than ever. Clearly, the sports car was a strategy, not a need, and the strategy was ineffective.

As with the sports car story, could buying a Mercedes-Benz be a way to fulfill a need for prestige or status? Or a need to impress others? These notions are certainly suggested by the advertisements for "high-end" cars. All needs are positive, universal, and general, and by this definition, I don't consider impressing others a universal need. Do all people need status to have a quality life? Is the need for status found everywhere—among all people? Can a person lead a high-quality life and not have a significant amount of social status? I think so. So, if social status is not a need, what is it? In NVC terms, we would say that a desire for social status is a strategy: a way to meet certain needs. The need it meets depends on the person: for some, social status might be a strategy for acceptance; for others, it might be a strategy for attaining self-respect, safety, belonging, or choice.

EXERCISE 3: Trying to Buy Love

Browse through the ads in popular magazines. Identify ads which seem to be addressing important underlying needs. For example, an ad for a car with an attractive woman in the photo. For each ad:

A. Identify how you feel when looking at it.
B. If you purchased the product, what needs might it meet for you? What needs might go unmet?
C. Identify the need or needs the ad is attempting to "sell" you based on the caption and visual message of the ad.
D. What in particular about the images and/or words stimulates your feelings and needs?
E. How do you feel when you think these needs might go unmet?

Example:
A. I'm looking at an ad for Bud Light that features a group of people all smiling and hanging out together. All of them I would consider attractive and sexy. Looking at the ad, I feel sad, envious, nervous, self-conscious, suspicious, and insecure.
B. The needs that I see the ad trying to sell are self-acceptance, fun, sexual expression, connection, stimulation, belonging, and beauty.
C. Everyone appears very confident and open in their poses. All the bodies are slim, muscular, and shapely. The group is mixed in gender and race suggesting to me that I will feel comfortable in a group of diverse people if I drink Bud Light. This implies to me that I will be sexually attractive and will meet other attractive people who are comfortable with their bodies and open to meeting others.
D. I would be extremely sad not to have my needs for self-acceptance, fun, sexual expression, connection, belonging, and beauty met. They are fundamental needs that I value highly.

However, I am also suspicious and not trusting that buying Bud Light will meet all those needs. I wish it was so easy as buying a particular drink!

A Need for Power?

Just as desiring social status can be confused with a need, I have heard this kind of thing said about people: "Bob needs to be in charge. He's bossy. A control freak—and power hungry!" But is having power over others a need? Do all people need such power? I don't think so. Like social status, "power-over" can be most accurately viewed as a strategy. For some people, it might be a means of meeting needs for security, respect, choice, or acceptance. Others might be trying to attain peace, order, confidence, self-acceptance, or safety by adopting this stance. We all need power and empowerment, as well as autonomy, choice, movement, and independence. Having power can be seen as having the capacity to meet our needs. If we had no power in our world, we would be unable to get out of bed in the morning! Or act on other choices to meet our needs. Exerting power *over* others, though, is a strategy. It is something we do to try to get something else—such as acceptance or respect. Power-over can also leave many needs unmet, including those for inclusion, mutual care, and transparency.

Intrinsic to power-over is a belief in scarcity, the belief that there's not enough power to go around—and we want to make sure our needs get met first. Power-over structures are typically hierarchical; they assume that the needs or concerns of some people are more important than those of others, or that those in power know what's best for those "below" them. Teachers decide what happens to students, bosses decide outcomes for employees, and bishops have authority over priests.

Contrast this with the "power-with" paradigm, in which the needs of all parties are considered vital and interdependent. The assumption is that there is no scarcity of power and thus no inherent conflict between needs. Thus both teachers and students want learning and growth to occur, and both value order, peace, and harmony, as well. All voices are needed in the dialogue, and through working together, we are likeliest to find strategies that will meet the needs of all. There may be occasions when, because of constraints of time or limitations of imagination, we do not identify a strategy that meets all needs, and when this happens we mourn any unmet needs. The holding and valuing of all needs is a constant in the power-with paradigm.

Approval and Self-Esteem—Who Needs Them?

Two other would-be needs that are not on the list of universal needs and that are often expressed in everyday conversation as needs are the desires for approval and self-esteem. Approval from others—their affirmation that you are a "good" person or have done something desirable or "good"—may seem like a need. Yet it is not.

We all have needs for making our own unique contributions to life and for being valued, appreciated, and seen. Approval, though, is in fact a judgment mixed up with needs: judgment of you and your behavior. Even though in the case of approval, the judgment is "positive," it is nonetheless a judgment. How satisfying is approval when it involves being judged by another? If we seek to align our behavior with our own values and needs, rather than with the approval of others, we have a much better chance of meeting those needs and increasing our quality of life.

Likewise, the list of universal needs does not contain the need for self-esteem, because self-esteem also involves judgment—judgment of ourselves. When I consider myself and decide, "I am a good, worthwhile, important person," I am not describing something I did that brings me pleasure. Rather, I am focusing on what I believe about myself and how I think I am as a person. Although the judgment in this case is about myself—and once again, it is "positive"—it is nevertheless a judgment, a point along the continuum of "good-bad" and an example of right-wrong thinking. If we can be "good" in some moments, we also can be "bad" in others. The practice of Nonviolent Communication invites us to step outside moral judgment to focus on needs met or unmet by specific words or actions. Rather than "globalizing" who we are or what we do "all the time," we "localize" behaviors and actions to specific needs met in this moment by specific words or actions.

Sometimes we behave in ways that are consistent with our most cherished values, and sometimes we do not—which leaves certain of our needs unmet. By evaluating whether our choices are consistent with our values, we can learn from our choices. Yet assessing whether our actions meet our needs is very different from judging ourselves for who we

I wanted to have sex and she didn't. I sure was frustrated!

—MATTHEW

My best friend has been seeing a man who I think is very manipulative and controlling. I have been telling her to break it off and pushing her really hard to leave him because I think it's such a bad relationship for her. We were barely talking to each other. After thinking about it, I realized that I was doing the same thing to her that he is—trying to get her to do what I want her to do. We sat down and talked, and she told me how much she wanted me to be there for her even if I don't agree with her choices in boyfriends. And how much she wants me to respect that she has to make the choices because it's her life—even if I disagree with her and even if she does make some mistakes and gets hurt along the way. The great thing is that now that I have stopped pushing about what to do and become more accepting of her right to choose, she is opening up more, telling me more about her own uncertainties and confusion about the relationship.

—SHEILA

are. Self-esteem is linked to this kind of evaluation. It is a *moral judgment* of my worth as a person. Even positive, moralistic self-judgments, such as "I'm an honest person," create a static view of ourselves and human behavior.

Some needs *related to* the concept of self-esteem are those for self-acceptance and self-respect. Self-acceptance is about accepting our choices and holding our needs as valuable even when we make choices that are inconsistent with our values or needs. This topic is covered in more detail in chapter 6. Similarly, self-respect is about holding dignity and care for ourselves; we do this outside of self-judgment. Both self-acceptance and self-respect can be seen as universal needs, experienced irrespective of others' assessments of our behavior.

When we evaluate how well a behavior or action aligns with our needs, we are making a *needs-based* or *values-based* judgment. In contrast to moral judgment, values-based judgment discerns how an action meets needs and is consistent with our larger values. This kind of needs-based judgment, or discernment, is crucial to getting clarity about what meets our needs and what doesn't; as such, it is different from right-wrong thinking or moral judgment. Marshall Rosenberg illustrates this principle with a story about a dog who is offered an apple. The dog has no interest in the apple; clearly, eating it would not meet his needs. At the same time, the dog is not thinking: "What an idiot—you just offered me an apple! Don't you know better?!" The dog knows: just because your words or actions leave my needs unmet, this does not mean that you are "wrong" or bad.

Balancing Everyone's Needs

Every behavior we engage in has the goal of meeting one or more life-fulfilling and universal needs. Of course, sometimes we discover that a behavior has unanticipated consequences that leave other needs unmet, which we may come to regret. This is why making choices in life can be challenging—we're juggling more than one need and not always confident we can meet them all. We may meet some needs while not realizing the ways in which our actions do not meet the needs of another group or person, or another area of our lives. Again, we can focus our assessment on whether needs have been met or not; this is different from moral judgment—a focus on our own or another's worth.

Not the Dynamite but the Detonator

One of the most important concepts in Nonviolent Communication is that we are responsible for our own feelings and needs. Other people's actions can contribute to meeting our needs and be the stimulus for our feelings. Ultimately, though, we are responsible for our emotional responses and for whether our needs are met or not. Just as we seek to step out of "right-wrong" thinking, we want to think outside "cause and effect," making a distinction between stimulus and cause.

While it is ultimately empowering and liberating, this concept of distinguishing stimulus from cause can also be difficult to understand or swallow at first. If you trigger a feeling in me, aren't you the one who caused it? It seems so clear—*you* are the one who made me angry! I was just fine until you cut me off on the road or made that stupid comment! And the more needs and pain are stimulated, the more seductive it becomes to blame someone else and find them responsible. Because our own emotional responses feel so automatic, immediate, and intense, it's easy to think that someone else has lit the fuse or turned the switch.

Yet while a car passing in front of you could understandably stimulate frustration and anger (and desires for consideration, awareness, and safety), that car and the person driving it cannot "make" you feel anything. No one can get inside your head and activate your feelings. Your feelings are your feelings—and your needs are your needs. And it is far likelier that your concerns will be heard and needs met if you can take responsibility for them.

As discussed earlier, our feelings occur in response to our experience of our needs being met or not met. While I might be angry or frustrated when I see a car run a red light, these are not the only responses possible. The strongest feelings could be fear, sadness, or concern. In each given moment, we can each experience a range of emotional responses; how we respond to particular circumstances is related to our own feelings and needs and our prior and larger life experience. Some emotional responses can be highly familiar and comfortable for each of us. We have our own histories of needs met and unmet, which can be restimulated by what we're experiencing in the present. And the circumstances stimulating our feelings and needs can, of course, change rapidly.

One way to test this principle is to consider how you respond to the same stimulus at different times. I know, for example, that a stimulus can affect me very differently depending on what else is going on for me that day. If I'm already feeling tired and anxious and someone says something I don't enjoy, I'll probably be more irritated than I would have been otherwise. This is especially true if the words remind me of what I'm already stressed about. In contrast, if I'm feeling self-connected, contented, and at ease, the words might have some "buzz," and I won't feel stung. My response is as much about what's going on for me—and my prior experiences and judgments— as what I'm experiencing in the present moment.

EXERCISE 4: Separating the Bee From the Sting

Think about a type of stimulus that occurs for you on a regular basis: perhaps words that someone you care about says, behaviors you see on the road while driving, circumstances at work or school, or even problems with your computer or another electronic device. Now think back to the last three times this kind of incident occurred and how you responded. While your response may have been similar on the three occasions, see if you can identify even shades of difference. Then consider larger circumstances that may have contributed to the quality and intensity of your response.

Example:

Now it's your chance to try . . .

Stimulus	Response	Circumstances/ Thoughts in Mind
Someone opens a car door when I'm cycling by.	Mild irritation, with some acceptance	This is the first time this has happened today; I've not ridden my bike for a week, and am excited about being out and enjoying the weather.
A car turns right in front of me, without indicating first; to avoid being hit, I jam on my brakes.	Frustration, anger, dismay	This is the second potential incident today! In this case, it was a close call! I really could have been hurt!
A truck drives by a construction site when water has collected on the road and, in passing within a foot of my bike, splashes muddy water all over my clothes.	Rage and despair	I really want drivers to see cyclists on the road and have some consideration and care! Why couldn't the driver slow down or wait for me to pass by before driving through the puddle?!?

Stimulus	Response	Circumstances/ Thoughts in Mind

Choice, Autonomy, and Responsibility

Taking responsibility for our response to stimuli does not mean
that others are not responsible for their actions. We may feel
very strongly that a particular action is not life serving, and feel
confident that many, if not most, people would agree with our
view. Yet while we may not like what we see, this doesn't mean we
have to make a moral, "right-wrong" judgment. By focusing on
the particular behavior, and how that behavior meets our needs or
not, we are far more likely to get our needs met and see a shift in
how we're feeling. No one likes to be judged or blamed, even if they
can see how a choice they made has contributed to others' pain or
suffering. We want understanding and to be seen for our intentions
and our humanity.

So we are all responsible for our actions. We can let people know whether a particular action is meeting our needs or not. We are also responsible for our own feelings and needs. This doesn't mean you need to change your feelings or disregard them; it means you have choices about how you will or will not go about meeting your needs, and how you will respond. This awareness can give you freedom as well as autonomy in how you respond to incidents and events in your life. It means you have choices about how you interpret the world and the behavior of others. You can see that all people are trying to meet needs, even in behavior that doesn't meet your own.

EXERCISE 5: Responsibility, Action, and Response

Think of an action you took that you feel some sadness or regret about, one that did not fully meet your needs or contribute to the well-being of others. Identify the action, the impact or result, how you're feeling when thinking about this, and needs your action met and did not meet.

Action	Impact/ Result	Feelings	Needs Met by Choice	Needs Unmet
Decided to go out for dinner and movie	Didn't reply to some work emails regarding a possible contract	Frustrated, disappointed, annoyed	Rest, fun, connection	Effectiveness, peace of mind, confidence around sustainability

More About Emotional Liberation

Being responsible for our own feelings and needs also means that we are not responsible for the feelings and needs of others. Those are their responsibility. Consider the following statement: "You didn't call me last week so I felt lonely and depressed." The implication is that you caused them to feel lonely and sad. By not calling, you are responsible for how the speaker is feeling. You are a real heel—or at least thoughtless and self-involved, since you "ruined their day."

From an NVC perspective, a more accurate statement would be "When you didn't call me last week, I felt lonely, sad, and depressed because I was really longing for companionship." This statement clearly shows the relationship between the feelings and the need and takes responsibility for both—your not calling is simply the stimulus. The sadness comes from wanting company: a need the speaker has. If the speaker hadn't been experiencing a need for companionship, they might have said, "When you didn't call me last week, I was relieved because I was needing rest and really wanting a break from all the socializing I've been doing." Note again that the events are identical—in both cases, you didn't call. Taking responsibility for what they are feeling, the speaker is also aware of their own needs. In the second example, by your not calling, the needs of the speaker were in fact met.

It is very important to express the needs that are being met in a given situation. The need to enrich the lives of others, to find a purpose or meaning in life through service to others, is one of the strongest (if not the strongest) of all universal needs. Yet there is always more than one way to meet any given need; needs are not strategy-specific. If someone is wanting connection and companionship, for example, this does not mean that you are the one who has to provide it, or to provide it at this moment. Hearing this need from another, you may offer to meet them later in the day or on the weekend; you may also be able to suggest another friend who might be willing to spend time with the person now. The need for companionship may even be satisfied simply by receiving an empathic response from you. Holding others responsible for our feelings and needs, and having only one strategy (or person) in mind to meet them, is like volunteering to be confined in a straitjacket— we immobilize ourselves with our limited options. We also can create unnecessary disagreement and conflict.

INTEGRATION: Questions and Exercises to Further Explore Chapter 2

A. What does it look like when we take responsibility for our own feelings and needs and state them clearly? For each of the following statements, jot a "Y" for yes if you think the speaker is taking responsibility, or an "N" for no if you think the speaker is not taking responsibility.

_____ 1. "You piss me off when you leave the dorm room unlocked."

_____ 2. "I feel sad when you say that because I want understanding, and I hear your words as an insult."

_____ 3. "I feel enraged when I don't see you looking at me when I'm talking."

_____ 4. "I'm disappointed that you won't go to the game with me, because I was hoping we could catch up."

_____ 5. "I feel angry because you said you'd help me with physics and then you didn't."

_____ 6. "I'm discouraged because I would have liked to have made my swimming times by now for the lifeguard exam."

_____ 7. "Sometimes the little comments my mom makes hurt me."

_____ 8. "I feel relieved that he won the election."

_____ 9. "I feel scared when I hear you raise your voice and use language that I consider profanity."

_____ 10. "I feel grateful that you had an extra umbrella, because the rain is getting heavier."

My responses for this exercise:

1. If you wrote "N," I agree. To me, the statement implies that the other person's behavior is responsible for the speaker's feelings. It does not convey the speaker's own thoughts or needs that cause those feelings. The speaker could have said, "I'm pissed off when you leave the room unlocked, because I am afraid my stuff will be stolen and I want my feelings to count for something."

2. If you put a "Y" next to this item, I agree. The speaker is acknowledging responsibility for their feelings. The speaker expresses the feeling (sad) and need (understanding), and also indicates that their need for understanding was stimulated by the interpretation or judgment that what the other person said was an insult. But the speaker "owns" the judgment, indicates that they *heard* the other person's statement as an insult, not claiming as fact that it *was* an insult.

3. If you put "N" next to this item, I agree. To express the underlying needs or thoughts, the speaker might have said, "I feel enraged when I don't see you looking at me when I'm talking, because I want to be seen and heard."

4. If you put a "Y" next to this item, I agree that the speaker is acknowledging responsibility for their feelings.

5. If you put an "N" next to this item, I agree. To express the needs or thoughts underlying their feelings, the speaker might have said, "I feel angry that you said you'd help me with physics and then didn't, because I have a strong need for reliability and dependability."

6. If you put a "Y" next to this item, I agree that the speaker is acknowledging responsibility for their feelings. The speaker is stating the want behind the discouragement—the desire to make the swimming times. Some might disagree because making swimming times can be seen as a strategy

for meeting needs for competence, acceptance, inclusion, or respect; to my ears, the speaker is taking responsibility.

7. If you put "N" next to this item, I agree. To express the needs or thoughts underlying their feelings, the speaker might have said, "Sometimes when my mother makes little comments I feel hurt, because I want appreciation and acceptance."

8. If you put "N" next to this item, I agree. To express the needs or thoughts underlying their feelings, the speaker might have said, "I feel relieved when I hear that he won the election, because I did not trust that the previous administration was looking out for our best interests."

9. If you put "N" next to this item, I agree. To express the needs or thoughts underlying their feelings, the speaker might have said, "I feel scared when I hear you raise your voice and use language that I consider profanity, because I am thinking that I might be in danger and I want to feel safe."

10. If you put "N" next to this item, I agree. To express the needs or thoughts underlying their feelings, the speaker might have said, "I feel grateful that you had an extra umbrella, because the rain is getting heavier, and I like to be dry and comfortable."

B. Strategies and needs can resemble layers of an onion, layered one upon the other over a core need. These core needs can often be obscured when mixed with strategies. Choose an object or outcome you want. Let's say it's an object, a car. Then complete this equation: "I need a car, because I need X." Then go to the next layer, "I need X, because I need Y." And then "I need Y, because I need Z." Keep going until you've reached the primary or core need. Regarding the car, for example, this might sound like:

- I need a car so that I can be popular.
- I need to be popular so that I can have friends.
- I need to have friends so I have companionship.
- I need companionship so I won't feel lonely.

In other words, I want companionship, and ease and confidence around not feeling lonely. Having reached this point, you may also wish to ask yourself, "What if I am lonely . . . ? What will happen?" Perhaps if you're lonely you won't feel connected with others, or safe. Doing this exercise, you can see that the car, being "popular," and having friends are all strategies. The core needs might be connection, safety, and community.

The key question then becomes: What are some other ways that I can meet these same needs?

Now try this exercise with an object or outcome that you are wanting:

I need_____ so that_____

I need_____ so that_____

I need_____ so that_____

Alternatively:

What if I don't get_____ or _____?

What will happen?

And:

What are three other ways that I can meet the same needs?

C. Our feelings and needs can be stimulated through direct contact with individuals and circumstances and also by hearing, seeing, or thinking about events and situations in the larger world.

Example:

Situation	Feelings	Needs Met/Unmet
U.S. in Iraq	sad, angry, worried	safety, consideration, honesty, awareness, care

D. Read the following quotations, the first from Joseph Goebbels, who was active in the Nazi Party during World War II, and the second by Richard Perle, a former member of the federal administration in the United States.

So total war is the demand of the hour . . . The danger facing us is enormous. The efforts we take to meet it must be just as enormous . . . The rest of Europe should at least work to support us. Those who do not understand this fight today will thank us on bended knee tomorrow that we took it on!

—JOSEPH GOEBBELS, February 18, 1943

If we just let our vision of the world go forth, and we embrace it entirely, and we don't try to piece together clever diplomacy but just wage a total war, our children will sing great songs about us years from now.

—RICHARD PERLE, January 31, 2002

Now answer the following questions:

1. What strategy (course of action) is each speaker suggesting?
2. How do you feel when reading about each strategy? What needs are "up" for you (met or unmet) by their words and stated intention?
3. What feelings do you imagine the speakers were attempting to stimulate in their audience? Is this different from the response you have had to their words? If so, why?
4. What feelings do you think were "up" for Goebbels and Perle when making these statements?
5. What needs do you imagine they were trying to meet?
6. While spoken nearly sixty years apart, how do both quotations refer to and make use of similar strategies—both in intended impact on the audience (a strategy in itself) and in the strategy suggested (specific course of action advocated)?

3

Really Listening

Seek first to understand, then to be understood.

—STEPHEN COVEY

How Could the Woman I Thought I Knew Be So Different?

Susan is a young woman living at home with her mother, working part time in an office and attending the local community college. In an interview, she told me the following:

> My mother is a very critical person. No matter what I do, it's not good enough. She doesn't like the way I dress, who my friends are, who I date, what I do in my spare time, how I drive. I'm ready to explode. I just don't want to go home anymore. It is so unpleasant. Every moment, she thinks I'm going to get pregnant. She's constantly riding me, watching me, checking up on me. I just wish she would get a life and give me a break!

After learning the basic principles of NVC, Susan decided to try using these new skills in talking with her mother. Now aware of feelings and needs, she was able to hear her mother and her concerns in a way she never had before. What she discovered amazed her:

After talking with my mother for half an hour and listening, really listening, as carefully as I could, I can't believe what I learned about her. I had no idea how scared she is for me. She feels like her life was cut short and not what it could have been, because she got pregnant young and never had a chance to go to college. She really does want the best for me. She worries a lot, because she loves me and is scared for my safety. She says that she will always be there for me, but she doesn't want me to "mess up" the way she did.

After years of conflict and misunderstanding, connecting with her mother in a new way changed the way Susan thought about her and her behavior. Susan commented about their exchange: "This was such an eye-opener. Before, I would always put my opinion in and tell her what I felt. And I never really heard her. I see her very differently now. And I am grateful for that. And for her."

What made the difference in how Susan heard her mother and perceived her mother's actions, enabling her to shift anger and impatience to compassion and gratitude? As we saw in the last two chapters, identifying what we are feeling and needing in any given moment can help us connect to what's most important to us. Listening for feelings and needs, Susan was able to hear that her mother is scared and worried. She was also able to understand her mother's urgent underlying need: peace of mind with respect to her daughter's future. She wants her daughter to have opportunities and choices that as a young person she didn't enjoy.

When Susan was fully able to understand her mother's hopes and fears, she could finally appreciate what had been motivating her mother's behavior for so many years. She also realized that their needs were not in conflict. Both of them want Susan to have choice and meaning in her life. And though the needs for safety and choice may be more salient or active at this time for Susan's mother than they are for Susan, it's not that these values are unimportant to Susan; she wants them too. Susan and her mother both want to be fully heard and to know that their concerns matter to each other. Each may see different choices or strategies (e.g., a college degree versus work experience or travel) as more or less likely than other strategies to fulfill the needs they value; their conflict is in the evaluation of different potential strategies, not at the level of needs.

Don't Just Do Something. Stand There!

Susan reported that she talked with her mother for "half an hour" and listened, "really" listened, "as carefully as I could." How do we "really listen" in this way? What organ do you use to listen? Most people will first say that they listen with their ears. And the ears do play a critical role in identifying words and discerning meaning from the utterances we hear. Upon reflection, though, people report their eyes, skin, and entire bodies are also important organs for listening. Our "gut" can give us a visceral response to what we're hearing; our skin, if it's tingling, cold, hot, or tight, can tell us something about what we're feeling. And if we're noticing tension, pain, or restriction in our bodies—or conversely, a sense of opening, relaxation, or release (most often in the shoulders, head, or chest)—this can indicate whether our needs are met or unmet.

How do we know when we're fully present to others and able to take in what they want us to know and understand? Being fully present involves more than eye contact and physical cues— although such behavior can indicate intent. It involves more than listening to the words we hear; we must take in the energy and intent behind the words. Listening in this way involves our whole bodies—not just our heads. And the primary organ involved in listening is the heart.

A colleague describes an experience she once had in another country. Because she was unfamiliar with the pronunciation patterns of the local people, she could not make out the *words* of a speaker who was clearly describing an experience of important personal meaning to her. Our colleague listened empathically to all the parts of the woman's expression: her posture, her movements, her facial expression, and the nonverbal characteristics of her speech. Though her words had not been understood, afterward the woman described how much she appreciated our colleague's empathic support.

Most of us are accustomed to listening just with our heads, to giving and receiving opinions, thoughts, and judgments. Rather than creating connection, companionship, and presence, "head-listening" usually leads to a degree of separation and disconnection. The "symptoms" of this disconnection can include numerous nonempathic responses, such as offering information, analysis, and advice. Most often, it is characterized by some form of agreement ("Yes, this is terrible. What can we do about it?") or disagreement (judgment, dismissal, minimizing, or denial). When we are disconnected in this way, we are not fully present to our own needs or the experience of the person we're wanting to attend to.

To listen with our whole bodies and get beyond good-bad, right-wrong thinking, we need to listen empathically to what is beneath a person's judgment or story. This means responding to the content or ideas a person is expressing and also the underlying feelings, values, and needs. The goal in listening empathically is not to solve a problem or get another to change their behavior. The goal is to connect with and understand at a heartfelt level what another person is experiencing. Often this kind of connection in itself can contribute to clarity and a change in how we and others approach a situation or experience.

Helping by Not Helping

How often do you feel fully heard and supported, that someone is fully present with you and your concerns? Based on a survey of three hundred adults I conducted, I would guess that most people rarely if ever get to enjoy this kind of experience. I asked the adults to imagine that they had heard the following statement from a friend: "I've got a big test tomorrow, and I just don't think I'm going to do very well." The table on pages 76–77 shows a number of ways people responded to the statement. As you can see, the most common was what we could call "advice giving." Some people suggested how the person might study, how he might get some rest or relaxation, or what to do if the exam didn't go well. None of the responses explored what the speaker might have been feeling or needing. Rather, the people responding were trying to "fix" the situation.

Reassurance Is Not Empathy

The next most common response was reassurance. The speaker was told that their feelings weren't "justified," that what they feared was not going to happen or wasn't true. When we reassure someone, our intention usually is to offer comfort and support. Unfortunately, it often has the opposite effect and closes off the conversation. So if Davita, in the example above, is worried about a test and I say, "You'll do just fine," I have no understanding of why she is worried and what it would mean for her to get a lower grade than she wanted. In giving her reassurance, I am not meeting her where she is in the present moment and her own experience. As such, I am unlikely to connect with her in an authentic way.

> *Because I've gotten mostly A's in school so far, nobody takes me seriously when I am worried about a test or assignment. They say, "Oh, Davita, you'll do just fine." They don't get it, and I wind up more upset than when I started.*
>
> —DAVITA

Sympathy Is Not Empathy

Another type of response people gave was a sympathetic one: "How awful. I feel terrible hearing that." When we see another person— especially someone we care about—expressing strong feelings, this can stimulate sympathetic feelings in us, feelings we may *believe* are similar to what the other person is experiencing. If we hear that someone feels sad, for example, we may feel sad ourselves. This is a sympathetic ("sameness of feeling" or "feeling together") response. When feeling this way, it can seem as though we're heart-connected with the other person, and certainly, at such moments our feelings are aroused. Yet in offering sympathy, while we provide some emotional companionship for the speaker, we are attending to our own needs and experience, not the feelings and needs of the other person. In doing so, we are not fully connecting or being fully present to that person. Have you ever told someone about a painful experience, only to find their reaction so strong that you shifted your attention to supporting *them?* This is an extreme example and it highlights that when we listen empathically, we want to maintain our attention on the feelings and needs of the speaker, staying open to connecting *with the speaker's feelings and needs, not our own.*

Your friend says "I've got a big test tomorrow, and I just don't think I am going to do very well." How would you respond? When we categorized students' responses, we found the following:	
A. "Just study as much as you can and then don't worry about it."	Advice-giving: Most common type of response
B. "Oh, you're smart, you'll do well."	Reassurance: Second most common type of response

The following types of responses were given less frequently.	
C. "Don't worry, it's silly to worry."	Denial of feelings
D. "There are lots of tests. That one doesn't count much."	Minimization
E. "If you think you have it bad, you should hear about my test schedule this week . . . "	I can top your story
F. "That's terrible. I feel so bad for you."	Sympathy
G. "Yeah, something like that happened to me last semester, and what I did was . . . "	Storytelling, comparing stories
H. "Let's go drinking and forget about it."	Avoidance
I. "I will help you study for it."	Offer of assistance
J. "Your problem is you're a compulsive worrier."	Diagnosis
K. "I think you worry a lot because you want to please your parents."	Analysis
L. "You should have studied all along."	Judgment

Storytelling and Comparison Are Not Empathy

Less commonly, students shared a story of their own. This can be a form of reassurance and advice giving through example. It can also be a way of trying to connect

I just hate seeing a guy cry. I will do anything to avoid that.

—MERRI

with the other person by showing that we understand what they are experiencing and that we're sympathetic. Intentionally or not, it can also have the effect of bringing the attention back to our own experience rather than keeping the focus (at least for the moment) on the person we want to support. Especially when someone is experiencing intense feelings, sharing an anecdote or comparing their situation to one of our own is unlikely to foster greater understanding or connection. Because it shifts the focus away from them, it can act as a form of minimization or denial.

EXERCISE 1: Other Than Empathy

Read the following statements and identify each as an example of fixing, advice giving, comparison, one-upmanship (I can top that story!), analysis, diagnosis, reassurance, minimization, avoidance, judgment, or sympathy. (Some statements may illustrate more than one kind of response.)

    A. "Well, why don't I help you get ready for the trip—then you'll have more time?"
        Type of nonempathy: _____

    B. "Wow, I'm really sorry to hear that. That's terrible."
        Type of nonempathy: _____

C. "That's nothing! You should have seen the test I had in
    chemistry last year!"
    Type of nonempathy: _____

D. "Maybe you're not making good choices because you're not
    getting enough sleep?"
    Type of nonempathy: _____

E. "I would talk to the professor. He'll give you an extension for
    sure."
    Type of nonempathy: _____

F. "But this isn't as bad as last year. At least in this room, you
    have heat!"
    Type of nonempathy: _____

G. "What a jerk! I'd be pissed off, too!"
    Type of nonempathy: _____

H. "Let me tell you about what happened to me when I drove to
    Florida, in this old truck, with you know, that guy who was
    so weird in that English class we took, who called himself
    Shakespeare. You won't believe this story!"
    Type of nonempathy: _____

I. "Just go to bed and don't think about it. You'll feel better in
    the morning."
    Type of nonempathy: _____

Putting the Shoe on the Other Foot

However we choose to respond to a person, there is nothing "wrong" with that choice. Sometimes hearing about your experience or how to fix a problem is just what a person wants. Such responses can meet needs for companionship, understanding, clarity, and support. Before choosing a communication strategy, however, you may wish to ask the person you're speaking to whether they would enjoy hearing advice or a story of your own, or whether they simply want someone to be with them and listen for the time being. Checking first can contribute to meeting needs for autonomy, awareness, and choice, and this can be especially important when a person is already aroused because their needs are not being met. Checking first can also help you focus on the other person and their needs in the moment.

In choosing how to respond, it can be helpful to first check in with yourself to see what your own feelings and needs are. If you feel distracted or distressed, you may not be able or willing to listen to what's going on for someone else. You may have heard this person express something similar before and, hearing what sounds to your ears like the same story again, you're feeling frustrated and tired. Without full awareness of why you're choosing to react in a particular way, you may respond with reassurance, advice, or another nonempathic response. This can be a strategy to communicate that you're not interested or available now, and that you want to attend to other needs. In such moments, however, rather than using nonempathy as a strategy, you can be honest and authentic about what's going on for you. "Sue, I'm hearing how anxious you are about your test tomorrow and that you'd like help preparing for it; I also have a paper due at five o'clock today that I'm really nervous about getting done on time. I want to focus on that." By expressing your own feelings and wants, you can attend to your needs for choice and self-care as well as accuracy, honesty, and integrity. You can also explore strategies that work for both of you. In this case, you might suggest, "Can I touch base with you about it after my paper is done?"

or "How about asking Brenda—she's in our class, as well." (For more about making requests, see chapter 5.)

A recent experience gave me insight into this matter. I was feeling discouraged about some choices I had made and how these choices were contributing to needs being left unmet in my life. I was feeling sad and shared my concerns with my mother. Her immediate response was to disagree with me. She pointed out examples of what she considered constructive decisions I'd made and how the decision in question had in fact contributed to some "positive" results in my life. As if reading my résumé, she then listed all the things I'd done in life. Hearing her, I felt more discouraged and depressed than ever—not to mention frustrated and overwhelmed!

What was happening in this situation? In sharing with my mother what was going on for me, I wanted companionship and support. I wanted understanding and to feel heard—for another human being to simply be present with me. I'm guessing that for her, it was very challenging to hear my pain. As a parent, she probably has a deep desire that I feel content with my life. Concerned about my well-being, she wanted to foster ease and acceptance and didn't know how. By giving me reassurance, she was in fact responding to her own fear and discomfort.

After I expressed my frustration that I didn't want reassurance, that instead I wanted companionship—for someone "to just be there" for me—she did listen, and her presence was a great gift. I'm sure it was challenging for her. In her listening, though, I experienced a sense of care and understanding. After I had fully expressed myself, my mood lifted.

Perhaps you can think of a time when you were distressed and someone wanted to "change" your feelings. Maybe all you wanted at the moment was their company and attention. Thinking of times like these can help you have more awareness and choice about how you respond to others. Do you want to listen empathically, with your heart? Or will you choose a strategy that may feel easier or more familiar—such as advice giving or fixing—that may not offer the support and companionship you want to give?

EXERCISE 2: Being There

Think of a recent situation where someone you know was
emotionally stimulated in some way (perhaps angry, sad, or
discouraged), they shared with you how they were feeling, and you
responded nonempathically. What were you feeling and needing at
that moment? What do you think their feelings and needs might
have been?

Situation (What I heard person say):	My feelings hearing this:	My needs hearing this:	Their feelings:	Their needs:

For Beginners

Most of us, of course, are accustomed to giving and receiving
nonempathic responses. At first, it can be very hard not to respond
in habitual ways. If we're stimulated by what we're hearing, it can be
especially easy to slip into analysis, disagreement, advice, or other
types of thought-based responses. For that reason, the sentence
frames that follow can be very useful for keeping us focused on
feelings and needs. This focus supports empathic connection.

Sentence Frames for Empathy Guesses

1. Are you feeling (insert feeling word here) because you're needing/wanting (insert need here)?

2. I am wondering if you're feeling (insert feeling word here) because you're needing/wanting (insert need here)?

3. Sounds like you're feeling (insert feeling word here) because you're needing/wanting (insert need here)?

4. I am guessing you're feeling (insert feeling word here) because you're needing/wanting (insert need here)?

5. So, you're feeling (insert feeling word here) because you're needing/wanting (insert need here)?

6. Is it that you're feeling (insert feeling word here) because you're needing/wanting (insert need here)?

Note: In some of these examples, inflection in voice tone indicates a question is being asked.

Three things are important to note about these frames. First, they are oriented toward the present. What are you feeling and needing *now?* You want to understand the person's experience in the present tense because that is what is "alive" and compelling for them at this moment: it is what they currently are experiencing. Sometimes a person's feelings may relate to thoughts about experiences in the past. Yet if a person is thinking or speaking about a past event, it is because that event still resonates with them now. So any statement we make, even about the past, can be framed in the present tense. This is what the "past as the present" frame looks like:

The Past as the Present:

When you think (present tense) about what happened ___ (years, months, days) ago, are you feeling ___ because you're needing ___ ?

Often when a person brings up the past, it's an indication of how much intensity and pain they may be holding about the present situation. If they're still thinking about something that happened in the past, it must still be bugging them—and their feelings may have gained in intensity since it's been bugging them for a while. There's a history of disconnection and unmet needs. This can be helpful to know in supporting them and can indicate the depth and intensity of feeling you may wish to "match" when listening empathically. You can meet intensity in your choice of words, tone of voice, and body language. If someone is shouting when expressing a judgment, whispering your empathy guess will probably not give them a sense of being heard, even if your words match their experience. To have a sense of being fully heard means to "get" where they are with the experience, including its intensity. Further, if the speaker does not give the present context when mentioning past experiences, it can be helpful to ask for that information when you are guessing their feelings and needs. This also fosters connection, bringing a past experience into the present.

EXERCISE 3: Bringing the Past Into the Present

For each statement about the past below, give a present-tense empathy guess.

Example:
> Past: "I failed a test last year."
> Present: "Thinking about that, are you especially nervous about this test you have tomorrow? Are you wanting to be seen for all the hard work you've put in this semester?"

A. Past: "The professor last year was never there during office hours, and when I went for help at the writing center, they said there were no times open."

Present: _____

B. Past: "He dropped all his other girlfriends without warning, too. He never told them why. Just said, 'Don't bother calling me anymore.' He did the same thing to me. What a jerk."
    Present: _____

C. Past: "I never made it on the team in high school either."
    Present: _____

D. Past: "What a loser. He lost a bunch of money gambling two years ago, too."
    Present: _____

E. Past: "I was really happy at my old job. Leaving was a big mistake—even with getting a raise."
    Present: _____

A Guess Is Just a Guess

The second point to remember is the tentative nature of empathic connection. We are not analyzing the other person or trying to "figure them out." Only the speaker knows what they are experiencing. We are trying to guess the nature of that experience and confirm whether or not our guesses are congruent with it. This is why we put our empathy guesses in the form of a question: "Are you feeling . . . because you're needing . . . ?" Alternatively, if we don't use a question, we can indicate openness by raising our intonation: "So, you're feeling . . . because you're wanting . . . ?" We can also add on a tag question to such statements: "Is that accurate?" "Does that match your experience?" Also, when we ask a question we needn't worry about getting it "right." The person we are listening empathically to will let us know if our guess matches their experience. Even if it doesn't, just our intention—our attempting to empathize—is enough to create connection. It is our willingness to be fully present with the other person that matters.

To support the person we're empathizing with in getting clear about what they want, it's also helpful to ask content-based questions, such as "Are you feeling sad because you're missing your family and wanting companionship and support?" Such questions facilitate connection and exploration more than an open-ended question such as "What are you feeling?" or "What do you want?" Common responses to questions like these, such as "I don't know" or "I'm not sure," just leave our conversation and connection at a dead end.

The question "Why do you feel that way?" is especially to be avoided. Since it asks for a reason or explanation, it is likely to elicit thoughts or cognitions rather than a connection with feelings and needs. And sometimes people interpret this kind of question as having to justify their feelings. When offering empathy, we want to foster acceptance and connection. Our feelings *are* our feelings; there is no need to justify or explain.

EXERCISE 4: Asking About Content

Go back to exercise 1 in this chapter (see page 78), which lists a number of nonempathic responses. Think of a situation that might have stimulated the response, and list the feelings and needs you think might be stimulated in the person. Then give a content-based empathy guess for each situation. You may wish to refer to the lists of feelings and universal needs as reference. The first one provides an example.

   A. Situation: person with a lot to do before a trip
       Feelings: stressed, overwhelmed
       Needs: space, support

Empathy guess: Are you feeling really stressed about the number of things you want to do before you leave for the airport? Are you needing support?

B. Situation: _____

Feelings: _____

Needs: _____

Empathy guess: _____

C. Situation: _____

Feelings: _____

Needs: _____

Empathy guess: _____

D. Situation: _____

Feelings: _____

Needs: _____

Empathy guess: _____

E. Situation: _____

Feelings: _____

Needs: _____

Empathy guess: _____

F. Situation: _____

Feelings: _____

Needs: _____

Empathy guess: _____

G. Situation: _____

Feelings: _____

Needs: _____

Empathy guess: _____

H. Situation: _____

Feelings: _____

Needs: _____

Empathy guess: _____

I. Situation: _____

Feelings: _____

Needs: _____

Empathy guess: _____

Walk on the Sunny Side

A third important point when responding empathically to others is that we want to identify what the person *wants*, not what the person *doesn't* want. This is like "walking on the sunny side"—focusing on the positive and moving forward. Just as the sun illuminates our surroundings, this contributes to greater clarity. It also increases connection and the chances that needs will get met, since we're focused on what we *are* wanting to experience. Notice the difference, for example, in saying to someone, "So you don't want noise here when you're working?" or asking, "So you're really longing for quiet so you can focus?" Rather than focusing on the problem—noise—we can focus on the solution or desire: in this case, quiet. Similarly, when making empathy guesses it's ideal to name the need in a positive statement. Rather than saying, "You're mad because your need for consideration is not being met" (focusing on the unmet need), it is more connecting to say, "You're mad because you're needing consideration." By giving an empathy guess in the negative, in some ways we're looping back to the original story or judgment— that something is "wrong"—rather than focusing on the life-serving need that is behind our being triggered and what's motivating our desires. We then can make a specific request to meet that positive need (see chapter 5 about requests).

EXERCISE 5: Sunny Side Up

For each of the following statements, what might you guess the person is feeling and needing?

A. "That was the rudest salesperson I have ever met. I can't believe they keep someone like that on staff to abuse customers!"
Feeling(s): _____
Need(s): _____

B. "It's hopeless. I'm never going to pass this course. It was so dumb of me to think that I could handle twenty credits in one semester and be in the band."
Feeling(s): _____
Need(s): _____

C. "My so-called friend is avoiding me ever since I lent him twenty dollars. I'll never trust him again. If he can't pay it back or doesn't intend to, I just wish he wouldn't lie about it."
Feeling(s): _____
Need(s): _____

D. "The stress is really getting to me. I am feeling so pressed— by my parents, my teachers, my job, and my girlfriend. I can't remember the last time I was able to just relax and unwind."
Feeling(s): _____
Need(s): _____

Short But Sweet

In offering empathy, it's also helpful to be succinct. Don't try to explain or justify your reflection. The goal is to help the speaker understand their feelings and needs. If you focus on the details of a story, it can be easy to "move into the head" and start analyzing. You don't usually need to know or understand all the details to create an empathic connection. And if you use more words than necessary, those listening can feel overwhelmed and have trouble tracking everything you've said. A rule of thumb is to try to keep your empathy guess to twenty words or less. Let's look at an example:

> *Your friend:* I can't believe Luke decided to end our relationship and doesn't want to talk about it. I sort of knew it had to end, but the timing is so difficult, what with my mother being sick and everything. He has meant so much to me for so long—I don't know how I am going to manage without him. Everything is just falling apart.
>
> *Your empathy—not as helpful:* So, I am wondering if, as a result of what he said, you are feeling sad because you really care about the relationship you've had and didn't want it to end in this way, especially with all the other things that are going on with you and given how long the two of you have been seeing each other?
>
> *Your empathy—more helpful:* Are you bummed he left because you're really wanting support right now?

EXERCISE 6: To the Heart of the Matter

For each of the following statements, make an empathy guess of twenty words or less.

A. "I just came from the bookstore and the books for my courses cost more than $500! How can they charge that kind of money? It's highway robbery!"

_____?

B. "My pants don't fit. I've put on fifteen pounds this year. I feel like a fat slob."

_____?

C. "Hey, guess what? I just got the promotion I wanted!"

_____?

D. "Sharon, I read your report and I can see that you put some effort into the formatting and style. However, the writing needs a lot of work. In several places, I can't figure out what you are trying to say—it just doesn't make sense!"

_____?

E. "Why can't you come home this weekend? It's your dad's birthday, and it's important to him."

_____?

Enjoy the "Talking Head" Show

When you first start offering empathy to others, you may feel a little baffled, and even completely lost, about guessing their feelings and needs. At first, it can almost seem like magic—how can you possibly know what someone's deepest emotions and desires are? People don't wear this information on their sleeves. When they're speaking, it's frequently about thoughts, opinions, and, often, judgment and name-calling. Finding a feeling or need in all the information tumbling out can be like looking for a needle in a haystack.

How do you start? Ironically, in listening for feelings and needs, often the best place to start is with the opinions, thoughts, and judgments being expressed: the "talking head show." As you may recall, "speaking from the head" means using thoughts, judgments, and cognitions—statements of blame, criticism, labeling, analysis, diagnosis, and the like. While this is not the level we want to stay on, such thoughts can provide important first clues to unmet needs.

Often we can find a clue in the root meaning of a word that comes up in a talking head show. If a person says, for example, "He's the most unsupportive person I've ever met!" the speaker probably wants care and support. While "unsupportive" is a judgment, "support" is a universal need. Similarly, if someone uses the words "dependent" and "uncaring," the needs that are up for them might be independence and care.

Words share roots with one another and also can be seen as belonging to cognitive "families." Awareness of these families and how some words have similar meanings (with connotational differences) can be helpful in listening empathically, especially if you connect the dots between strategy words that are similar to feelings and needs words. If someone says, for example, "I'm sick of this job! I never get any help!" it's likely the speaker wants support. "Assistance," "help," "guidance," and "direction" all refer to particular and related strategies. They are all similar in meaning to the universal need: "support."

In addition to looking at the root meaning of a word and its "family," it can be helpful to look for its opposite and/or what universal need would "satisfy" the feeling or judgment being named. If someone is screaming: "I can't stand the noise! I just need a break from it," it's safe to guess they're craving quiet, movement, and relief. The opposite of "noise" is quiet, and if you want a "break," you probably want a change in the situation (movement) so you can change your experience (giving you relief). Similarly, if the names you have for someone are "stubborn" and "pigheaded," you may want mutuality, openness, and consideration. If you're feeling hungry, what would satisfy this? Nourishment. If you're feeling tired, you could want rest. If you're bored, you could want stimulation and/or challenge.

Again, when we're "empathy guessing," we can't know for sure what's going on for the other person. Watching the talking heads show—all the labels, opinions, and judgments that come rushing out—can help us connect with the person's underlying feelings and needs.

EXERCISE 7: Unearthing Needs in Roots and Oppositions

Part One

Look at the following judgments and labels. Based on the root of the word, guess what need might be up for a person using such a judgment. To help think of the needs, you may wish to refer to the universal needs list on page 368.

Judgment	Need
A. Caring	_____
B. Untrustworthy	_____
C. Inconsiderate	_____
D. Kind	_____
E. Unsupportive	_____
F. Disconnected	_____
G. Uncommunicative	_____
H. Meaningless	_____
I. Unclear	_____
J. Ineffectual	_____

Part Two

Look at the following judgments and labels. Based on the opposite of each word or word set, guess the possible needs of a person using such a judgment. Again, you may find it helpful to refer to the universal needs list. Space is provided to guess two or three needs that may fit for each set.

A. Mean, cruel, vicious _____   _____   _____

B. Tired, exhausted, spent _____   _____   _____

C. Anxious, worried, tense _____   _____   _____

D. Selfish, self-centered, self-serving _____   _____   _____

E. Cramped, crowded, overwhelmed _____   _____   _____

F. Critical, judgmental, demanding _____   _____   _____

G. Disgusting, ugly, distasteful _____   _____   _____

H. Meaningless, pointless, irrational _____   _____   _____

I. Shortsighted, thoughtless, unaware _____   _____   _____

J. Finished, perfect, complete _____   _____   _____

Walking in Another Person's Shoes

There's an old saying that before judging another person, you need to walk a mile in their shoes. This concept is also helpful in listening empathically. Based on what you hear the person expressing, what do you imagine they're feeling or needing? Think, for example, about someone who has an important presentation at work the next day and has not, in their opinion, sufficiently prepared. What would you be feeling in this circumstance? Take a moment to imagine it. What sensations do your feel in your body? Perhaps heat, pressure, or restriction? How are you feeling? Perhaps anxious, worried, tense? Maybe the needs most "up" for you are effectiveness, ease, confidence, and relief? By placing yourself in a similar situation in your mind's eye, you can imagine a "bridge" from your own experience to that of another. Your experience may not match what the other person is experiencing, yet by using your imagination in this way, you can begin to guess what their experience might be— and offer them empathy.

Empathizing Across Cultural Differences

Within any given language and culture there are numerous dialects and subcultures, each with different expectations and levels of experience in talking about feelings and needs. In Jewish culture, for example, it is considered acceptable to share personal feelings somewhat freely and in some detail. In Asian or Native American cultures, such sharing may come less readily. With co-workers we may talk less about our feelings than with family or friends. We may notice a difference when talking with those who are younger or older. When speaking with those who are less comfortable talking about their feelings and needs, empathy guesses are especially helpful. Even if your guess does not match what is going on for the person, it gives the speaker something to start with and "chew on"—a starting point with which to reflect on their own experience.

In some environments, such as at work, you may find it helpful to guess about needs only. If you recall, our needs are the driving energy of life; our feelings simply connect us to this energy. Among those who practice Nonviolent Communication, there is the belief that 90 percent of the power of empathy is associated with empathizing with needs, and 10 percent is associated with empathizing with feelings.

Regardless of who you're speaking to, you'll want to adjust your language and manner of expression to match theirs. Feelings, for example, vary in intensity and flavor. "Nervous" has a far different level of intensity than "terrified," while both words describe being anxious or fearful. In choosing which word to use, you may wish to balance two considerations: What, in your estimation, best matches the person's current experience? Are they just scared or, in fact, terrified? And what word will they be most comfortable hearing to foster trust and connection? If someone is feeling vulnerable or unsafe, or simply uncomfortable talking about feelings, you may wish to guess "lower" on the level of intensity. Using modifiers (such as "little," "a bit," "very," "extremely," "really") can also be helpful in adjusting the pitch of your guess. "A little nervous," for example, conveys a lower level of intensity and pitch than "very nervous."

In a similar way, you can choose words describing needs that go shallower or deeper. For example, in a work environment, you may not want to guess that a person needs "safety," even if you sense this is the need at play, if you imagine this need goes to a depth that might be uncomfortable for the person to discuss at work. To support trust and connection, you might guess instead that the person is wanting consideration and care. While not getting to the deepest root of a person's fear or pain, connecting in "shallower waters" can still create connection and understanding. What's most important is not the words you use—it's the intention you hold.

In some cases, where you are just not sure what words would support connection, you might wish to use silent empathy. In silent empathy, you focus on understanding the speaker's feelings and needs, and your intention to connect is expressed by being present and attentive and listening with your whole body. No words are needed when you are really tuned in to the other person. Can you remember a time when someone listened to you intently, with caring? That was silent empathy.

EXERCISE 8: Changing Pitch

Part One

For each of the following word pairs below, representing "high" and "low" feelings in terms of intensity, add other feeling words that complete the range. You can also use modifiers to increase and decrease intensity. Some words may be quite close in meaning.

Example: Anxious; nervous; scared; afraid; frightened; terrified; stricken with fear

A. Happy _____ecstatic

B. Sad _____seriously depressed

C. Irritated _____furious

Part Two

Look at the lists of feelings on page 367. Choose a group of words not included in part one and put the words in order of feeling intensity. You may also wish to notice which words you consider synonyms. For example, happy and glad could be considered to have a similar "pitch" (in terms of intensity) and meaning; jubilant, in contrast, would have a much higher level of intensity than "happy."

Going Deeper

When listening empathically to someone, take your time. As you guess their feelings and needs, you will start to hear phrases like "Yes, exactly" or "Absolutely" or "Yeah, yeah." These responses indicate that the person is really connecting with the needs underlying their feelings. Initially, you are likely to observe a flurry of words, as they are eager to explain and clarify for themselves what is going on for them. Continue with the process. You may be amazed by what unfolds and the range of feelings and needs that emerges. Take your time and keep empathizing until you sense that the person feels complete and "done."

Why do you want to keep guessing until the person feels complete? Often, it is only in reaching the "core" need that a person feels fully heard. And they may not become aware of the "core" need until feeling heard about the "constellation" of needs surrounding it. Have you ever seen those wooden, stacked Russian doll sets?

When you open one doll, another, smaller one is inside that one, and another inside that until you reach the last doll at the center. This is one way to think about finding the core need. Sometimes we can use one need as a strategy for another (community, for example, can be a strategy for safety). It is only by empathizing with the first need that we can become aware of a need related to it or beneath it.

When people are upset about something, they will often move from one point to the next without stopping. In such cases, it can be very helpful to interject and ask that they pause for a moment, giving you a chance to connect and offer them an empathy guess. Otherwise, as a listener you can easily get lost in the level of detail, losing connection and clarity. When interrupting to foster understanding, it's helpful to state what you're feeling and needing. "Can you pause for a moment? I'm feeling overwhelmed with all that I'm hearing, and I really want to understand what you're saying." When both parties pause to take a breath, it can really help slow things down, contributing to both the movement and clarity of communication.

When Do You End?

After a while the speed with which the person is speaking will slow and you are likely to observe a calming, easing, or dissipation of tension. This may include a physical shift, indicated by a deep sigh; a change of facial expression; or a repositioning of their body. Now you might wish to ask, "Is there anything more you would like to say?" You can also follow up by asking, "What's going on for you now?" This is a reminder for the speaker to check in with what they are feeling in the moment; it can help them see whether they are "complete" with what they have been sharing. Even if you choose to simply sit in quiet empathy, the speaker will let you know when they are done.

Even before you sense that the empathy process is complete, it's helpful to pace things and to take your time. Careful attention can speed up the process of understanding.

When Is It My Turn?

When a speaker feels "complete"—they have finished sharing what's most alive for them—they often want to hear what is going on for you. They may have a need for shared experience, or reassurance that you are accepting of them and their feelings. If you have been caught in a conflict with the person you're listening empathically to, it is usually at this point—after they feel fully heard—that they will be most interested in hearing what you are feeling and needing. In fact, after receiving the gift of empathy from you, they will probably be eager to hear about your experience.

If the person is not able or willing to hear your concerns, this is a sure sign they're feeling incomplete in the empathy they need. If you can, go back to the steps described above, focusing on what's alive in them. If you are feeling too stimulated or fatigued to do so, you may wish to take a break to get some empathy for yourself or to practice self-empathy (see chapter 6) before continuing. If your own needs are not being met, it can be difficult if not impossible to be empathic to another. This is a basic principle, "empathy before education," that we will explore in the next section.

Empathy Before Education: Attending to One's "Cup" Before Filling It With Another's

If you have a cup full of water and attempt to pour in the contents of another, the water will spill over; there is simply insufficient room to hold the contents of both. Similarly, if two people are stimulated—

angry, frustrated, or hurt—and one wants to give the other "a piece of their mind," it will be difficult if not impossible for the first to hear the second. Like the cups of water, they are too full of their own feelings and needs to have the space to hold the experience of the other. In Nonviolent Communication, this principle is known as "empathy before education." If we want to "educate" someone about our own experience (our feelings and needs), we want to see that they get the empathy and "hearing" they need first.

This principle was discovered firsthand by a man, Barry, who was learning Nonviolent Communication and had recently joined a new faith community. He found himself in a group of congregation members, all of whom were opposed to a woman being able to choose to have an abortion, while he was not opposed. A tense situation ensued:

> The group got into an argument about abortion being murder or not. My standpoint was firmly pro-choice—"It's a woman's body and her choice." Another person's viewpoint was that abortion is "baby killing." "God makes that choice— not you." I had a hard time relating to her, or even hearing her for that matter. We were in a heated argument, to say the least, when I finally realized this was getting me nowhere. I decided to stop talking and only listen, but *really* listen—not how I'd been listening before. Before, I was listening, but only with my own idea in the back of my head. I was literally waiting for her to stop talking so I could elaborate on my position. Now I cleared my head and heard her completely. I realized she was very firm in her opinion, which did have some good points that I had not been able to see before. And although I disagreed with her, I had to give her credit for her opinion and allow her to think the way she wanted to.

Barry realized that since the other person felt so strongly, there was no way she would be able to hear his viewpoint and concerns.

Putting his own opinions aside for the moment, he chose to hear the other person in a way he had not been able to before. What was the result? A shift occurred:

> After I listened without speaking for some time, she seemed to be in shock that I was finally quiet; I think she appreciated my listening and hearing her out. She was then willing to hear me, so I spoke. I explained my ideas, and I said, "I understand and respect your opinion," which made her happy and allowed her to open up to my ideas. By the end of the conversation, she admitted that perhaps her way of thinking was old-fashioned, but that was how she was raised, and she wanted to give some thought to others' opinions. I was really impressed with how well Nonviolent Communication worked in this situation. I was able to open my own mind and able to do the same with somebody else.

By empathizing with the other person first and fully hearing her concerns, Barry opened the way for the other person to hear his concerns, too. This is what we mean by empathy before education. Before Barry could "educate" regarding his own views, the person he was speaking with first needed to have the sense of being heard.

Sometimes, of course, our own feelings and needs are so "up" that it's difficult to hear what's going on for another person. In that case, we need to get some empathy or practice self-empathy before proceeding. We need to empty our own cup before we can receive more from others.

But I Want to Help!

When empathizing, we are connecting with the person's internal experience; we are not doing anything directed toward changing that experience or the outside world. At first, this can be frustrating.

We're accustomed in our culture to taking action—to changing, fixing, and taking charge. When someone is in need or in pain, it can be challenging to simply be present with what they are feeling and needing. We want movement and relief. Empathy can seem like a detour or "delayed gratification."

Yet as you gain experience in practicing empathy, you'll see that it is also an effective strategy for creating change. An immediate shift can occur in what you think about a situation, how you feel about it, and how you relate to others. From this connection, other strategies may emerge that are far more effective in meeting needs than those that would have been chosen if empathy had not first occurred. You can, of course, give reassurance and advice any time you want. You probably will find, though, that sharing experiences and moving to strategies will be much more effective *after* you have listened empathically.

Why is this so? Empathizing first gives you more information about what's actually happening for your friend, rather than just your interpretation. It's easy to think that we see exactly what's going on in a situation for another person. Sometimes, based on what we know about them and/or our own experience, we may in fact have a clear idea. Yet human beings can respond to the same stimulus in a variety of ways. We have no way of knowing for sure what their experience is unless we empathize first. We can best support them if we see the situation from their perspective: walk in their shoes.

If suggestions come to mind and you wish to share similar experiences, save these for *after* listening empathically. Then you can ask questions such as "Would you like to hear of a similar experience that I had?" and "Would you like some suggestions about how to handle the situation?" Once your friend has fully expressed their concerns and been fully heard, they will be more interested and probably grateful to hear any ideas you may wish to share.

Will Other People Think I'm Weird or That I Talk Strangely?

In the beginning, people may be suspicious of your new way of communicating with Nonviolent Communication. "What is this different way of talking all about? Is this some kind of technique you're trying out on me?" If this kind of question or complaint comes up, you may wish to respond with transparency: "Yes, I do want to improve our relationship, to feel closer, to deal with our conflicts more effectively. It may sound different, and it's my way of wanting to understand better what's going on for you and for us to hear each other." In being transparent, you're sharing the needs you're hoping to meet (effectiveness, ease, intimacy, and connection) through using NVC, and by doing so, you are already taking a step toward empathy and connection. And hearing the needs you're hoping to meet, the person you're speaking with is likely to understand and appreciate why you may be trying a new way to communicate.

As you learn NVC and put it into practice, those around you will see that you are now able to listen and express yourself more effectively. They will probably also notice that you are better able to stay in a conversation that previously would have broken down into misunderstanding and disagreement. As you gain skill in practicing NVC, you can also begin using a "colloquial" or "street" form that doesn't strictly follow the model and yet still focuses on feelings and needs (see chapter 10). Empathy, though, is not really about the words—it's about the intention to hear the other person, to understand the other person's experience at the deepest level possible. And sometimes the best type of empathic response is no words at all. When we do speak, it is often not the words we use but our tone of voice and how we position our bodies when relating to the other person that most communicates our interest, compassion, and intent.

A Cautionary Warning!

Rome wasn't built in a day. When you are first starting out with NVC, you may not want to change your way of talking with people with whom you have the most intimate or challenging relationships. This may be the time to just *think about* feelings and needs in your interactions. Practice for a while on those more distant from you—or by practicing self-empathy (see chapter 6). The challenge with most intimate relationships is that these are the people who know you the best, and they will be struck by the change in the way you are speaking. If you have had a lot of conflict with them, they may not have a lot of trust and may think you are trying to manipulate them to your advantage. Trying to connect in this case is like attempting to run a marathon on the first day you start jogging. Give yourself a chance to learn the skills and practice before you try out for the Olympics!

This doesn't mean you can't start using your new skills immediately. Marshall Rosenberg is fond of saying that anything worth doing is worth doing badly. In other words, if we wait until we can do something perfectly, that day may never arrive! By practicing NVC and putting it to use, you will gain confidence and fluency. And just as when learning a foreign language, knowing a little NVC is better than knowing none at all. Even casual contact can benefit from NVC consciousness and skills. If you're nervous about starting out, start with absolute strangers. I have found NVC very helpful when traveling, in making my needs clear and in requesting help when dealing with people in "official" capacities—such as those with banks, schools, and other institutions. I also find it helpful to practice NVC in everyday conversations that are free of tension or disconnection. Whenever we are discussing something that matters to us, listening empathically supports clarity, connection, and depth of understanding.

Finally, it is important to remember that the frames we've suggested here are simply a road map for creating an empathic

© 2005 Sam Zavieh

connection. The four signs along the road are observations, feelings, needs, and requests. (Observations and requests are covered in later chapters.) These steps, when you're conscious of them, can greatly contribute to empathic connection even when you're not speaking and giving silent empathy. Regardless of the words or frames you use, keep the focus on the feelings and needs of the speaker. If you are not willing or able to guess both, the most important to focus on is usually the needs.

INTEGRATION: Further Exercises to Explore Chapter 3

Put an "E" next to each item if you think that Person Two is responding empathically to Person One; write a "J" if you think it's judgment or evaluation. If you do not think Person Two is responding empathically, write a response that you consider to be empathic, as empathy has been described in this chapter, focusing on feelings and needs.

_____ 1. Person One: "How could I be so stupid, leaving my wallet at the bar?"
Person Two: "Nobody is perfect, man; stop being so hard on yourself."

_____ 2. Person One: "Honestly, all the rich city kids should leave this school. Let them go to a fancy private school."
Person Two: "Do you really think that would fix anything?"

_____ 3. Person One: "You aren't Mr. Know-It-All."
Person Two: "Are you frustrated because you want to be acknowledged for what you know?"

_____ 4. Person One: "I think you take me for granted. If I transferred schools and left, how the heck would you live without me?"
Person Two: "That's a lie. I don't take you for granted."

_____ 5. Person One: "How could you say something so mean?"
Person Two: "Are you angry because you want more
consideration and care in how you're spoken to?"

_____ 6. Person One: "My boyfriend is making me mad!
Whenever I cry, he just calls me a baby and walks away."
Person Two: "Do you think he should stay and comfort
you?"

_____ 7. Person One. "I'm so down. I haven't had a relationship
for six months. I look so fat."
Person Two. "Are you discouraged—wanting someone
you can be close with?"

_____ 8. Person One. "I'm worried about this semester. I'm
taking four upper-level classes, and they seem so hard.
I feel like I should change majors."
Person Two: "Are you anxious because you would like
the semester to be a bit easier?"

_____ 9. Person One: "When my family comes to visit me
without letting me know, I get so pissed. I feel like they
don't think I have a social life."
Person Two: "I know what you mean. My parents do
the same thing and I could kill them."

_____ 10. Person One: "I didn't like how you rowed today's race.
I wanted to see the stroke rating up higher. It seems
like all the training help we did together was useless."
Person Two: "I know you're upset. I just didn't feel in
the groove."

My answers to this exercise:

1. If you put a "J" next to this item, I agree. I interpret Person
Two's behavior as telling Person One how they should think
about themselves, and as an attempt at offering reassurance.
A response I consider empathic would be "Are you ticked off

because you want to take care of things that are important to you?" The feeling guessed is "ticked off" and the needs guessed are awareness and caring: remembering to take care of things that are important.

2. If you put a "J" next to this item, I agree. I interpret Person Two's question as about Person One's thoughts rather than their feelings and needs. A response I would consider empathic is "Are you angry because you value respect for all people, regardless of their financial situation?" The feeling guessed is anger and the need, respect.

3. If you put an "E" next to this item, I am in agreement. The guess included the feeling of frustration and the need for acknowledgment, to be seen for who he is.

4. If you put a "J" next to this item, I'm in agreement. I see Person Two as arguing with Person One's judgments, not receiving empathically. A response I would consider empathic is "Are you hurt and do you want to know that you matter, that you make a difference?" The feeling is hurt and the needs guessed are to matter, to count, to have a purpose.

5. If you put an "E" next to this item, I agree. The feeling is anger and the needs are consideration and care.

6. If you put a "J" next to this item, I'm in agreement. I see Person Two as asking about Person One's thoughts and judgments about what the girlfriend should do. A response I would consider empathic is "So you're angry and want acceptance for how you express yourself?" The feeling guessed is anger and the need is acceptance.

7. If you put an "E" next to this item, I agree. The feeling guessed is discouraged and the need is for closeness or intimacy.

8. If you put an "E" next to this item, I am in agreement. The feeling guessed is anxious and the need is ease.

9. If you put a "J" next to this item, I agree. Person Two is saying that he has the same experience and feelings as Person One, and this is not empathy. A response I would consider empathic is "Are you irritated because you want to make your own decisions about how you spend your time?" The feeling here is irritated, the needs guessed are choice and autonomy.

10. If you put a "J" next to this item, I'm in agreement. Person Two is explaining his perspective, not inquiring about Person One's feelings and needs. A response I would consider empathic is "Are you disappointed because you want to know that your efforts make a difference in how the team does?" The feeling guessed here is disappointment and the needs are contribution and being seen.

4

Creating Shared Reality
via Observations

There is no more difficult art to acquire than the art of observation, and for some men, it is quite difficult to record an observation in brief and plain language.

—WILLIAM OSLER, nineteenth-century Canadian physician

Mario: We need to talk. You're not doing your share around the house. It's not fair that I do everything!

Jake: What are you talking about? I do my share. I don't think you even notice what I do.

In the above dialogue, Mario and Jake are arguing about household chores, and they certainly see the situation differently. One thinks he does "everything"; the other thinks he "does his fair share." In the end, without clarity about what's actually happened, it's unlikely they'll reach any understanding or way forward. What exactly has each of them observed about the housekeeping? What are their *observations*?

An observation is a statement about what you or another has seen or heard, free of any evaluation, judgment, or blame. Imagine you're speaking with a detective about what happened. All the detective wants from you is the "who, what, when, and where," not your

reading or interpretation of actions or events. Or imagine yourself a
fly on the wall, or someone with a video camera capturing the scene.
What exactly does the fly see or the camera record? Even better,
imagine that you're a fly on the wall *with* a camcorder: as impartial as
a fly with the ability to record what you're seeing and hearing.

Clear observation is a key element in resolving conflict and
supporting clarity and shared understanding. Have you ever been
in an argument and realized you and the other person actually *did*
agree? The problem was not in the principles—your values—or
even in the preferred strategy for supporting those values. Rather,
you disagreed over terms, or how you described a situation, not
the situation itself. "Ah, that's what you meant," you say once the
situation becomes clear. "I thought you meant something else!"
Perhaps the reason it had been difficult to hear each other was that
judgments or interpretations were mixed in with observations,
making it hard to see the situation clearly.

You may be thinking, "What's so hard about making
observations? I'm a fair and accurate person. I don't exaggerate. I say
it like it is!" Yet even when we have the best of intentions, judgment
can creep into how we see and describe things. We think our version
of what happened is the "truth"—it seems so obvious and clear to
us!—that what actually happened, on an objective, "just the facts"
level, becomes distorted or obscured.

Let's look at an example. Let's say you were supposed to meet a
friend at 2 p.m. at the cinema. He doesn't arrive until 2:15. You're
irritated because this has happened before—in fact, nearly every
time you've met him. You might say in such a situation, "You're late
again—as usual!" At first glance, this could seem to be an observation.
It's true that he has been late more than once. Yet "late" is an
assessment. The observation is in the details *behind* the assessment.
How do you know he's late? He arrived fifteen minutes after the time
you agreed upon. Click! That's the observation: it's exactly what both
of you would see if it were captured on a video camera.

Are there any other judgments in the statement, "You're late

again—*as usual?* How would a camera record "again" and "usual?"
If you were using a camcorder each time you met, it might record
his arriving at the coffee shop twenty minutes after the agreed-upon
time ten days ago and twenty-five minutes after the agreed-upon
time for lunch a month ago. Add to this today's meeting. So your
observation might be "The last three times we've met, you've arrived
between fifteen and twenty-five minutes after the time we agreed
upon." That's the observation: exactly what happened.

Why do we want to translate words like "always" and "usually"
(adverbs) and words like "late" (adjectives) into clear observations?
In effect, "again" and "usual" offer shorthand versions of our
experience; they are summaries (colored by our opinions),
not descriptions of what actually happened in this instance.
Grammatically, words like "always," "usually," "never," "sometimes,"
"good," "wrong," and "late" (for more examples, see the table on
page 114) are all modifiers and forms of evaluation or judgment.
When used to summarize our experience, they lack specificity
and concreteness. When you say "always," do you mean he's *never*
arrived at the agreed-upon time, not once? Do three times in two
weeks make an "always?" Would you have used "again" if the last
time he was "late" was two months ago? A year ago? A decade ago?
Would you consider him late if he'd arrived within five minutes? Two
minutes? Two seconds? Perhaps you would not consider two seconds
"late" worth mentioning. Would five or ten minutes matter to you
if the situation were a job interview? What if it were your wedding?
How about if you were meeting some friends to go out? You may
think this is splitting hairs, yet definitions of "late" vary widely
between cultures, individuals within the same culture, and even for
the same individual in different situations. The point is that when we
refer to something or someone as "late," what we're really expressing
is that the time the person arrived left some of our needs unmet.

If you recall our discussion about right-and-wrong thinking,
one of the primary elements of this limiting worldview is that
behavior and life are static. You are what you are all the time; it's

not what you're *doing*, but who you *are* that's causing the problem. By using general and evaluative words, you are in fact damning other people (including yourself and those you care about) to a kind of frozen eternity. No one enjoys being stuck in this cold, desolate place. And in a universe of "always" and "never," what room is there for change?

Some Words That Imply Judgment			
All	Always	Constantly	Ever
Extremely	Never	None	Often
Rarely	Repeatedly	Too	Very

EXERCISE 1: Distinguishing Observations From Evaluations

Mark each of the following statements as an "O" if you think it is an observation, or "E" for evaluation, judgment, interpretation, or conclusion. If you mark "E," translate the evaluation into an observation.

_____ A. "Tina stayed in her house for two days."

_____ B. "Bob fixed my computer last night."

_____ C. "John didn't ask why I called him."

_____ D. "My mother is a giving person."

My responses for this exercise:

A. If you marked this item "O," I agree that an observation was expressed without having an evaluation mixed with it.

B. I see this as an evaluation. In my mind, "fixed" is a matter of opinion. I remember a dispute with an auto repair center that claimed it had fixed my car. I did not agree; I did agree that it had replaced some parts. In this B statement, an example of an observation might be "Bob did a great job of fixing my computer last night."

C. If you marked "O," I agree that it expresses an observation without having an evaluation mixed with it.

D. I believe that "a giving person" is an evaluation. An observation without evaluation might be "For the last three years, my mother has volunteered at a homeless shelter one day a week."

EXERCISE 2: Tracking Judgments

For a few hours or a day this week, carry a small notebook or some index cards with you. Write down any judgments you notice yourself making during that time about yourself, others, or the world.

When I started paying attention to the judgments I was making, it was almost overwhelming. Every time I see someone, I'm thinking about how they're dressed, what they're doing, whether I trust them or like them. Or else I'm thinking about me and whether I'm doing something wrong.

—MARY BETH

A. What do you notice about your judgments? Is there a pattern?

B. Were there more judgments about yourself or others?

C. Were the judgments mostly "positive" or "negative"? (About needs met or unmet?)

D. How do your judgments generalize ("globalize") a situation or make it static?

E. Translate each judgment into observations, feelings, and needs. Remember when making observations, you need to imagine having a camcorder and include only that which would be recorded on video and audio. Check that your observations are free of adjectives and adverbs.

Taking Full Responsibility for What We See and Hear

There's a third element to an observation you may have noticed—perhaps the most important and dramatic aspect of all. When we are making a judgment about another person, we're talking about *them—and that's the focus.* "*You're* always late!" If we're focused on someone else rather than what's going on inside ourselves (our own observations, feelings, and needs), the likelihood of a judgment occurring increases by a quantum leap. A pure observation, in contrast, will concern *our* experience. In the classical NVC model, it starts with an "I" phrase such as "When I see . . . ," "When I hear . . . ," or "When I think about . . . " Even though you may be seeing, hearing, or thinking about another person's action, when you start out in the first person, you're taking responsibility for and ownership of what you're seeing and hearing.

In my experience, at least half of all conflicts occur simply as a result of lack of information, or misinformation. Nine times out of ten, people don't clarify or confirm what they're seeing or hearing. As a result, they're drawing conclusions about something that may in fact not have happened (or actually did happen when they thought it didn't). This is why it can be helpful to take full responsibility for what we're seeing and hearing. I recently attended an NVC program, for example, during which I made a few points. Later someone told me he was disappointed I wasn't included more in the conversation. This surprised me. I told him I had seen myself as very included, especially given that the facilitator had not known I was going to attend and we had never met before. When I shared this, the whole situation shifted for the person. He'd assumed that the facilitator and I had known each other for years and that we were both leading the program together! He became excited about the way I'd been included. What had changed? The information and how he was seeing things. By starting our observations with an "I" statement, including observations about what we're thinking, we can take full responsibility for our experiences.

EXERCISE 3: Taking Responsibility for Our Experience

    A. Think of a judgment, opinion, or evaluation that you've made. How was this based on a particular interpretation or reading of events? Did the information you had change at any point? How did that impact your subsequent judgment?

    B. Look at a judgment you wrote down in your judgment journal about someone else. How does it involve blaming another person? Rewrite it as an observation, using a phrase such as "When I see . . ." or "When I hear . . ." or "When I think about . . ." How does starting in that way change the quality of what you're reporting and lead to taking more responsibility for your experience?

First Aid for Observations: Your Inner Video Camera . . . and "PLATO"

Every week for several years, a woman attending an NVC practice group I led would say, "My boss is an idiot—and that's an observation!" Is it really an observation to say that someone is an "idiot?" What actions or behaviors do you think she experienced with her boss that led her to have this opinion of him? What would the observation be? What would a camcorder show?

Similarly, I was once teaching a group about observations and asked for an example. A person in the group who was a vegan (she eats neither meat nor dairy products) enthusiastically offered, "The vegetarians in my house are polluting my butter knife!" Wanting to support her in coming up with what I would consider an observation, I asked her: "What does this look like? What would a camcorder catch on film about the butter knife?" To this she emphatically replied, "The vegetarians are *contaminating* my butter knife!" If you imagine that you had a camcorder, what do you think you would *see* happening? What was being done to the butter knife in this situation, with the vegetarians and the vegans sharing a meal?

The video camera idea is more than a theory: it really works! Let's put it into practice. Imagine you have an actual camcorder in your hands, and "see" and "hear" in your mind's eye what it is capturing. When I applied this practice to the butter knife, I immediately got clear: the vegetarians had taken a knife that the person in the group used for spreading soy margarine and used it for dairy butter. For the vegan, this was the form of "contamination." Watching the scene through the camcorder's lens, all I saw was that a butter knife had been moved.

Regarding the "idiot" boss, it was clear that the woman attending the practice group didn't like the way the boss was managing and handling things. When we applied the camcorder technique, we got concrete details. Several times, the boss asked for details regarding a client they were working with, and each time, after receiving the notes, he could not locate them and asked for them again. In another incident, a woman named Pema joined the staff; after four months, the boss was heard several times pronouncing the person's name "Pammy." If we were using our camcorder, we would find numerous other observations that led to the woman having judgments of her boss. The judgment "idiot," just like the words "good," "bad," "best," and "contaminated," lack specificity. We really have no idea what is being described with these words until we get observations. All we learn from the judgment words is the intensity of the emotional trigger the speaker is experiencing.

To locate the level of specificity we seek, in addition to the camcorder practice, it can be helpful to include PLATO in our observations: person, location, action, time, and object. When we say that three times this week the vegetarians in the household took a knife that was at the table to use with the dairy butter, we have in this observation: person (the vegetarians), location (at the table), action (used), time (three times this week), and object (knife, soy margarine, and dairy butter). With this level of detail, we have a clear and concrete observation. PLATO helps us to include all that a camcorder would record.

Regarding the example of the person being late to the cinema, the observation also includes PLATO: "The last three times we've met, you've arrived between fifteen and twenty-five minutes after the time we agreed upon." We have person ("we" and "you"), location (implied—at the cinema and other places), action (met), and time (fifteen to twenty-five minutes late). In this case, there is no object (as there was in the butter knife example). Even if every element of PLATO is not present, to arrive at a clear observation, it is still helpful to include as much of PLATO as we can.*

EXERCISE 4: Including Your Friend PLATO

A. Look at the observations regarding the woman's boss who was called an idiot. Identify PLATO in each one.
B. Go back to some judgments you recorded in your judgment journal. Translate one or two judgments, making sure to include PLATO.
C. How is using PLATO similar to using a camcorder when coming up with observations?

Owning Judgments

Shazam: You're driving too fast!
Terri: No, I'm not.
Shazam: Stop yelling!
Terri: What makes you think I'm yelling?!

---

* It is my understanding that Miki Kashtan of Bay NVC first developed this concept of PLATO to support coming up with clear, positive, and doable requests. I also think it works well with creating clear observations.

Sometimes it's challenging to convert a judgment to an observation. It requires equipment, for example, to measure volume, speed, or time with accuracy. If someone is walking or cycling "too fast" for you and you don't have a speedometer, how do you put time into your observation? And how do you know how fast is "too" fast? When road conditions are icy or wet, driving at the posted speed limit can seem "too" fast. What if you say someone is talking "too loud"? It's not as if you have a volume meter with numbers on it to reference. We may find a poem or another work of art wistful, sad, and moving, yet how do we give "observables" for the complexity of that experience?

In all these cases, we can often still put PLATO into our observations to make them concrete. For example, you could say to someone, "You're driving about two times as fast as I feel comfortable with, given the road conditions." Or "You're speaking at about a third of the volume I need to hear you easily." It can also be helpful to "own" the judgment, to indicate that the event or behavior is not what you enjoy or value. This "ownership" takes your words out of the realm of moralistic judgment and shows your view for what it is: a preference or value. You can "own" a judgment by adding a tag to your statement, such as "In my opinion . . . ," or "In my judgment . . . ," or "I would consider that (to be) X." So, for example, Shazam could have said, "In my opinion, we're driving way too fast to be safe given the curves on this road." Similarly, when describing a work of art, you could comment, "For me, that's the most moving and beautiful work I've seen in this show—look at those colors!" Taking ownership of our judgments in this way is different from saying "This is the best piece in the show."

If someone gives you a judgment or evaluation, you can also clarify the situation by offering an observation, or at least owning your own assessment. For example, when Shazam said, "Stop yelling!" Terri could have replied: "I'm surprised to hear you say that. I wouldn't consider this 'yelling.' And I'm willing to lower my voice if that would help you feel more comfortable." A shorthand way of taking ownership of our judgments is to use a feeling word to describe how we're experiencing the situation. For example, rather than saying, "That's an obnoxious comment to make," we could say, "I'm irritated hearing that . . ." and then share what needs are left unmet for us.

EXERCISE 5: Owning Our Judgments

Take each judgment below and rewrite it so that the person speaking is taking responsibility for the judgment they're making, shifting the statement from judgment to opinion. Try using feeling words.

Example:
    Judgment: "That's a stupid thing to say."
    Ownership: "I'm irritated hearing that . . ."

    A. Judgment: "Beethoven's Ninth Symphony is inspirational and uplifting."
        Opinion: _____

    B. Judgment: "There's no better sport than women's basketball."
        Opinion: _____

    C. Judgment: "Stop bothering me!"
        Opinion: _____

    D. Judgment: "Can't you move any faster?"
        Opinion: _____

Flying Solo With Observations

While the NVC model includes four steps—observations, feelings, needs, and requests—I often find that just practicing the observation step can be helpful in itself. When I'm triggered by something that happens, I simply keep bringing my attention back to the observation until I find a level of perspective and calm. For example, say someone bumps into me on the street when they walk by. My judgments and stories might spiral out: *How can they be so inconsiderate? Why did they push me? Didn't they see me? What am I, chopped chicken liver? Why didn't they say, "Excuse me"?* At those moments, I can remind myself exactly what happened: someone walked into me. On an observation level, that's all that happened. Everything else, including the word "pushed" and my calling them "inconsiderate," is an interpretation and a judgment. The more I go into my judgments and stories, escalating and globalizing what happened, the more agitated I can become. If I repeatedly bring back what happened to the observation, I can separate out what happened from my interpretations, which really have nothing to do with what happened.

In a similar fashion, if I'm talking to someone who has been emotionally triggered and is in a place of judgment, bringing what they are saying back to an observation can also be grounding. For example, someone says to you, "You never listen to me!" Rather than disagreeing or giving your side, you could simply make a guess about what the observation is. "You've asked me several times not to bring up this topic when we're trying to get out of the house, right?" Once the person has let you know the observation "fits," you can make a feelings and needs guess. "And I bet that's really frustrating because you've asked me this several times?" and "You want to trust that I can track things like this?" Even if you don't get to the feelings and needs steps, clarifying the observation can contribute to the other person experiencing being heard and understood. Other forms of inviting an observation in this situation could include asking the speaker for an example: "I just heard you say that I never listen to you. Can you give me an example so I can get what you mean?" Or inversely, when expressing your own needs: "I'm wondering if you can think of one time that I did hear you? I'd like some balance and perspective—and shared understanding—of the number of times that I have listened to you and understood what you were saying."

Expanding the Road Map

In the last chapter, we suggested a "classical NVC" formula to use as a road map when first using NVC. The NVC model includes four basic steps: observations, feelings, needs, and requests (OFNR). In the next chapter, we will look at requests in detail. For the moment, however, our road map looks like the following:

The NVC Model—First 3 Steps

Observation(s): When I see/hear/think about _____
_____ (observation),
Feeling(s): I am feeling _____ (feeling), because
Need(s): I'm needing _____ (need).

Take Two

How does the NVC model sound when put together? Suppose your boss came to you and said, "I can't believe how irresponsible you are! Is it too much to return a phone call to someone?" Imagine that, rather than a judgment, your boss offered a clear observation, feeling, need, and request:

> I just heard from Mr. Smith that he left two phone messages last week and hasn't heard back (observation). I'm concerned about this (feeling), especially given how important a client he is for us. I want the company to be sustainable—I also want a level of responsiveness in how we do business (needs). I'm wondering what happened on your end—did you get those messages? (request)

How does hearing a clear observation, along with feelings, needs, and a request, shift the way you hear this concern? You probably have more clarity and understanding about the situation and what's actually happened, at least from your boss's perspective. Hearing what your boss is feeling and needing, you may also have some understanding about why she is so agitated and concerned.

Regardless of where the conversation goes from here, by starting out with a clear observation we at least know what is being discussed. We can see "apples from oranges." A clear observation creates a strong foundation for supporting connection and understanding. Looking at the example above, the observation makes clear what the trigger is for your boss. Perhaps you have information your boss doesn't have, such as that you were out sick the week before. Or perhaps you have returned Mr. Smith's calls and you're baffled as to why he's not received your messages. Regardless of what's happened, by exchanging observations, much of the "charge" can be taken out of challenging conversations.

If you think about it, judgments and evaluations can be seen as mixing up the four steps of the NVC model and jamming them together. When we have a strong opinion, the energy behind the judgment is our feeling; what triggered our feeling is the observation; and what we're really longing to experience in that moment is the need being met. By expressing our experience via observations, feelings, and needs—and then making a request to meet our needs— we are simply stating our experience in a way that it can be easily heard and understood.

In the next chapter, in which we focus on requests, you will get to practice the whole model together in its entirety. First, though, here are two more exercises to help you further integrate this chapter.

INTEGRATION: Questions and Exercises to Further Explore Chapter 4

A. Mark each of the following statements as an "O" if you think it is an observation or an "E" if you think it is an evaluation, judgment, interpretation, or conclusion. If you mark "E," compose an observation for the situation.

    _____ 1.   "Amber often sleeps around."
    _____ 2.   "Dan is confused."
    _____ 3.   "My friend arrived late for our lunch meeting."
    _____ 4.   "My son usually doesn't shower."
    _____ 5.   "Denise thinks she looks better in black."
    _____ 6.   "My stepmom complains for no reason."

My responses for this exercise:

1. I believe that "sleeps around" is an evaluation. An observation free of evaluation might be "Amber has gone home with three different guys this week."
2. I see "confused" as an evaluation. An observation without evaluation might be "Last week, Dan said he wants to leave the company and start his own business, and this week he says he is working hard to get the promotion he hopes to get."
3. I consider "late" as an evaluation. An observation might be "My friend arrived at 12:20 p.m., and the email said we would meet at noon."
4. I believe that "usually" is an evaluation. An observation without evaluation might be "My son showered four times this month."
5. A pure observation in this case would be "Denise said, 'I think I look better in black'" or "I heard Denise say that she thinks she looks better in black."
6. I believe that "for no reason" and "complains" are evaluations. An observation without evaluation might be "At the restaurant last night, my stepmom described something she disliked about each of the dishes that was served, and ate all that was on her plate."

B. Look at the photos on the following page. Give a judgment about each and then an observation. In giving observations, make them as specific as possible and make sure to include PLATO.

C. Think of a situation that you found challenging. Take a large piece of paper and at the top, write your judgment about what happened. Then imagine that you had a camcorder and were using "stop frame"—with stills from the video you recorded. Draw a simple picture from each "still" of what happened. Based on the stills, write at the bottom of your paper an observation free of evaluation.

D. Listen to the news or read a story in the newspaper or online. Find a judgment that someone has given—perhaps about politics, the economy, or social or cultural issues. Based on the context in the news article, write an observation free of evaluation based on the judgment provided.

E. Think of someone in your life from whom you hear judgments and evaluations. Practice writing a dialogue in which you hear them share a judgment. Then practice in the dialogue requesting an observation such as "I hear you saying X . . .; can you give me an example of when you've heard me say that?"

F. Think of a situation where you've given opinions and didn't acknowledge doing so. Go back and write down versions of your opinions where you take responsibility for them, such as "In my view . . ." or "The way I say this is . . ."

5

Fostering Trust and Collaboration: The Power of Requests

*Cats seem to go on the principle that it never does
any harm to ask for what you want.*

—JOSEPH WOOD KRUTCH

As we saw in chapter 4, by making use of observations we can foster shared understanding about each person's experience. This creates the foundation for hearing each other's feelings and needs, furthering empathic connection. The last step of the model, requests, brings this connection and shared understanding to completion and explores how the needs of all parties might be addressed. Making requests—which involves openness to others' needs and strategies while also holding your own needs as vital—is a crucial practice in fostering collaboration.

In many ways, observations and requests are similar; they are like bookends at either end of the NVC process. Observations involve an objective, concrete description of what you *have* experienced; requests, in turn, involve a clear, positive, and doable account of what you'd *like* to see happen. Both observations and requests concern the exterior, outside world—the ways in which needs can be met. Feelings and needs, in contrast, concern our internal terrain.

You can imagine the interplay of these external and internal experiences by imagining an infinity symbol. One loop represents your internal world of feelings and needs, and the other represents your observations and requests of the external world. There is a continual flow between the two.

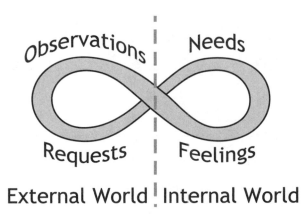

Observations | Needs

Requests | Feelings

External World | Internal World

Source illustration by Hadassah Hill

Without a clear request, neither party can know for sure what would contribute to meeting the needs and fostering the well-being of the other: the loop or cycle is left incomplete. We all have a desire to contribute in life; by making and hearing requests, we explore what will best meet our needs and those of others.

In this chapter, we will focus on the intention behind requests and then explore several types of requests as practiced in the NVC model: connection requests, strategy requests (clear, positive, and doable), and group requests. Each kind of request is about seeing how we can meet needs and hold everyone's needs with care. Ultimately, as is the case with every step of the NVC model, requests are about fostering connection.

What Is the Essence of a Request?

The key element of a request is neither the form it takes nor its content; it is intention. A request comes from a place of openness and curiosity and a genuine caring about the concerns of both parties. It's about flexibility with respect to *how* your needs are met while caring that both *your* needs and the needs of the *other* matter. When we have strong attachment to a particular strategy, we run into the potential for misunderstanding, conflict, and even violence. If we have the mistaken belief that only *this* particular strategy can meet our needs, we can become desperate if others don't agree or act on that strategy. In the end, it is our own responsibility to see that our needs are met.

In this spirit, the key requirement for the request step of the NVC model is that the request be *free of demand*. In NVC, we acknowledge this openness by beginning requests with the phrase, "Would you be willing to . . .?" This tagline expresses the spirit of curiosity and invitation we want to embody when making requests. As we will explore in detail in this chapter, another way to confirm the spirit of a request is to check whether we are open to hearing "no" in response to our question. If we are unwilling to hear "no," we are not truly making a request; we are making a demand. And who likes to hear ultimatums or demands?

Freeing Ourselves and Others From Demands

Demands can take various forms: the words we use, our body language, and our tone of voice. Most often, in words, demands are stated with phrases such as "You have to . . . ," "You must . . . ," or "You should . . ." Demands can also take the form of stated or implied punishment, threats, or consequences (positive and negative), often making use of collocations such as "If you don't do X then I'll . . . " or

" . . . you'll have to . . ." Demand is especially likely to creep in when one person is in a position of authority, power, or control—when there is a power differential. This can be seen when a parent says to a child, "Eat your vegetables and you'll get dessert" or "Listen to me or else!" We can also see power differentials expressed at work: "If you work every weekend this month and get the project done, you'll all get a bonus" or "If you do this once more, you're fired!" Demand can also creep into our most intimate relationships, the place we most want to believe our needs matter. If we perceive that they don't, we can become especially fearful, disappointed, and forceful: "If you don't listen to me (or do X), then why should I ___?" or "If you really loved me, you would . . ."

Sometimes in our own eyes, our demands can seem reasonable, "fair," and necessary. Our urgency may seem justified. "You have to stop smoking—you're ruining your health!" or "Don't take the job—it's bad for your career!" Yet take a moment and consider how often there is true urgency. If I saw flames and smelled smoke, I am sure I would not say, "The house is on fire. Would you be willing to leave the building?" I would probably shout, with great urgency: "Fire! Get out of the house!" If someone is crossing the street into the path of an oncoming car, I'd also use an imperative: "Pay attention!" "Watch out!" These kinds of moments, though, are rare in life. A trainer I know works in a hospital where the staff is integrating NVC into its work. While they often deal with life-and-death situations, even ER staff has found that the need for imperative demands—when injury might otherwise occur—is rare (perhaps occurring 10 percent of the time).

Take a moment to think about how you experience demands. Do you enjoy being told what to do, especially in a forceful way, with urgency or threatened consequences? When you hear a demand associated with an idea, are you more open or closed to it? Given that we value autonomy and choice, when we hear demands (in any form) we are likely to go into a place of disagreement, resistance, and—especially over time—rebellion.

I see this regularly in workplaces and in couples and families. Often, the lack of a perceived choice can lead to what I would consider passive resistance and lack of communication. In work environments, for example, a person will not complete a task, or will pass it on to someone else without comment. A staff person says one thing and does another, changes departments, or quits. In couples and families, this can lead to what I call "fire walls." Young children throw temper tantrums, teenagers do the opposite of what their parents are telling them to do (even if the behavior is dangerous), and with couples, I hear expressions such as "I've had enough! I'm not listening to you anymore!" At first, making a demand can seem an effective way to meet needs. In the end, though, no one's needs are met when demands are at play. Maintaining the intention and awareness of *holding all needs with care* (ours and those of others, in a spirit of collaboration) dramatically impacts the quality and outcome of the decisions we make.

Ultimately, demands often backfire, leading to the opposite result of what we want (immediately and/or in the long term). If someone hears or interprets a demand in our words or actions—if they sense they're going to be punished, even in a mild way, for not giving us what we want—they're more likely to refuse our request or comply begrudgingly. Do we really want the people in our lives to take actions they are not inspired or motivated to take? If they do, it may us give some ease in the immediate moment. In the long run, though, it is likely to leave needs unmet, including our own.

In this context, as an NVC trainer, I often ask two questions that help me come up with "juicy" (appealing) and truly connected requests: *What do we want someone to do? And why do we want them to do it?* Unless both questions are addressed, the end result is often unsatisfactory. Imagine, for example, you are a parent who wants your child to complete a homework assignment. Do you want the child to do their homework because they want their allowance, or they want to go out with friends? Or would you like them to complete it because you want them to value learning? In a work environment, do you want someone to complete a task because they think they "have to" or because they see how their work is meaningful and contributes to the organization?

A Recipe for Requests

Marshall Rosenberg has written the following instructions regarding requests. These guidelines—which you may wish to hang up somewhere in your home or workplace—offer a handy reminder of the principles we are exploring:

> *Please do not fulfill my request*:
>   Out of guilt, shame, fear, duty, or obligation;
>   because you think you "should";
>   to gain my affection or acceptance;
>   because you are afraid of how I'll react if you don't.

> *Please fulfill my request only if*:
>   You are giving from the heart . . . joyfully.
>   You are doing it from a need to contribute;
>   it meets some other need or value of yours.

Inspired by this spirit of requests, Conal Elliot has created a brief formula to support making requests from a place of true openness and inquiry. The next time you're making a request, consider whether you can imagine making the following statement:

> It would really meet my need for (state need here) if you would be willing to (state request here), and I am totally open to meeting my need in other ways if that doesn't work for you.

Even without speaking this phrase aloud with another person, by trying out this formula before speaking, you can check that your request is truly a request and that you are, in fact, open to hearing "no."

EXERCISE 1: Living Free of Demands

A. Think of a situation where you made a demand. What was the end result? How did your making a demand impact the quality of your connection with the other person and/or the outcome?

B. Now think of a situation where you heard a demand. How did hearing a demand impact your willingness to take action?

C. Think of a demand you have made that has a "should" or "have to" in it. Translate that "should" into observations, feelings, and needs. Then write down a request including the words "Would you be willing . . .?" For example, concerning smoking, you could write: "When I see how much you're smoking, I'm really concerned about your health—I care about you. I wonder if you'd be willing to talk with me about it?"

D. Think of something you'd like to see happen, such as a child in your family interacting differently with a sibling or a colleague handling something differently at work. Ask yourself the two "juicy request" questions: *What do you want this person to do? and Why do you want them to do it?* In answering the second question, you may wish to look at the needs list (see page 368) and focus on the needs that would be met for you.

E. Reread the formula for requests that Marshal Rosenberg created. Imagine that every action in your home, workplace, community, or faith-based organization was conducted in this spirit. How would this impact the quality of work, connection, trust, and collaboration in these communities?

F. With some demands, you can hear the caring underneath someone's urgency (such as in the example above regarding smoking). In this case, the demand is really a cry for help: a cry for attention and action. Think of such a demand that you've heard from someone in your life. What feelings and needs are underneath that demand?

G. Take a moment and imagine hearing an urgent "have to" or "should" in someone's voice. How do you feel hearing that, including in your body? Now take a moment and imagine hearing a request from someone who first shared their feelings and needs and then said, "Would you be willing to . . .?" How do you feel now, including in your body?

Connecting Through Requests

Once we are aligned with the true spirit of requests, the spirit of openness and collaboration, we can focus on the main objective: connection. This is most often achieved through starting with what we call a "connection request." A connection request checks in about some aspect of a person's present experience: what they are thinking, feeling, needing, or understanding. This shared experience moves discussions forward and creates clarity around next steps, including action steps. Connection requests are especially useful when there is conflict, or strong feelings have been stimulated in either party.

There are two basic kinds of connection requests. One is called reflecting (or mirroring) and is a recap of what you've heard someone say in terms of content. By reflecting you can ensure you've made yourself clear on a cognitive level, or that you have clearly heard what the other person has said. The other kind of connection request is about feelings or response: what's going on for the other person when they hear what's "up" for you. This second kind of connection request can be grouped under "checking-in" requests. We will explore each kind of connection request in turn.

Reflecting Thoughts

Sometimes, especially if a situation is charged or if you're not sure you've heard someone with clarity, it can be helpful to reflect back a person's thoughts or judgments before listening empathically. Reflecting in this way can alleviate one of the most common forms of miscommunication: simply mishearing what another person has said. Such "mishearings" and "misunderstandings" can easily lead to disconnection and conflict. What might you do if the listener reflects back a message very different from what you intended? Consider this example between Jill and her husband, Ryan.

> *Jill:* When you spent most of last night talking with the other women and didn't spend more than ten minutes with me, I was pretty upset. I wanted to be with you and to have fun together. I didn't want to leave the party and make a "scene." But I wasn't enjoying myself. I was hurt. That was why I decided to walk home and left. I'm feeling nervous—our relationship is very important to me, and I really want to make sure I'm being clear. Could you tell me what you just heard me say?
>
> *Ryan:* Well, you're saying that I made you leave?

Jill sees that Ryan has fulfilled her request; he told her what he heard, and she is grateful for that. Now it's clear that there is a discrepancy between what she wanted to communicate and what he heard, and this allows her to address this fundamental gap in understanding without blaming him for "misunderstanding" or herself for "speaking unclearly." She also has an opportunity to express herself again, and to see if there is now congruence between what she wanted to communicate and what he took in. The next round of conversation might go like this:

Jill: Thanks for telling me what you heard. What I want to say and be heard around is that I chose to leave. And I really want you to understand what was going on for me and why I made that decision.

Rather than saying, "See, you just don't listen" or "But I didn't say that," Jill can simply let Ryan know that what he reflected back does not match what she wants to communicate.

When reflecting, it's helpful to use "I" statements and take responsibility for what you're hearing. After all, it's not until you've checked with someone that you can know for sure if you've heard what they wanted to express. Rather than beginning with "You said . . .," you can start with "What I'm hearing is . . ." or "What I heard you say is . . ." and then reflect back the content. In doing so, you are giving a summary or "headline" version of what you heard the person say (so the conversation can move forward). It can also be helpful to frame your connection request by sharing what you're feeling and needing when you offer or request a reflection: "I'm nervous about how many words I just used to explain and want to make sure I'm making this clear. Could you tell me what you've heard me say?"

Reflection can support our conversations in many different ways. Here are a few of them, along with examples of both requesting and offering reflection.

Different Uses of Reflection

Clarity (Wanting to check what you heard or what others heard you say)

Requesting: I'm noticing the number of words I've used, and am not sure I've made this clear. Could you tell me back what you heard me say?

Offering: I'm feeling a little overwhelmed with what I've
heard. Can I tell you back what I've heard so far, to
make sure I got it?

Accuracy (Revisiting what's been said)

Requesting: I'm hearing you respond to something that
doesn't match what I recall saying. So I'm wondering
if we could pause for a moment and just check what
you heard me say a moment ago?

Offering: You know, I'm hearing you say something now that
sounds different from what I heard before. Can I
check with you that I'm getting it?

Pacing/Being Heard (Wanting to slow down the pace of the
conversation, foster connection)

Requesting: Would you be willing to tell me what you've
heard me say so far? I appreciate that I'm sharing a
lot with you and want to see what I'm getting across
. . . and how it's being heard.

Offering: I'm noticing the pace of our conversation and
feeling concerned, really wanting us to hear each
other and be connected. I'm wondering if we could
just take a breath and then I can tell you what I've
heard so far?

Integration (Taking in new learning, including from empathy)

Requesting: Wow. This is really big for me. I want to make
sure I'm taking it in. Could you tell me back what
you heard me say, to help me digest it?

Offering: I think this is a really important piece. So I want to
reflect this back to you, to support your integrating
it, and really taking it in . . .

Note that reflection is often used in tandem with other NVC
support skills such as interruption, taking a breath, and self-empathy.
All of these supports can help pace conversations and support

connection. Also, while we refer to this practice here as "reflection," you can use different words to describe it, depending on who you are speaking to. Sometimes at work, for example, I might say, "Can you recap this for me?" or when wanting to be colloquial (such as when speaking with youth), I might say, "Can someone give me a headline on what I just said?" Regardless of how you refer to reflection, practicing it can help support clarity, connection, and understanding.

EXERCISE 2: Reflecting on Reflection

A. Think back to a conversation where misunderstanding or disconnection occurred. How might it have been helpful to reflect back what one or both parties were saying to support clarity, shared understanding, and/or pacing?

B. Think of a conversation you engaged in today. Write down three reflection requests you could have made during that conversation, along with the feelings and needs that would have prompted each request.

C. Reflection requests can go both ways: offered and requested. Take the three reflection requests you wrote for number two above and switch the direction: if you were offering to reflect, change the request so that you were asking the other person to reflect. For example:

Original: Would you be willing to tell me what you just heard me say? I'm concerned with how complicated I've made all this, and am not sure it's clear.

Reversed direction: I'm getting a bit lost with the number of details I've heard and am not sure I'm clear about what you're saying. Can I tell it back to you to make sure I'm understanding you?

Connection Requests for Checking In

Reflection requests are just one way to foster shared understanding and connection. We can also inquire about how a person is feeling: whether they have a sense of being heard and are ready to hear our views, and whether they're ready to move on to another topic, among other examples. These kinds of connection requests can be grouped under "checking in"—getting a "weather report" on what is going on for the other person. The classic way of checking in is to simply ask: "How do you feel, hearing me say this?" The following are some other reasons to check in with connection requests and examples of how you might do so.

Different Uses of Connection Requests

A. *More information:* Are you open to hearing an idea? Can I tell you a bit more about this?

B. *Completion:* Are you complete with what you wanted to share? Is there anything else you want to add?

C. *Soliciting opinions:* I'm wondering what you think about this? What are your thoughts?

D. *Setting the bar:* Do you object to this plan? Are you uncomfortable with this? Is this something you could imagine doing?

E. *General check-in:* How is this sounding to you? How does this land with you? What's up for you hearing this? Are you OK with this plan?

Connection requests, whatever their form, are key to holding the mind-set and intention of NVC, which is about fostering collaboration and win-win solutions. It is through connection requests that we discover the ways in which our experience and view of things resonate with the other person. It's also how we become aware of their feelings and needs and how they're seeing things. From this shared understanding, we can explore strategies and find those that truly work for both parties, embodying the full expression of requests and arriving at requests both parties can energetically say "yes!" to. Often, even when we have the best of intentions, conversations break down because one person moves prematurely into a strategy. Or one person agrees to something that they're not fully on board with, which impacts the relationship moving forward and how the strategy is implemented. Connection requests offer the best assurance that both parties are moving forward in a unified, concordant way.

EXERCISE 3: Connecting With Connection Requests

A. Think of a situation you're unhappy about. Write an observation (O) and then your feelings (F) and needs (N). Then write three possible connection requests you could make after sharing an observation, feeling, and need.

B. Think of a conflict, or a conversation that didn't go as well as you would have liked. Looking back on it, did one or both parties move prematurely to a strategy? How would making a connection request have supported a better outcome?

The overall purposes of connection requests are to increase trust and understanding between parties and to keep the dialogue open until a mutually satisfying solution can be found. If you are confident about the quality of connection, you may instead wish to go directly to a strategy, offering a solution-oriented or action request: for example, "Would you be willing to return this book to the library for me today?" If the proposed solution request does not work impeccably for both parties, then it is time to return to connection requests: requesting reflection or check-ins to ensure that both parties hear each other and can hold with care the other's needs.

Making Powerful Requests

Once trust and understanding around each person's feelings and needs are established, it's natural and organic to move to strategy or action requests. In fact, not moving to action steps at this point can be frustrating and disconnecting. As Marshall Rosenberg has commented, sharing our needs without making a request creates a form of hell, because we all deeply desire to contribute to life and to others' well-being. Hearing about someone's needs, especially when expressing feelings associated with unmet needs, can quickly become overwhelming and, ultimately, can be heard as a judgment or demand. If you don't include a request in your communication, it may feel unresolved and incomplete.

Let me share an example. Once I was working with a couple who had come to see me for support in their relationship. One of them repeated several times that he wanted caring: "Caring! Caring! Is that too much to ask? I just want caring!" I could only imagine how many times his wife had heard this before. He'd learned a bit about NVC and was familiar with the needs part of the model. He hadn't, though, included an observation or a request. As a result, he was "stuck" on this need, without it being fully heard or met.

When I asked him, "What would that *look* like?" we easily came up with a request. He was fatigued with the number of times he'd started to tell his wife a story, only to have her interrupt him with something that was going on with her instead. He saw these interruptions as proof that she didn't care. His request was simple: the next time he started to tell a story, he wanted to complete his story before she offered to share something about her day. While this single act may not have completely addressed his desire for caring in the relationship, it was surprisingly relieving and powerful, especially considering the number of times he'd spoken about this need before without indicating a clear way for his wife to contribute to meeting it.

Making Requests Real: Clear, Positive, Doable, and Present-Oriented

To be effective, it is important that action requests are *clear, positive, doable,* and *present-oriented,* or CPDP. When action requests meet the CPDP criteria, they are both easier to hear and easier to act upon. We will consider each of these qualities in turn.

Specificity Supports Clarity

The first quality, clarity, refers to the extent to which different people hearing the same request have a similar understanding of what the requester would like to see happen. When requests are vague or general instead of clear or concrete, we may be unsure whether or not the request has been fulfilled. Say a parent says to a child, "I want you to be respectful of your grandparents when we visit." What does that mean? The child may think he is being respectful, while the parent doesn't think so. How can either of them tell? What would that look like? Does the parent want the child to assist the grandmother in the kitchen with the dirty dishes? Does she want him to ask permission before leaving the dining table? Or does she want him to refrain from speaking when the grandparent is speaking and say "excuse me" before he does speak? Coming up with a clear and concrete request is a helpful way to get clarity about what *you* want; it then helps the other person fulfill the request.

Sometimes, when there is a lack of specificity or understanding about what is actually being requested, it may seem impossible to even attempt to fulfill it. Let's say, for example, that Juanita is upset with Mark because he arrives later for their dates than she likes. So she asks him, "Can you please be on time?" What is her definition of "on time" and how does that compare with his? As we discussed earlier, there are huge individual and cultural differences in the meaning of "late" and "on time." To make this clear and concrete, she could formulate her request this way: "Can you meet me next time within ten minutes of the time we've agreed?" Or she might say, "It's really troubling me how many times you're arrived ten to fifteen minutes after the time we've agreed to meet. I'm wondering if you'd be open to talking about this?"

Let's look at another example. Ted's father is angry because Ted has maxed out his credit cards and doesn't have money for textbooks for the spring semester. He tells Ted he wants him "to be responsible." What would that consist of? Might there be differences of opinion between Ted and his father about whether he had fulfilled the request? If instead, the request is specific and without a judgment, Ted is likely to be far more willing and able to act on his father's wishes.

I've also heard similar kinds of "nonrequests" in work situations. When working with an organization, I heard that during a review session a supervisor had said he wanted the employee to "show more teamwork." The employee was confused, especially because he thought he already was a "team player." He asked the boss, "What do you mean by teamwork?" and the boss replied, "You know—teamwork!" What would have supported clarity here is a clear observation (about what had happened to prompt this vague request) or, since the supervisor wanted a change in behavior, a clear request. He could have said, for example, "The next time you're working on a project, I'd love for you to check with two other people impacted by it to see if what you're planning works for them."

To help make requests specific and concrete in this way, we can include the same elements we use for observations: PLATO (person, location, action, time, and object). Let's look at the example of Ted again. When his father says he wants him to be "responsible," there is a person (Ted), yet no action ("being" is not an action; it is a verb that links to an adjective or predicate adjective, in this case, "responsible"). There is no time, location, or object. A request that is clear and concrete and has all the elements of PLATO could include, for example, Ted creating a budget before the next semester starts, or his agreeing to take on a part-time job during the next semester so he will have sufficient funds to buy books. The request could simply be that Tim make a time during the next week to hear his father's concerns and consider some strategies that might work for both of them. Each of these has PLATO in it.

Think Positive

When a request is positive, we're asking for something we *do* want rather than something we *don't want*. Why is this important? Positivity in requests contributes greatly to clarity. If I ask you to go get us some ice cream and tell you I don't want vanilla, there may be dozens of other flavors available. It would be very easy for you to bring back another flavor that I also don't like. In contrast, if I ask for chocolate, rocky road, or mint chip, you have a clear idea of what I want. Unless none of those flavors are available, it will be quite clear and easy to meet my request.

Let's look at a more complex example. Say you're concerned about tripping over something and you want some order in your room. You request that your partner pick her clothes up off the floor. If you ask her not to leave her clothes on the floor, next week she might very well leave her books on the floor. You would have an even better chance of seeing your needs met if you simply asked her to keep the floor clear of any objects so you can have a sense of safety and avoid falling.

In addition to gaining clarity and concreteness, by stating our request in a positive way, we're inviting ourselves and others to move *toward* what we want. It also helps us get clear about what we truly *do* want. It can take a bit more effort and imagination than simply focusing on what we don't want—what's not working. It greatly increases the odds, though, that we will get to experience what we truly desire in life.

EXERCISE 4: Making Requests Crystal Clear

Part One

To practice identifying and expressing clear requests, place a checkmark next to any of the following statements in which you think the speaker is requesting that a positive, specific action be done. Create a clear and concrete request for statements you leave unchecked.

_____ A. "I want you to pay attention to me."

_____ B. "I'd like you to tell me what you consider the high point of your day."

_____ C. "I'd like you to be more sure of yourself when you talk."

_____ D. "I want you to tell me why you take drugs."

My responses for this exercise:

A. This item lacks clarity and specificity for me. The speaker could have said, for example, "Would you be willing to make eye contact with me when I'm talking and then recap what you heard me say?"

B. If you checked this item, I agree that the statement clearly expresses what the speaker is requesting. Although I might have a different idea of what the highlight of the day was for them, in this request the speaker is specifically asking the other person to describe what they experienced as the high point.

C. This request lacks clarity regarding a specific action. The speaker could have said, "I'm wondering about your taking a course in public speaking, which I think might contribute to your self-confidence."

D. I am not sure the listener would know when they had completed telling why they use drugs. The speaker could have said, "I would like you to tell me two things you enjoy about using drugs."

Part Two
Translate each negative statement into a positive, doable request.

Example:
"Stop making noise!"
Request: "Would you be willing to turn the radio down to half its current volume and close the door?"

Now you can try:
    A. "Can't you give up smoking?"
        Request: _____
    B. "I don't want you to break any more dishes. They're expensive!"
        Request: _____
    C. "Jimmy, can you stop climbing that tree? It's too small—you'll break a branch!"
        Request: _____

Part Three
    A. Think of some requests you frequently make at home or at work. Are they clear/concrete and positive? If not, practice reframing them in this way, either on paper or in your imagination. How do you think the outcome could be different?
    B. Think of something you recently asked for while making use of a negative. What happened? How might the result have been different with a positive request?

Do-Ability: Because We Want Real Change

Often when we ask people to do something, there is a quality, implied or explicit, of eternity. "I don't want you to say that again!" "Will you take the trash out from now on?" "I want to know that you'll always love me." This, in effect, makes what we're asking for un-doable, since no one can with integrity agree to never or always do something. If we are following PLATO as a guideline in making clear, positive, doable, and present-focused requests, the time element we include—with time frames such as "this week," "this month," "this year," or "the next time"—is what makes our request doable.

Let's go back to the example being on time. Beyond definitions of "on time," let's say that Juanita's request was "I want you to be on time in the future." How is Mark to understand "on time in the future"? Does that mean for the rest of his life and in every situation? Maybe this is what Juanita would like, but for Mark to fulfill such a request is probably unrealistic. Even with the best of intentions, he may again arrive after the agreed-upon time on occasion—caught in traffic or held up at work. Setting an unrealistic goal will most likely lead to frustration for both parties, and further judgment and disconnection. "You said you wouldn't be late anymore, and here you are, late again!" When we're upset about something and wanting relief, it can be natural to want a lifetime insurance policy and permanent change. What is most likely to create change, though, is a doable next step that will raise awareness and bring us closer to the behavior happening consistently. It's also more likely that the person we're making the request of can say a full-hearted "yes" and actually act on what they are agreeing to.

So what would a clear, specific request sound like in this case? Juanita might ask, "Would you be willing to make a commitment now to arrive within ten minutes of the agreed-upon time the next time we meet, or else call me?" or "I'm wondering if, next time, you could think about your workday and come up with two or three ideas that would support you in leaving the office in sufficient time to meet me?" or "The next time you're meeting me during rush hour, could you allow an extra fifteen minutes for travel time?" In these requests, Juanita is not asking absolutely for Mark to arrive "on time" for the rest of his life. She's also not asking that he always call. Rather, she's asking for a "commitment" that he be willing to call if he's running ten minutes behind the time agreed upon. Again, if Juanita simply asked, "Would you be willing to call me if you're running late?" this would leave us back at square one, since we wouldn't have her definition of "late." Mark might not consider it necessary to call until twenty minutes have passed.

Do-ability means feasibility within the realm of possibility. There's no point, for example, in asking someone to go to the moon unless they work for NASA and are scheduled for a flight. And sometimes more mundane, closer-to-earth requests are not doable because of their lack of clarity or specificity. "I want you to love me the way I love you!" would not be a doable request. How would either person know if this were achieved? How much does one person love the other? It all comes down to requesting something a person can do now that will contribute to the well-being of another. We want to form requests that can be fulfilled and are life enriching. A doable request in this case might sound like "Would you be willing to tell me how you're feeling about me?" or "I've mentioned several times that I really enjoyed your company today . . . I'm wondering if you enjoyed our time together?"

It's About Now

To be effective, we also want requests to concern actions in the present, things the other person can do *right now, in this moment* that would meet needs. So Ted's father might ask, "Would you be willing to agree now to talk about your budget for the coming semester and how you plan to stick to it?" or, more simply, "Would you be willing to make a commitment to stay within your budget for the coming semester?" While the budget concerns the next semester (fifteen weeks into the future), Ted's father makes requests regarding the budget that can be fulfilled now: a commitment or an agreement about the budget. Potentially, there may be a commitment to talk further if the agreement they reach does not appear to be working.

EXERCISE 5: Making Requests Doable

Transform each of the following requests into clear, positive, doable, and present-orientated requests:

A. "We need more teamwork around here."
B. "From now on, will you do the dishes?"
C. "Moving forward, you've got to handle these reports differently."
D. "I don't want you to talk to me that way!"
E. "Can you just relax a little? Let go of it."

Hearing the "Yes" Behind the "No"

Even when you make the most specific, positive, and present-oriented request, you never know for sure if the other party will agree to fulfill it or not. That's what makes it a request.

The spirit of a request comes with the understanding that, as human beings, we enjoy contributing to the well-being of others; few things are more satisfying in life. The only time this is *un*satisfying is when we perceive a conflict of strategies: if a particular strategy for meeting the needs of another conflicts with strategies to meet all or some of our own needs. Holding this understanding in our awareness, when a person says "no" to a request, we can hear this "no" in a new way. It is not a "no" to our needs or to us personally; instead, it is a "yes" to needs the other person is seeking to meet. Because we care about their needs as well as our own, we can empathize with them to understand what those needs might be. Since needs are never in conflict—only the strategies we choose—we can seek strategies that work for all, or at least that hold everyone's needs with care and consideration.

EXERCISE 6: Finding the "Yes" in "No"

Read the following requests and the "no" replies. For each "no," give an empathy guess (Are you feeling . . . because you're needing . . .?) and then another request.

Example:
   "Hey, Tom, I'm really tired, and I have an exam tomorrow."
   "Would you be willing to do the dishes tonight?"
   "No—I have a test too!"
An empathy guess and new request might sound like this: "Hm, sounds like you're also stressed out. How about we leave the dishes tonight, and I'll wash them tomorrow afternoon after my test? If that grosses you out, maybe you could just rinse them tonight and I'll wash, dry, and put them away tomorrow?"

Now it's your turn:
   A.   "I have a petition here asking that the state close the Indian
        Point nuclear power plant. This plant is 25 miles from
        New York City and a recent study by Columbia University
        suggests it could be vulnerable to earthquakes."
           "I don't like to sign petitions unless I really know what
        they're about."
           Empathy guess and new request: _____

   B.   "Umm, baby, I'm feeling really sexy. Why don't we skip that
        concert and just stay in tonight?"
           "Actually, I was really looking forward to the concert."
           Empathy guess and new request: _____

   C.   "Can you type up these five letters before you leave work
        today?"
           "It's 4 p.m. now, and there's no way I can get five letters
        typed before 5. And I have to drive my son to his hockey game
        tonight and can't be late—so I can't do overtime today."
           Empathy guess and new request: _____

A Different Game From Compromise

Many of us have learned that getting along with people involves compromise: "You have to give a little to get a little." "You can't have it one way." "Sometimes you win, sometimes you don't." Behind such statements is the belief that it's not possible for two (or more) people to get what they really want at the same time. This belief, ultimately, is based on scarcity and, in my view, is a limited way of seeing the world and human needs and interactions.

In this book, we take a different approach. We want to avoid compromise and sacrifice. Too often, people give up on their needs quickly. They don't bother to check in with themselves: how do I really feel about this? Will it work for me in a way I can feel happy about? Are there some other strategies that we can think of that might meet both our needs? Do I really understand fully the needs that are on the table for the other person in this situation?

When people make agreements by compromising or sacrificing genuine needs, they may not be able to comply with the compromise, at least not for an extended period. Having unmet needs, they may fall into resentment or retaliation. The apparent agreement will ultimately be undermined, to everyone's detriment. As an old saying goes, when you compromise, each person gets to keep half the resentment. True collaboration involves putting our own needs on the table, making connection requests to understand others' needs and perspectives, and then coming up with strategies (clear, positive, doable, and present-focused) that can work for everyone.

EXERCISE 7: Choice or No Choice?

Part One
Discuss the following questions with another person. You can also respond in writing in your journal.

A. Think of a time when you agreed to do something that you really didn't want to do. What was it?

B. Did you do it? Did you do it wholeheartedly, with energy and enthusiasm? Or did you do a half-baked job that didn't really satisfy anyone?

C. Did you feel resentful to others who you felt "left you no choice?" Or did you find a way to comply with the request so that the experience proved to be a positive one for you?

D. How would the situation have been different if you had had a chance to openly discuss what was up for you about the situation and to be heard about the needs you had that weren't being met?

E. To what extent do you think you had a full and accurate understanding of the other person's needs in the situation, the life-enriching desires that were so important to them? How might you have felt about continuing to dialogue for mutually acceptable alternatives if you'd had that full understanding?

Part Two

World history gives repeated examples of what happens when one group of people's needs are met and not another's. World War I, for example, was supposed to be the war to end all wars. Yet after the war, the German people were left with little economic means to meet their needs; as a result of high inflation, a wheelbarrow of deutschmarks was insufficient to buy even a loaf of bread. Some historians have written about how such conditions contributed to Germany starting World War II. Think of a historical or recent event where, based on what you know about the event, you're confident that the needs of all parties were not met. Then give some concrete examples of how this may have led to resentment and/or retaliation.

Event	Parties Involved	Needs Not Met	Retaliation/ Resentment

Dogging for Your Needs: An Alternative to Compromise

We've discussed being open to hearing "no," listening to the "yes" behind the "no," and avoiding compromise. Finding win-win solutions involves being as open as possible to what strategies you will accept. It also means you never stop "dogging" for your needs, maintaining a gentle and persistent attentiveness in bringing your needs to the table and seeing that they are attended to while also empathizing with others as they seek to fulfill their needs.

Want some inspiration for being such a needs hound? No one does this "dogging" better than my cat! When she wants affection and attention, she will try to climb on my lap, even if my laptop is sitting there! If that doesn't work, she will rub her head against my arm or lie down next to me, purring loudly. She has similar ways of expressing her needs when she's hungry or feeling bored and wanting to play. Unlike many humans I know, she is well able to "dog" for her needs. And if her needs are not met in a particular way, she does not seem to hold a grudge or make any judgments. She's open to different strategies! If a cat can "dog" for her needs so well, certainly we humans can too!

In a way, dogging for your own needs while holding concern for the needs of others is like patting your head and rubbing your tummy at the same time. While wanting to hear and meet the needs of others, you don't want to give up on that tummy rubbing; looking to meet all needs includes yours. At first, this can seem like a challenging balancing act, especially if you're experiencing your own feelings and needs fairly intensely. In the next chapter, we look at a particular skill, self-empathy, that can greatly support you in staying "on your feet" while engaging in the dance of Compassionate Communication.

The Duck Criterion

Never comply with a request until you can do so with the joy of a small child feeding a hungry duck.

—MARSHALL B. ROSENBERG

Since we're accustomed to compromising in our culture and taking second best, how can we feel confident that everyone is *really* satisfied? A key tool in this process is a highly advanced technology known as the "hungry duck" test. How does this technology work?

You can ask someone how they feel about a particular strategy, and they might say, "Yes, that's fine by me." Yet when they agree to that strategy, do they have the enthusiasm, excitement, and joy of a small child feeding a hungry duck? To make sure, Judith Lasater, an NVC practitioner and yoga teacher, has proposed using the "duck index" in negotiations. When considering whether to fulfill a request, parties rate how they feel about doing so on a scale from one to ten, where ten is "the joy of a small child feeding a hungry duck" and one is "no joy at all." The rating, which may be done silently or aloud, provides clarity about the needs of both parties and whether everyone's needs have been considered.

If you can't relate to a hungry duck, imagine a time in your life when you did an action out of complete delight and choice. There was nothing you would love to do more at that moment. Perhaps you were working on an art project for someone you love, helping a small child with a task, or playing your hardest with your team so you could achieve a goal. At that moment, you felt content, satisfied, and fully alive—as if you'd just enjoyed the most delicious and nourishing meal possible or were standing outside on a beautiful day looking at a majestic view. It's that kind of satisfaction and energy that you want when you reach an agreement. If all parties involved are not feeling full, satisfied, delighted, and energetic, there are still needs to be addressed.

This "delight, not compromise" or "hungry duck" scale can be especially helpful when negotiating between friends or intimate

partners. In these kinds of relationships, we may be accustomed—
out of desiring ease, harmony, and consideration—to "go along with
things." If we truly want intimacy with those we love and want to
be fully present to who we are and what we want in the moment,
the hungry duck index can help. You can use the index in both
"directions"—to assess whether you're fully happy with a request,
and to make sure that those you are making requests of are truly and
joyfully saying yes.

The hungry duck index can also be useful in expressing how
much one person wants a particular outcome. Let's take a peek at
an interaction between Shelley, who wants to go to a special lecture
tomorrow night at the local community center, and her partner,
Alan, who Shelley hopes will attend with her.

Shelley: Hey, Alan, do you remember the talk I told you about
on how we can support conservation through the utility
payments we make? It's tonight at the community center.
How about going to it with me?

Alan: I don't know. I was thinking of relaxing and watching TV.

Shelley: Hmm, can you tell me a little more about how you're
feeling? I'd like to understand what's going on for you,
since I'd love for you to come along.

Alan: Well, I'm feeling achy and drowsy. I've got a mild
headache, and I'm having trouble keeping my eyes open.

Shelley: You sound pretty tired. So on a scale from one to ten,
with ten being "yes," how close are you to saying "yes!"?

Alan: Sort of a three.

Shelley: OK, thanks for elaborating. I guess I'm partly with
you on this. In some ways, I'd like to relax tonight too,
which sort of makes the idea of going a three for me
also. I'm also excited about there being something we
can do to support energy independence and protect the
environment. That's a nine to me. And I'd really like you
to come with me—I enjoy your company so much—so

that's a ten! Plus I'd like your input, since we pay the
utilities together.

Alan: Hmm, you know, hearing that, I feel differently now. I
care about the energy problem too. And I am especially
happy hearing how much you'd like my company. We
always have fun together. And maybe afterward we could
stop at the office supply store and I could pick up some
things I need for tomorrow. That would be an extra
bonus that would really help me out, to have it taken care
of. What do you think?

Shelley: Sounds great! Thanks for being open to this. I think
tomorrow night we're both free, and we can just hang out
and relax.

Once Alan hears how much his attending the talk would please
Shelley, he experiences a shift in his interest level; his enthusiasm for
attending with Shelley genuinely changes, and he offers a strategy
that might also meet his needs (stopping by the office supply store).
This is different from doing something because Shelley wants him
to or because he feels guilty or sad about saying "no." He won't do it
from a sense of coercion, fear, judgment, obligation, or compromise.
Rather, Alan changes his position out of a spirit of shared
companionship, enjoyment, and mutual benefit.

Suppose Alan's feelings didn't shift? Maybe he decides he'd really
prefer to stay home that night. Shelley might choose to empathize
with Alan's feelings and needs, finding out what he is saying "yes" to
by not going. She might learn he's been feeling run down for a while
and is concerned about doing too much and getting sick. Shelley
might experience a shift in her experience when she hears this
because she cares about his health too. She might also discover some
alternative strategies, such as going to the presentation and taping it
or taking notes so she can share the information with Alan later. She
could find out whether the presentation will be offered on another
day, or ask a friend to attend with her. Among our needs are caring,

support, and connection with each other. The appeal of different strategies can deepen or lessen for us as we gain understanding of what will truly contribute to happiness and well-being.

The Fist and the Open Hand

In addition to thinking about the hungry duck index when making requests, it may also be helpful to think about a fist versus an open hand. When making demands, we are in effect in the energy and mode of a closed fist: boxing for our needs (with force or coercion) rather than "dogging" for them. When we act from a place of a closed fist, we are restricted, in a combative mode, lacking openness. How can we accept what someone is offering with fists clenched? Feeling anxious and lacking trust about our needs mattering or being met, we, too, clench up. Our needs and a single way of meeting them also harden up in the form of a fist: "Either we do it this way, or else"—and the "or else" can take myriad forms. Whenever this "demand energy" is present (an urgency and lack of trust around meeting needs), there will be that fist—even if there are no physical consequences and we use words only. Demands are a kind of power-over rather than power-with; the closed fist epitomizes that kind of "bullying" fear energy.

A request, in contrast, is an open hand. We're not clenching, holding our hand close to our body in fear or self-defense. Rather, we are extending, reaching arm and hand out with openness toward another. In our open hand is something we would like to offer, and with an open hand, we are also in a position to receive. We are sharing our values and needs, offering what matters to us most as a kind of gift, and trusting that others will see, hear, and value our needs. From the position of an open hand, we can best invite dialogue, and both offer and receive strategies. An open hand is the stance of mutual understanding and collaboration.

Can I be strong enough as a person to be separate from the other? Can I be a sturdy respecter of my own feelings, my own needs, as well as his? Can I own and, if need be, express my own feelings as something belonging to me and separate from his feelings? Am I strong enough in my own separateness that I will not be downcast by his depression, frightened by his fear, not engulfed by his dependency?

—CARL ROGERS,
On Becoming a Person

The next time you're in dialogue with someone, check in with yourself. Are you in the metaphorical stance of a closed fist, arms crossed in refusal or resistance? If so, this may be a time when you want to practice self-empathy or request that someone listen empathically to your feelings and needs. Or are you, alternatively, in the energy of an open hand, ready and willing to hear the needs of others and to explore strategies that will work for both of you? Historically in the West, people used their right hand to hold the hilt of the sword at their hip for self-protection. The tradition of shaking hands in greeting was a literal way to indicate friendship and trust, since in shaking hands, both of you had to release your hold on your weapons and meet each other with peaceful intentions. Inspired by this image, I find it helpful to check in with myself: Am I approaching this person and situation with the energy and attitude of clenched fists, ready to place my hand on my sword? Or am I ready to greet them with an open hand?

The Dance of Compassion

A dialogue of openness, to which at least one person comes with an outreached hand, aware of consciously caring for both parties' feelings and needs, can be seen as a kind of dance. The dance moves between sharing and hearing experiences (observations), honest expression of feelings and needs, and empathy—hearing the feelings and needs of the other. It also involves a dance around strategies: offering and receiving strategies, dogging for our needs, and being open to hearing "no." These NVC steps and practices are all supported by making connection requests; pacing and clarifying conversations by reflecting; slowing down dialogues at times by pausing or taking a breath; and checking in with ourselves, including our bodies, to support self-connection, see how we're feeling, and determine whether our needs are being met. The primary goals of practicing NVC are understanding and connection; the four basic steps (OFNR) and related "support" steps we have explored all contribute to connection and collaboration:

Connecting with energy of needs as met

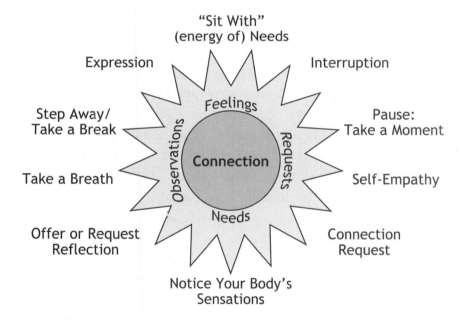

The whole NVC model, with different support practices, supports understanding, connection, trust, and collaboration

Source illustration by Hadassah Hill

Finding an Abundance of Strategies

When we're feeling attached to a particular strategy, one way to generate openness is to generate as many different strategies for meeting our needs as possible. We can create a cornucopia of possibilities looking at all the PLATO (person, location, action, time, object) variations. Rather than being attached to one particular person meeting our needs, for example, who else in our lives can we think of to support us in meeting our needs, including ourselves? Is there a specific action we're attached to? What other action (or time or location or object) also meets our needs?

Alternatively, sometimes when I'm frustrated or disappointed about someone's response or how a situation has left needs unmet for me, I like to practice shifting my attention to needs met. Every time I do, my perspective and mood shift. For example, if I'm disappointed about a friend cancelling plans to meet me, I can check in about needs that *are* being met by this change. I might find it meets my needs for spaciousness and ease around taking care of some tasks that have been on my mind to attend to at home. It may also give me an opportunity to enjoy listening to a new CD while carrying out those tasks. No matter how challenging a situation is—and I tend to see the glass half empty in life rather than half full!—I can find *some* needs that are being met.

One NVC practitioner, Gail Taylor, has said, "There are ten thousand strategies to meet a need." While at first we may struggle to see so many possibilities, being attached to only one or two strategies is certainly limiting, and it can be seen as acting from a place of scarcity. A limitation of strategies, in effect, is a crisis of imagination, and we are a profoundly visionary and creative species. Just pause for a moment to consider all we have created! If we've found a way to split atoms, unravel DNA, and create spaceships (not to mention other complex technologies such as creating written languages, making chocolate, and inventing hundreds of musical instruments), we can certainly find alternative strategies in any given circumstance. Our greatest resource is an awareness of possibility.

If you're stuck on one solution, you may want to ask others, including the person with whom you are seeking to collaborate, for support in generating possibilities. We often fall into thinking we're the only ones who can figure something out: a lonely state rife with pressure. I have been repeatedly inspired by solutions young children come up with when they have a sense that their needs matter and they understand the needs of others impacted by a situation. A mother attending an NVC course, for example, was concerned about her three-year-old son throwing sand at a playground, worried that it might get in the eyes of other children and hurt them. After she offered her son an empathy guess—"You're having fun throwing sand, aren't you?"—and shared her concern for the other children in the sandbox, her son came up with a solution on his own: to throw the sand into a bucket.

I repeatedly see a similar phenomenon in organizations and at workplaces. Those in a position of leadership who are unhappy with how something is going will make decisions, including decisions that impact others, and are then dissatisfied with the results. Given their position, they see themselves as responsible for fixing or solving the issue. When they invite input, however, including from the very people who, in the leaders' minds, are contributing to the challenging situation in the first place, they often find surprising solutions. While valuing teamwork and collaboration, they may still forget to take this most basic step: "This is what I see going on. These are the needs I see on the table—for me, you, and the team. What do you see? Are there concerns or needs that I'm missing? And given all that's at play, what ideas do you have to resolve this—what will address everyone's needs?" This is what true collaboration and a generative approach to possibility look like. Believing that we are the ones who have to figure out or solve everything is another form of demand—a demand of ourselves.

EXERCISE 8: Broadening Our Horizons

A. Felice has had a rough week at work and wants to relax and connect with others on the weekend.
   1. What are fifteen different ways Felice could meet her needs for relaxation and connection?
   2. Can you imagine fifty more ways she could meet those needs? How about a hundred?
   3. What was it like imagining so many different possibilities? How did it affect your feelings about any one strategy?
B. Think of a situation where you were in conflict with someone. Was one person or more attached to a particular strategy (solution) or interpretation?
C. Think of something you'd really like. What needs would this meet for you? Think of at least three other ways the same needs might be met.
D. Think of an ongoing conflict or challenging situation. What are all the needs at play that you see for yourself and others? Whom could you invite, including those directly involved in the situation, to support you in generating diverse solutions?

All Together—Again

In the last chapter, when discussing observations, we presented the first three steps of the NVC model: observations, feelings, and needs. We've now added the fourth and final element: requests.

Let's look at an entire dialogue in which every step of the process is included. Here is the situation: Jane and Adam are two adults in their sixties, both divorced. Jane invites Adam to a party, and Adam is sensing that Jane likes him romantically. He doesn't want to "lead her on" and is concerned that agreeing to go to the party with Jane would do that. In this dialogue, an informal or colloquial use of the

---

The NVC Model—4 Steps

Observation(s): When I see/hear/think about _____
_____ (observation),
Feeling(s): I am feeling _____ (feeling), because
Need(s): I'm needing _____ (need).
Request(s): Would you be willing to _____ ?

NVC model is used. While you don't see the classic form—"Are you feeling . . . because you're needing . . . ?"—an awareness of feelings and needs informs the discussion and there is a frequent use of observations and requests. At times, when judgments are made, they are "owned" as such. While reading the dialogue, see if you can spot where each step of the model is being practiced.

Jane: Hey, Adam, Doug's having a party with some dancing Saturday night at this house. Do you want to go? I think it'll be fun.

Adam: Hmm. Well, thanks for the invite. I'm pleased you'd like to go with me. Let me think about this for a minute. (Pause.) Well, actually, I am feeling a bit hesitant. Would you like to know why?

Jane: Well, I guess so; I am curious.

Adam: OK. Well, I really enjoy our friendship and doing things with you. And this is a little hard to say, because I do care about you and your feelings. And I am thinking that you might be interested in something more intimate. Am I on target about that?

Jane: Well, yeah, sort of, I'd like that.

Adam: Well, I appreciate your honesty. And I'm also very flattered because I do think you're attractive—and an amazing person. And I also want to be honest, especially because I care about you. I enjoy your company very much, and for whatever reason, I'm just not feeling romantically attracted to you in a way that I imagine you are looking for. Maybe it's because I need more time to integrate all that's been involved for me in getting divorced. This is really hard for me to share, and I'm concerned how you're hearing it. Could you tell me what you've heard me say?

Jane: Yeah. You don't think I'm attractive enough for a dating type of relationship! You want someone sexier.

Adam: Hmmm. Thanks so much for telling me what you heard. I really, really value you as a friend and your feelings are important to me. And I think I'm not expressing myself clearly. Would it be OK with you if I tried again?

Jane: (Looking down and frowning, she nods agreement.)

Adam: I value our friendship very much and I care about you. Being with you is fun, and I feel supported and understood. And for me, for whatever reason, the chemistry isn't there. Heaven knows that doesn't mean there's anything wrong with you—or with me. You are a great person. It just means that I don't feel that way, at least at the present. How do you feel hearing this?

Jane: I'm disappointed. I guess I also appreciate your honesty.

Adam: And is the disappointment about wanting someone special in your life?

Jane: Well, of course! I really miss that. I like having company, and that kind of intimacy with someone.

Adam: I know what you mean. Intimacy and closeness are big needs of mine too.

Jane: Hmmm. Well, I am disappointed that it's not happening between us; at the same time, I'm glad we talked. I value your honesty and I am feeling more confident about our friendship. I appreciate being able to talk frankly like this.

Adam: I'm relieved to hear that. I care about you and our friendship. I really want it to continue. I appreciate your openness to hearing this, and your understanding. And I'd still like to go to the party with you—if you're open to our going as friends?

Jane: Sure. (Smiling) As long as you know I may be on the lookout for other romantic possibilities . . .

Adam: Of course!

No matter how you slice it, this is a challenging situation: one person wanting a romantic relationship with the other and the other person not desiring it. At the close of the dialogue, Adam empathizes with Jane's desire for intimacy. He can well understand it because he has the same need. Yet it would not meet his needs for integrity or honesty to act on those needs in relation to Jane. Jane's disappointment comes from her longing for an intimate relationship. Because she feels Adam has fully heard her, Jane feels renewed connection with her friend and even gratitude for the kind of the relationship they do have.

A Graphic Overview

Now we will introduce you to a visual summary of the Nonviolent Communication model that we call the Compassionate Communication model, seen on pages 168–70. As the model illustrates, our senses take in events in the outside world as well as internal stimuli, and we interpret those events based upon our experience, learning, history, and culture. We consciously choose some of these interpretations, while others occur automatically without conscious awareness: for example, people who have experienced trauma may have uncontrolled flashbacks when in contact with certain stimuli. As a result of this processing, in our current experience, we experience our needs as met or unmet or our values as being represented or not represented. This causes us to have certain feelings. As "choosers," we evaluate potential strategies to meet needs and choose one based upon:

A Model of Compassionate Communication

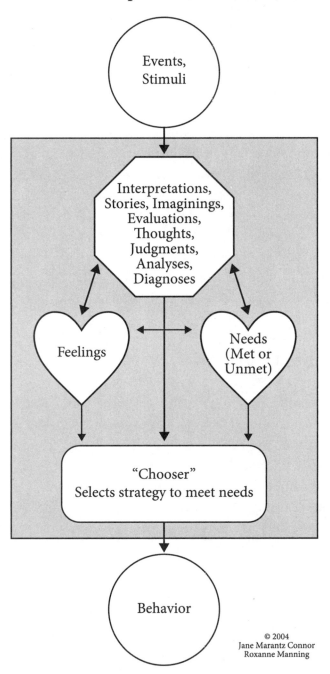

© 2004
Jane Marantz Connor
Roxanne Manning

A Model of Compassionate Communication

Notes on the Model

For heart-to-heart connection, it is best to talk only of feelings and needs.

Events and stimuli:
1. Events and stimuli are frequently external and observable, but can also be internal (e.g., hunger pang)
2. Events and stimuli are interpreted on the basis of:
   - Experience
   - Learning
   - Culture
   - History

Needs:
1. Needs may be experienced as met or unmet, depending on our interpretation of events.
2. When we experience needs as met, positive feelings are stimulated.
3. When we experience needs as unmet, negative feelings are stimulated.

Feelings:
1. Positive feelings, stimulated by met needs include:
   - Joy
   - Contentment
   - Excitement
2. Negative feelings, stimulated by unmet needs include:
   - Frustration
   - Sadness
   - Fear

Chooser:
1. The strategy selected by the chooser is that which best serves our needs but is impacted by our interpretations and feelings.
2. The strategy selected by the "chooser" is influenced by:
   - Experience
   - Learning
   - History
   - Culture, etc.

Making interpretations, focusing on feelings and needs, and choosing strategies are often internal processes that are not visible.

- The stimuli we have been exposed to
- The interpretations we make of the processed versions of these stimuli
- Our experience of our needs as met or unmet
- The feelings thus stimulated in us

The strategy we choose may or may not result in behavior that is observable to others.

·:❊:·

We've covered a lot of ground in this chapter, describing and exploring a number of key concepts in NVC, including

- The distinction between a request and a demand
- Connection requests, including both reflection and "check-in" requests
- Finding connection when hearing "no"
- Making clear, positive, doable, and present-focused requests

It is understandable if your head is spinning, and you're still integrating all that you've read. For most of us, developing facility with the language and intentions of NVC takes time, repeated exposure to the basic principles, and practice living this process, receiving feedback, and trying again. Luckily, it is a skill you can practice anytime and anywhere, both silently and aloud. As is the case with many skills and practices—whether it is meditation, martial arts, or golf or tennis—you can always go deeper. NVC is a lifelong endeavor. To support you further in your practice, we close with two exercises that apply the concepts explored in the first four chapters of the book. Then, in the next chapter, we will delve into self-empathy, a practice that supports self-connection, choice, and presence in practicing NVC with others.

INTEGRATION: Questions and Exercises to Further Explore Chapter 5

A. To obtain practice identifying and expressing clear requests, place a checkmark next to any of the following statements in which you think the speaker is requesting that a doable, specific action be undertaken. Compose a request for any statement that you do not check.

_____ 1. "I'd like you to respect that I am different from you."

_____ 2. "I'd like you to tell me how you feel about my wanting to break up with you."

_____ 3. "I would like you to do the tasks that you sign up for each week."

_____ 4. "I'd like to understand you better."

_____ 5. "I would like you to show me a little more courtesy."

_____ 6. "I'd like us to go out and have fun more often."

My responses for this exercise:

1. I don't believe this sentence clearly requests a specific action. The speaker could have said, "The next time you're aware of wanting to comment on a choice I've made, I'd like you to pause for a moment and reflect on what needs you'd be meeting by making that comment."
2. If you checked this item, I agree that the statement clearly expresses what the speaker is requesting.
3. If you checked this item, I agree that the statement clearly expresses what the speaker is requesting.
4. I don't believe this sentence clearly requests a specific action. The phrase "understand you better" is vague. The speaker could have said, "I'd like to meet this week for coffee so that I can learn more about you and your perspective on things."
5. I don't believe this sentence clearly requests a specific action. The phrase "a little more courtesy" is vague. The speaker could have said, "The next time you'd like to borrow some clothes, I'd like you to check with me first."
6. I do not believe that the phrase "more often" clearly identifies the specific action being requested. Instead, the speaker could have said, "I'd like us to go see our favorite band play at the café this Thursday."

B. There is no inherent conflict between people's needs; at the same time, it can be challenging to find strategies that meet all needs. Therefore, it can be very helpful to practice brainstorming strategies and requests. Generating a significant number can help reduce the attachment to any single request or strategy. To practice this concept, you may wish to try the following exercise, especially in a group: brainstorming is often energized when multiple people participate. Remember: with brainstorming, the idea is to generate as many ideas as possible and not to evaluate the ideas until the generating phase is complete.

1. Think of a situation of conflict between two people. (One of these could be you.)
2. What are your feelings and needs in the situation?
3. What are the other person's feelings and needs in the situation?
4. Brainstorm as many strategies or requests as you can that might meet the needs of both parties.

6

Empathy in the Fast Lane:
Self-Empathy and Choice

All kinds of thoughts are always clamoring inside you.
Many different feelings arise and subside. Many memories haunt or
please you. How you respond to these things, from moment to moment,
how you maintain your inner world, creates your destiny.

—GURUMAYI CHIDVILASANANDA

In oneself lies the whole world and if you know how to look and learn,
the door is there and the key is in your hand. Nobody on earth can
give you either the key or the door to open, except yourself.

—JIDDU KRISHNAMURTI, twentieth-century Indian philosopher

What lies behind us and what lies before us are tiny
matters compared to what lies within us.

—HENRY STANLEY HASKINS

In the first five chapters, we focused on how to empathize with others. We explored a view of the world where everyone's needs, including our own, can be seen as valuable. Yet how does one attend to one's own needs while also attending to others' needs? This is the task we take up in this chapter, via the practice of self-empathy. As you will see, self-empathy has broad applications. It is useful in responding to judgment, regret, and indecision and supports self-acceptance and self-understanding. It is helpful both when responding to our own inner "bugs" or demons and when interacting with others.

When something another person says or does emotionally triggers us, it can be challenging to respond with compassion or even full awareness or choice. If your own empathy "battery" is low, it is hard to be present or care for another. By practicing self-empathy and becoming aware of your own feelings and needs in the moment, you can "recharge" your empathy reserve. Gaining greater self-connection increases your ability to be present and respond with compassion and choice. Developing your own self-empathy practice and finding ways to identify, respect, and honor your deepest longings will also contribute in important ways to your sense of inner peace and joy and your ability to relate to others with confidence and freedom.

The "Reverse Golden Rule"

Around the world, regardless of language or culture, the golden rule is the same: "Do unto others as you would see done unto yourself." The opposite, which my former colleague and professor of rhetoric Lois Einhorn calls the "reverse golden rule," is also true: "Do unto yourself as you would see done unto others." If we practice empathy and compassion for those around us, we will also want to practice compassion for ourselves, because harmony in relationships requires care for the needs of *all* people. Yet many people find they most frequently speak to themselves with a voice that is critical and harsh; they may believe that caring about their own needs is "selfish" and will lead to disapproval and disconnection from others.

As has been described, empathy and self-empathy are two sides of the same coin; if we are not engaged in self-compassion and self-care, it is impossible to sustain empathy for those around us. On airplane flights we're told that if there's a change in cabin pressure, we need to put our own oxygen masks on first before helping others. Similarly, if you don't get the empathy you need first, how can you be present to someone else? Only when your cup is full—when you're getting the empathy you need—can you be fully available to receive messages from others, including the most challenging messages of criticism, demand, or blame.

Empathy Directed Inward

As you might guess, practicing self-empathy is in many ways similar to giving empathy to others. The only difference is that rather than focusing on others' feelings and needs, for the moment you turn your empathy "antennae" inward toward yourself. You ask yourself, "Am I feeling _____ because I'm needing _____?" and link your feelings and needs to clear observations and requests. You can complete these steps in your mind, by speaking aloud (to yourself or another person—ideally, not the person who triggered your response), or by writing them down. Some people like to keep a self-empathy journal to create a regular practice of self-empathy.

Four Steps of Self-Empathy

Seeing, hearing, thinking about _____ (Observation)

I'm feeling _____ (Feeling)

… because I'm needing _____ (Need)

Aware of the above, I would like to _____ (Request)

As with all empathy, you want to focus on what's "electric" (energetic and true for you) in the present moment. So while you may be concerned with past actions and regret, you talk about your experience in the present tense. You could say, for example, "Thinking about _____ (any past event), I'm feeling _____." After beginning with this phrase, you would continue through the rest of the model, identifying what you need and any request or strategy you may have to meet it. In taking these steps, you can become aware of how the past still "lives" in the present.

In practicing self-empathy, it may seem odd at first to make a request of yourself. In talking to yourself, of course, you may not make a formal request: "Self, would you be willing . . ." Rather, having connected with your feelings and needs, the request step is simply an opportunity to consider what you may wish to do at this point to support meeting your needs.

Because it can be difficult for people to change the way they do things just by connecting with an *intention* to change, it can be helpful to make a clear, positive, doable request for yourself. For example, if you notice that you feel sluggish and want more energy, rather than telling yourself, "I want to exercise more," a clear, positive, doable request for yourself might include deciding this week to exercise three days for twenty minutes each day, or asking a friend to exercise with you, or deciding that you will have called three local gyms to find out about their schedules and fees by the end of the week. The particular strategy you choose is wide open; what's important is making a clear, positive, doable step to move your intention and your needs forward. For more on making clear, positive, doable requests, see chapter 5.

Sometimes I just want someone to listen and be there for me. And then I remember that I can listen and be there for myself.

—STEPHANIE

When practicing self-empathy, it's helpful first to check in with your body. See if you notice any tension, pressure, restriction, or heat, and where these sensations are. Do you notice this sensation in your back, jaw, head, or chest? During the process, after identifying your feelings and needs, check in with your body again and see if you notice any shift in your physical sensations. If you sigh or experience some other relief of tension you're holding, this is often an indication that you've connected deeply with your feelings and needs. You may also wish to check in again with your feelings to see if there has been a shift.

Sometimes when I check in with myself at the start of practicing self-empathy, I'll choose a number between one and ten to indicate my tension or stress level at that moment, with ten being most stressed and one indicating that I am most at ease or relaxed. After I practice self-empathy, I check in again to see where I am now. If I'm still at a five or a six, I may further explore what I'm feeling and needing, since my practice of self-empathy may be incomplete.

It's also very important when practicing self-empathy to take in the full energy of the need as met. Once you've identified your top needs, you can do this by taking a moment to sit with each one and remember a time when it was met for you. Or you can imagine the need as fully met in your life, also imagining how this feels in your body. When you connect with the need as met, you can take the full value or "nourishment" of that need, experience a shift (including in your body), and enter a different mind-set and energy when responding to the initial trigger.* If you read over the needs list on page 368 as if it were simply a shopping list and do not connect fully with the need as you experience it, as met, you may receive little benefit from practicing self-empathy. Our visceral memory and experience of needs met give us self-connection, insight, forward movement, and relief in the practice of NVC.

---

* I would like to acknowledge CNVC Certified Trainer Robert Gonzalez, who has developed and advocated this practice in the NVC network of connecting with the "beauty" of the need, which we refer to here as the "energy" of the need, as met.

EXERCISE 1: Seeing Our Judgments, Creating Compassion

A. Think about a recent choice or behavior you're unhappy about. Describe it objectively in a few words or sentences (this is the observation step).

B. What judgments do you have of yourself about this choice or behavior? Write these down too. (Paying attention to your judgments can help you discover the feelings and needs underneath them.)

C. Thinking about what happened and the judgments you have of yourself about it, now identify what you are feeling and needing. Write down three to five feelings and needs.

D. Check in with yourself: has connecting with your feelings and needs created any ease or shift for you, including in your body? If you notice that your body is still tense or restricted, you may wish to go back to the earlier steps and see if there are any judgments, feelings, or needs that you'd like to further explore. Remember to connect with the energy of the need as met in this process by remembering or imagining the need being fully met and experiencing this met need on a somatic (sensory) level.

Self-Pity Is a Different Game

I was brought up to think that you have to be strong and just not let things get to you. Anything else is a sign of weakness.

—PHILLIP, a student

When people first hear about self-empathy, they can confuse it with self-pity, or "feeling sorry for yourself." Yet these are remarkably different activities. Self-empathy is healing and empowering, focusing on our primary needs in life and how to meet them.

It is about taking responsibility for our feelings, not blaming others for them. It is a celebration of who we are, what we most value, and the choices we have. Self-pity, in contrast, involves seeing ourselves as victims and not taking responsibility for our feelings. It is about judging ourselves and taking away our choice and power.

Let's look at an example. Two friends decide to go to Florida for a snorkeling and diving trip. They invite their friend Vincent to come along too. Vincent would love to go: he's just learned how to dive and is eager to practice; he also really enjoys hanging out with these friends. At the same time, he has made a commitment to himself this year to pay off his credit card debt and start saving money to buy an apartment. Vincent feels disappointed and discouraged about not going. This is the second time he's skipped a trip like this. Self-pity in this case could sound like this:

> It's not fair. How come I can't go? What makes them better than me?

> I deserve better. I should have the same chance to go that they do.

> How come I never have enough money? If only my parents had helped me out more. This all started with my taking out too many loans when I was in college.

Self-empathy, by contrast, could sound like this:

> Thinking about the trip, I'm really disappointed. I'd love to go, have fun, and relax and be with my friends. I also would like to learn more about diving and get more experience.

> Thinking about the trip, though, I also feel really anxious. This debt has been hanging over me for months—I really want the relief of being done with it. I'm also excited about my plan

of saving up a deposit to buy an apartment. I feel happy and energized thinking about that. I really want a nicer place to live and more space—and the security that owning my own place can give me.

In the statements involving self-pity, Vincent focuses on what he lacks. He sees himself as less than others ("What makes them better than me?"), compares his situation to his friends' ("I should have the same chance that they do"), blames himself ("How come I never have enough money?"), and finds the cause of his predicament in circumstances outside himself—that his parents didn't help him more and so he took out student loans. Vincent sees himself and his life as static and unchanging: he never gets enough and life is unfair.

In practicing self-empathy, Vincent identifies the needs that are stimulating his feelings of sadness and disappointment: needs for choice, relaxation, connection, and inclusion. He appreciates how much he values these qualities and desires them in his life. He also sees the choice he does have; by choosing to skip the trip and pay off his debt, he gains confidence in his goal of owning an apartment. Valuing all his needs, he may also come up with other strategies to meet them. He may choose to take a day off from work to do something fun with friends locally, or choose to do something fun and relaxing after work, or to take an intermediate diving course locally to deepen his skill while also sticking to the budget he wants to keep.

Ironically, it is when we are stuck in self-pity that we most need empathy. When we pity ourselves, we are likely to feel discouraged and hopeless, even despairing. Finding that the cause of our distress is outside ourselves, and engaging in a fixed view of ourselves and the world, we have little or no confidence that things can change. Through self-empathy, the hope and movement we want can occur. We can focus on what we want in life, mourn our needs that are not fully met, and choose actions that will best serve us. In doing so, we can enjoy self-acceptance, choice, and empowerment.

EXERCISE 2: Breaking Free of Self-Pity

Part One
Reread the statements where Vincent is engaging in self-pity; imagine that you are him. How do you feel, including in your body, when reading and reflecting on statements of self-pity? Next, read over the statements where he is practicing self-empathy. How are the self-pity statements different energetically from self-empathy?

Part Two
Think back to a recent situation when you were feeling sorry for yourself (self-pity).
  A. Describe the situation in one or two sentences.
  B. When you are engaging in self-pity and thinking about this situation, what judgments do you have of yourself or others?
  C. How are you feeling?
  D. What needs are you aware of?
  E. Has practicing self-empathy given you any insight or relief?

Self-Empathy for Our "Mistakes"

In addition to self-pity, we can all at times experience self-judgment, regret, and shame regarding a choice we have made. At the time we made it, given the needs, information, and internal resources we had, a particular action may have seemed the best (or only) course to take. In the end, however, we find that it did not meet all our needs or have the impact we wanted. In these moments, it can be easy to engage in self-criticism: "How can I have been so stupid?"

Sometimes I can't believe how hard I am on myself —I don't like the way I look, the way I talk, or the way I laugh. I don't even like the way I criticize myself so much.

—ANONYMOUS STUDENT

"Why do I always make the same mistakes?" "I should have listened to what my friends advised." We are in pain about our actions and the decisions we made. We may also be concerned about how others might see our actions and whether they are judging us or our behavior.

At times like these, because you are in pain, it can be hard to have compassion and understanding for yourself. Perhaps you even find yourself thinking, "I don't deserve compassion" or "I should suffer for what I did." Such thinking is familiar because it's what we've learned in our culture. Blame-thinking comes from a dominant belief that punishment and suffering are necessary for getting people to do what they "should" do, for learning and growth, and for restoring harmony when people have experienced harm. We may be afraid that if we don't "punish" ourselves, we'll make a "wrong" decision again. We engage in self-blame because we want effectiveness, learning, movement, and hope.

Of course, we can meet all these needs without judging or blaming ourselves, via self-empathy and understanding. In fact, research and other evidence show that punishment and "should" thinking do not lead to long-term change and the kinds of connections that enrich life and generate positive feelings. Rather, this kind of self-talk leads to further internal suffering and to other needs being unmet, including those for choice, self-acceptance, respect, and autonomy. In effect, telling ourselves that we "should do" or "should have done" something differently is just like someone else giving us a "should." Telling ourselves what we should or must do without identifying the life-serving, positive reasons that such an action would be meaningful to us can easily lead to resistance and rebellion. No one wants to be told what to do—even by themselves!

Further, holding a fixed, static view of ourselves—that we are a certain kind of person or will never change ("that's just how I am: lazy, thoughtless, and self-centered")—can make it even more challenging to imagine and create change. It reinforces the behavior we want to change and is discouraging rather than motivating. While I haven't seen a specific study on this, I would think that statistically, the more likely it is that we tell ourselves a "should" about something (that we should stop smoking, lose weight, spend less money, or spend more time with our families), the less likely it is that we will actually move in the direction we want. This goes back to the old adage of carrot and stick: should thinking is a big stick; connecting with our core values and what we want to generate and experience in life is a big, juicy carrot!

EXERCISE 3: Freeing Ourselves From Shoulds

Part One

What do you tell yourself that you should or shouldn't do? Think of some recent or current situations where you might talk to yourself in this way and complete the following statements:

    A. "I never should have _____."

    B. "I shouldn't be so _____."

    C. "I shouldn't always be _____."

    D. "I should have known better than to have _____."

Part Two

    A. When you're telling yourself each of these shoulds, how are you feeling?

    B. What needs are "up" for you?

Part Three

Did you feel a change energetically between telling yourself shoulds and connecting to your feelings and needs? How do you experience each in your body?

Two Parts of Ourselves: The Chooser and the Educator

In thinking about self-judgment, blame, and shoulds, some people find it helpful to think of two parts of ourselves: the *chooser* and the *educator* (sometimes also called our "internal critic" or "loyal soldier"). The

Don't "should" on me!

—BUMPER STICKER

chooser is the part of ourselves that made a choice, thinking it was life-serving. The educator is the part of ourselves that is disappointed or even scared or frustrated when thinking about the choice and its impact. The educator wants us to learn from our choices so we can be more confident about decisions we make in the future.

Think back to the last time you made a decision that you now regret. Your chooser probably wants understanding for the choice you made; your educator is the internal voice that's impatient or unhappy with that choice. When your chooser and educator are in the midst of an internal conflict, what's most helpful is to listen empathically to each in turn. What were you feeling and needing when you made the choice? You made it in an effort to meet your needs. What is your educator feeling and needing when thinking about that choice and its results?

It can also be helpful to think about the two questions we've raised before in this book: What do we want in life, and how do we want to get it? We all have needs for effectiveness, competence, meaning, and contribution. Self-empathy offers a way for us to determine whether our choices are effective *and* to learn and grow from these choices in a way that's fully consistent with our values.

Let's look at a real-life example of how self-empathy and listening to what both our chooser and educator have to say offer clarity, relief, and change.

Over the last few years, I've been renovating a house that I bought with my parents. During the renovation, I've experienced numerous challenges with several contractors, including two different contractors taking deposits and not finishing or even starting the job, or working to the standards I'd like. After saving up again to finish the job, I recently hired a third contractor. I was very happy with how their work was progressing, so I made a second payment—and the next day, they called to say they weren't showing up for work! "Oh no," I was thinking, "I've made the same mistake again!" A lot of self-judgment came up for me: "How could I have done this again?" "Won't I ever learn?" "I'm too trusting!" "I should have thought this through more, based on all the other experiences I've had!" It was very painful for me to imagine that I'd ended up in the same kind of situation as I had with the previous contractors.

Listening to my educator, it was clear what she wanted: peace of mind (about the job being completed and having the funds to do so). She also wanted hope about learning, self-development, and growth, as well as closure and relief around the whole situation. Self-trust was the "big" core need for me: wanting to trust that I was holding my own needs with care (rather than simply the needs of the contractors).

I also took time to notice what needs my chooser wanted to meet by the choice I'd made. I was so happy and relieved with the quality of work the new contractors had produced and how quickly they were completing it. I made a second payment because I wanted to recognize them and show my appreciation. "Finally—contractors I can rely on!" This was the positive judgment that had driven my writing them a second check, perhaps prematurely and in an amount that was larger than the percentage our agreement called for at that phase of the job.

Once I connected with all these needs and listened deeply to both my educator and chooser, I took a deep breath and noticed I was feeling much more relaxed. From this place of ease, I stepped back, looked at the big picture, and asked myself a question: what did I really want to see happen in this situation now? I realized what

I most longed for was a "positive" experience: the work completed and done to the standard I desired, and trust and ease with the contractors. I wanted relief from any "drama": freedom from fear, self-judgment, or tension (wanting harmony, peace, flow, trust, and ease). In brief, I wanted a different experience from what I had before, both around the quality of the work and the professional relationship.

When I connected to these core needs, something surprising happened for me. I remembered that regardless of what the contractors did or did not do, I still had a choice in how I responded. It was not just their actions that impacted the outcome; it was how I *responded* to their actions. I also remembered that I didn't know what would happen next; the contractors might very well turn up for work tomorrow. I realized that I was, in effect, reacting to a "what if" based on previous experiences. Maybe the reason they had given for not coming (that all their workers had the flu) was true. I also had an insight about how my words and choices may have contributed to past situations. Each time, because I saw myself as powerless, I was so nervous that I assumed the worst about each contractor. This influenced how I'd dealt with each situation: my fear drove a quality of demand and desperation. Seeing this gave me new compassion for the previous contractors. It also led me to consider what I wanted to do differently *now*, in this situation.

I decided not to challenge the contractors' story about why they weren't showing up. Instead I called back and left a message saying how much I appreciated the work they had done, and that I looked forward to seeing them the next day. And sure enough, the next day they did turn up, and they finished the job over the following week. I also decided that regardless of how happy I was with the work, I would make no further payment until the job was finished and the architect had signed off on it.

While the contractors may have turned up and finished the job anyway, it was truly liberating for me to practice self-empathy and listen to my chooser and my educator in this situation. I gained new insight and peace about what had happened before and found self-acceptance and peace about what was happening now. I also believe this led to my responding to the contractors very differently from the way I had in past situations, and that this in turn supported the quality of the work relationship I wanted with them, making it more likely they would be happy to return to the work site and complete their tasks as agreed.

Exercise 4: Listening to Your Chooser and Educator

Think of a recent choice you made that you are unhappy about. On a piece of paper, describe what happened (the choice you made) in one to three sentences. Now make two lists, one marked "Chooser" and one marked "Educator." Under each list, write down all the thoughts and judgments that each part of you had about the situation. Now translate these judgments into feelings and needs. After completing this process, you may wish to consider how you want to proceed now, given all your feelings and needs. How did listening to your chooser and educator give you insight or relief?

Mourning Unmet Needs—Celebrating What Matters

In my experience with the contractors, I had an opportunity to mourn choices I'd made with previous contractors: to become aware of my regret and needs unmet. By doing so, I became deeply aware of what I really valued in the situation and what I wanted to experience next. In the practice of Nonviolent Communication, mourning is a conscious process of focusing on our unmet needs and appreciating how much we value those needs in our life. It involves deepening our awareness of how we are enriched when these needs are met and how much we want these qualities to be present for us and for everyone. Through the process of mourning, we come full circle from a place of grieving or loss to celebrating what matters most to us.

Have you ever had the experience of missing or losing something and, through that loss, more fully appreciating its value? When we mourn the loss of a loved one, for example, we are in effect celebrating their life and all the ways they contributed to us and the world. When we engage in mourning unmet needs, we go through a similar process regarding choices we've made. This can involve simply thinking about and reflecting on the importance of these values, or imagining situations in which they have been fully lived and how much we enjoyed that experience. It can also involve nonverbal rumination, reflecting on images or even bodily experiences associated with the needs we hold dear.

Mourning unmet needs is very different from recrimination or self-blame. Habitually, many of us go quickly from feeling "bad" about a choice we've made (self-conscious or sad) to judgment or self-blame, followed by a rapid-fire apology or reactive new strategy. The practice of mourning offers much deeper closure, understanding, and self-acceptance. Mourning and celebrating needs met and unmet by our choices are two different ways of acknowledging what we most want and value in life. Awareness of our needs can play a key role in our making choices that more fully meet our needs.

EXERCISE 5: Mourning Needs Met and Unmet by a Choice

Part One
Go back to the situation you worked on in exercise 3. Take a few minutes to fully sit with the value of each of the needs you identified. Imagine each need as fully met in your life, perhaps reflecting on

a moment when that need was met or imagining what it would be like and how it would feel, including in your body, for that need to be fully met. When imagining the need as met, check in with your body to see how it responds—see whether you experience lightness, release, or relaxation in any way. Once you have experienced a shift of this kind, it can be helpful to consider what you may wish to do now to act on, or at least hold with care, these needs that matter to you so much.

Part Two

Three months ago, Sylvester took a part-time job in addition to his full-time job because he wanted to increase his income. Now he feels overwhelmed and discouraged; nothing is going well. He's having trouble getting to work on time because he's so tired, his relationship with his partner has deteriorated significantly, and he's stopped going to the softball games he used to enjoy with his friends.

    A. What needs might he have been trying to meet when he decided to accept the part-time job?

    B. What needs appear to be unmet by that choice?

EXERCISE 6: Shifting Self-Judgments to Self-Empathy

Part One

Think of three actions you took or behaviors you engaged in the last week that you did not like and/or are feeling frustrated, sad, or disappointed about. For each, describe the behavior or what you saw yourself doing (observation), any judgments you have about what you did, how you feel when thinking about what you did, and the needs unmet by the action or behavior. Here is an example:

Observation (What I did)	Self-Judgments (Thoughts about what I did)	Feelings about what I did	Needs unmet by what I did
Told one of my children, "Be quiet!" with a volume and tone I didn't like	I was harsh, mean, unfair, unreasonable, and not modeling the kind of behavior I want my children to learn	Sad, discouraged, regretful, heavy-hearted	Care, consideration, awareness, self-connection, choice, integrity

Part Two

Looking at each of the three situations you have identified, would you be as critical of someone else as you are of yourself? If not, why? If you would be less critical, what might you be thinking about the other person and/or the situation that gives you more understanding and compassion? What stories are you telling yourself about your own behavior that's leading you to engage in self-judgment?

Part Three

While sitting with how you feel about each situation you described in part one, and the needs left unmet, can you think of a request you could make of yourself? Regarding the example of raising your voice to a child, you might write, "The next time I'm aware of being really angry and impatient, I'd like to try taking 'time out'—stepping out of the room for five minutes—to cool down and reconnect with my feelings and needs."

Embarrassment, Fear, and Shame: Dealing With Double Judgment

Sometimes when we say or do things that are inconsistent with our values, we feel self-conscious, embarrassed, or sheepish. At these moments, we may not have met our own needs for living our values, making conscious choices, or acting with consideration for others. We may feel vulnerable and prone to fear or shame, wondering what others might think of us. This can be especially true if we fear punishment or "consequences." At such times, we may be wanting acceptance, understanding, security, and trust in relation to others. In practicing self-empathy, it can be helpful to look at all our needs, including those unmet by our actions and the needs possibly unmet by being observed and, perhaps, judged.

Let's look at an example. Tim has been considered the star of his college basketball team and one of the top scorers throughout the year. After many years, his team has finally made it to the division championships. He knows that his coach, teammates, and the whole school are counting on him. During overtime, in the last minute of the game, he drops the ball, and the other team wins. When he thinks about losing the game, Tim feels sad, disappointed, discouraged, insecure, dismayed, and even shocked. By dropping the ball, he has not met his own needs for competency, effectiveness, and contribution. Thinking about what happened and how others may be judging him, he is feeling nervous, scared, disconnected, and vulnerable. These feelings are associated with needs for trust, acceptance, understanding, and support. Aware of both his own feelings and needs and those that others might have, Tim is more empowered to connect with others about his fears and get the connection and support he wants. He might say to his coach, for example:

I'm still in shock. I can't believe I dropped the ball at the last minute—especially after getting so many points earlier in the game. I really thought I'd make the difference for the team this year. I'm also a little nervous—I wonder what you're thinking about what happened?

Regardless of what Tim's coach or anyone else is thinking, by asking in this way Tim can connect with others and find out what judgments they might, in fact, be holding. In this example, Tim offers his own feelings and needs and then also shares that he's nervous about the coach's response and would like to know what he's thinking.

In my experience, as someone who has struggled with fear of judgment for most of my life, I have found that 99.9 percent of the time, what people are actually thinking is light years from what I fear. They are usually thinking of their own issues and concerns. For example, Tim's coach may be worried that his contract is in jeopardy of not being renewed and wondering if the team losing will affect the renewal of his contract. Rather than experiencing anger or contempt from people whose judgment I fear, I usually find understanding and compassion. In the rare cases I do hear judgment, I can choose to self-empathize silently in order to calm my own distress and then empathize with what the other person is feeling and needing. To illustrate, Tim and his coach could have the following dialogue after Tim's statement and inquiry:

> Coach (sharing his judgments of Tim aloud): You blew it— you froze just when the team needed you! And we'd talked about how to handle situations like that—you should have jumped in sooner!
>
> Tim (empathizing silently with himself): Wow! When I hear the coach say, "You blew it!" I'm frustrated and mad. I know I missed the last shot, but I really helped the team a lot this year—I don't think we'd have made it this far without

my moves. I'd love some appreciation for all that I did do
for the team.

Tim (empathizing with the coach—also silently, to himself): I
bet he's really disappointed because we were so close
to winning the championship and this is the first time
we got this close since he became coach. Now we have
to win the next two games. I can understand why he's
frustrated, and I know a lot is riding on this for him.

Tim (empathizing out loud with the coach): Yeah, I know this is
very upsetting for you. You really had high hopes of our
winning the championship this year, and now you're
probably nervous about whether we'll make it or not.

Coach: Yes, that's true. I didn't mean to snap at you—it's just we
were so close, and this game would have sealed it for us! I
know you were trying your best.

Once the coach has a sense of being understood, he is better
able to understand what might be going on for Tim. Tim is able
to find the space to empathize with the coach because he has
self-empathized first, mourning his own unmet needs and then
guessing what feelings and needs might be "up" for the coach.
Finding common ground in shared perspectives makes for renewed
understanding and connection. When Tim asks the coach about his
experience and names his own discomfort about what happened, he
opens up space for dialogue, and to address misunderstandings.

EXERCISE 7: Taming Double Judgment

Think of an action you took that you were unhappy with and that you
fear others may be judging. What are your own judgments, feelings,
and needs in relation to the choice you made? What judgments do
you think others might have and how do you feel thinking about these
judgments? What needs are "up" for you regarding the judgments?

First, describe the situation in one to two sentences. Then list:

My judgments of my actions

My feelings about my actions

My needs "up" in relation to my actions

Judgment(s) I fear others may have

How I feel thinking about these judgments

Needs "up" thinking about these judgments

Self-Empathy for Full Choice

I could make things the way I want if I could figure out what I want.

—ANDREW

In addition to fostering compassion for choices we've made and supporting us in resolving differences with others, self-empathy can help us make choices in the present. In doing so, it's helpful to remember that our needs are not in competition. All needs are life serving and valuable. In practicing self-empathy and doing a "needs-meter reading," we are not pitting one need against another and judging or rating them. Rather, we are taking a needs "inventory"—placing all our needs out on the table where we can see and appreciate them and noticing which ones are most "up" at this point in time. One way to do this when making a decision is write on a piece of paper the different strategies we are considering and then make a list of the needs met or unmet by each strategy. We can then sit with the energy of the needs as met (including noticing the response somatically), discern which needs we will choose to act on in this moment, and mourn any needs unmet by our choice. In the following exercise, you see an example of what this process can look like.

EXERCISE 8: Making Needs-Meeting Choices

Grace was in her senior year of college and not sure what to do: part of her thought she should get a job to start her career and bring in money. She also thought it could be helpful to do further study and get a higher degree. And part of her was longing for the meaning and adventure of working abroad for a year as a volunteer.

Situation: What to do after finishing college			
	Strategy A: Grad school	Strategy B: Job	Strategy C: Join Peace Corps
Feelings thinking about strategy	Excited, stimulated, nervous, eager	Hesitant, bored, accepting, excited	Excited, scared, inspired, curious
Needs met by strategy	Learning, challenge, growth, community, meaning, self-development, hope (about choices/ opportunities in the future)	Sustainability, security, choice (from having financial resources), confidence, independence, challenge, growth, develop-ment, learning	Purpose, adventure, challenge, choice, growth/ learning, meaning, contribution, engagement with the world, aliveness
Needs unmet by strategy	Financial sus-tainability and independence in the short-term, lack of spacious-ness with focus/ intensity of grad school, predict-ability, ease	Purpose, adventure, growth, learning	Security, safety, predictability, ease, comfort, financial sustainability (at least for term of service)

After sitting with all her needs in this way and noticing energetically her feelings, sensations, and needs regarding each choice, Grace decided to apply for a volunteer position abroad. She noticed that the needs met around this choice were most "alive" for her; she also accepted that the needs unmet (such as for financial sustainability/ease during her Peace Corps service) are needs that she was willing to live with as unmet to gain this life experience. In sitting with her needs, she especially noticed the response in her body concerning each choice and the needs met or unmet. When thinking about volunteering abroad, she noticed a lightness in her heart area and a burst of energy that extended into her limbs. While there was some anxiety (experienced as tightness in her stomach), it did not have the same level of intensity as her feelings of excitement.

Now it's your turn to do a "needs-meter." Think of a decision you want to make and that perhaps you are even torn about.

A. On a sheet of paper, write down the different strategies you are considering.
B. Below each strategy, write down how you are feeling about each one. Then sit with your feelings. What sensations and energy do you notice in your body? To connect with your feelings, you may find it helpful to use your imagination. Visualize taking the course of action you're considering. Imagine in your mind's eye going through each step involved. Imagining the action in this way, what feelings, sensations, eagerness, or willingness do you observe?
C. After connecting with your feelings thoroughly in this way, consider what needs would be met by taking each action. Name each need and reflect on how much you would value experiencing fulfillment of that need. You can also imagine holding one need that would be met in your left hand and another need in your right and "weigh" the aliveness of each need for you in this moment.
D. Once you've completed the above steps, check in with

yourself to see if you have clarity or a changed perception about which strategy you'd prefer. If you don't, you may wish to go back and check to see that you've fully identified all the feelings and needs at play.

E. When you're clear about which strategy you would like to choose, check to see if any needs will go unmet. If so, honor them. Sit with how much you value those particular needs and how much you want to experience them in your life. You may wish to consider your openness to meeting those needs in another way at the moment, or at a future time with a different strategy. This reflection and consideration of all the relevant needs is an important step to feeling peace and ease about the choice you make.

F. Did you find this exercise helpful? Has it given you some new insights, including about making decisions and holding all your own needs with care? Note these on the sheet of paper.

Taking Responsibility for Our Choices

Sometimes it's easy to think we have no choice, that there are things we *have* to do. When I think in this way, I remind myself of an old saying: "No one can take from you that which is really yours." Your autonomy—your ability to choose—is always yours. In some situations, you may wish that you had more or different choices, but there are always choices. To look at an everyday example, consider the following dialogue:

Tim: Shoot—I have to go to work tomorrow.
Jack: What would happen if you didn't go to work?
Tim: Well, I'd get fired.
Jack: So, you are choosing to go to work because you want the security of keeping your job?
Tim: Well, yeah, I guess I am.

If you are thinking in terms of reward and punishment, you may feel you have no choice. If you don't go to work, you will lose your job: that, in effect, can be viewed as a "punishment" (as our society often frames it) or, at least, a consequence. Yet going to work or not is a strategy to meet your *own* needs. It is these needs—not the demand or threat of retribution—that you're responding to and acting on when you choose to go to work.

Ultimately, we all have a choice in how we respond even in the most dire circumstances. Viktor Frankl, psychiatrist and author of *Man's Search for Meaning*, observed when in the Nazi concentration camps, for example, that people (even under such extreme and limited conditions) exercised choice in how they dealt with their environment. They chose, for example, to cooperate or compete with their fellow inmates and made different choices in how they responded to the guards, many of whom were acting in ways that would be considered harsh. Some in the camps, even under the most inhumane of circumstances, managed to act from a spirit of compassion.

It may be challenging to remember the choices we have. If we are anticipating or experiencing needs unmet, and don't like any of the options we see, it may feel like we have little choice or none at all. By checking in with ourselves about what needs we *are* meeting—or seeking to meet—by a strategy we take, we can remember what we're saying "yes" to and take responsibility for our choices, as well as any unmet needs. This is often also the first step in coming up with other strategies that can meet our needs. Regarding the dialogue about the job, for example, if you are aware of how much you dislike going to your job and the needs it helps you meet—and doesn't, this can be the first step in exploring other ways to meet the same needs, such as, perhaps, looking for a different job, considering what changes or requests you could make about the current job, working part time, or other strategies. Regardless of what you choose, it is empowering and even sometimes liberating to take full responsibility for your choices and the needs they meet, and to mourn any needs that are unmet by the strategies you engage in.

EXERCISE 9: Uncovering Choices

The following exercise will give you practice in translating "have to" statements into statements reflecting choices you have and the needs you may meet in your choices.

Statement	Consequence of doing the opposite	Translation into a positive choice statement/Needs met
"I have to go home this weekend or my mother will kill me."	"If I don't go home this weekend, my mother may be hurt and disappointed. We've been planning this visit for weeks and she told me she's looking forward to it."	"I am choosing to go home this weekend because I know it will please my mom and I enjoy that. Needs met for contribution, care, connection."
"I have to write a paper this weekend."		
"I have to go to work."		
"I have to call my boyfriend."		

Empathic and Nonempathic Choices

One of the most liberating and creative ideas in NVC is that we have choice in how we hear others and how we respond to them. When a person gives us a message, especially one that we consider critical, there are two choice points:

- Do we focus on the other person or on ourselves?
- Do we respond empathically (about feelings and needs) or nonempathically (with judgment, evaluation, and blame)?

When combined, these two choice points lead to four types of possible response:

Four Types of Response (Empathic and Nonempathic):			
Stimulus:	Focus on:	Nonempathic Response: Blame, judgment, disconnection	Empathic Response: Focus on feelings and needs
Parent says, "Your grades are so low I wonder why you are in school if you're not going to do your best."	Self	Blaming self: "I'm a failure. I don't deserve to be in school."	Empathizing with self: "I'm really sad and pained, urgently wanting some understanding and support."
	Other	Blaming other: "You're so unfair. You don't have a clue what I have to put up with."	Empathizing with other: "Are you upset and worried because you're wanting to trust that I'm going to be OK with the choices I'm making?"

With each conversation we engage in, these choice points occur. Will you respond in a nonlife connecting way, from a place of criticism and blame? Or will you respond with empathy? How will you direct your energy at the moment, toward another or toward yourself? In the course of a dialogue, this focus of attention will repeatedly shift. At one moment, you may want to empathize with yourself; in the next, you may choose to focus on the person(s) you're engaging with.

EXERCISE 10: Four Ways of Responding—Awareness and Choice

Read about the following situation and then complete the four types of possible responses (focus on self versus other, and focus on judgment versus feelings and needs).

> At a party, Dan tells a joke about a white man having sex with two "Oriental" women. Peter says, "The correct term is 'Asian American,' and I don't think it's funny! It's racist and offensive!"
> What are four ways Dan could respond in this situation? Give a sample response for each kind of reply:
> (*Note:* These responses could be actually spoken aloud or just said silently to oneself.)

    A. Blaming self
    B. Blaming other
    C. Empathizing with self
    D. Empathizing with other

The Fourfold Path of Compassion

In any given moment, we can choose to respond with compassion or not. In the preceding table, we saw two ways of responding compassionately: with empathy directed toward oneself (self-empathy) and with empathy directed toward another (receiving with empathy). There are two other forms we can choose from. Often we think of self-empathy as being a silent, private process, and responding to another empathically as a verbally expressed response. We can also choose to vocally share what is going on within us, describing our observations, feelings, needs, and requests to another (this is honest self-expression). And we can listen empathically to others without speaking or responding (offering silent empathy). Overall, the four ways of compassionate response vary in two ways. Is my empathy focused on myself or another? And is it silent or spoken?

Four Types of Compassionate Responses			
		Manner of Expression	
		Silent	Spoken
Focus on	Self	(Silent) Self-Empathy	Honest Expression
Experience of	Other	(Silent) Empathy	Empathic Response to Other

The four possible kinds of compassionate responses (to ourselves or others; silently or voiced) complete a "dance." When communicating with compassion, we move back and forth (and back again) between these different "steps," depending on what we imagine will most contribute to clarity, movement, ease, understanding, and connection. With this mix of empathy, we may also wish to offer observations (including reflecting what we've heard the other person say or requesting that they recap what they've heard from us) and explore strategies (requests) that address everyone's needs. Including observations and requests with feelings and needs completes the whole four-part practice of Nonviolent Communication.

EXERCISE 11: The Four-Step Dance of Compassion

Read about the following situation and then complete the four kinds of responses possible when practicing Compassionate Communication.

Jennifer is differently abled and uses a wheelchair. A group she's involved with is having a social gathering at a restaurant that's not wheelchair accessible. She raises this concern with the organizer of the event and is told: "It's nothing personal. We want everyone to come. But with the size group that we have, this was the only place that was available."

What are the four compassionate ways that Jennifer could respond in this situation? Give a sample response for each kind of reply described in the Four Types of Compassionate Responses in the table on page 204.

Who's Up Next?

When responding compassionately, how do we decide whom to focus on first, and when? And how do we decide whether to use empathy or self-expression?

When working to resolve a conflict, we want to go where the greatest "heat" or energy is. Which person or group is most "up" in their feelings and needs? Who is most angry, critical, or defensive? Who needs to be heard first? That is the person we start with, whether it is ourselves or the other party. This goes back to the principle of empathy before education. If one person or party is feeling riled up and on edge, it will be difficult if not impossible for them to hear anyone else's concerns, take them in, and respond compassionately. So we seek to establish a connection with the other person through empathic listening before trying to educate them about the impact of their choices on us or about how we're seeing things.

In determining who's the "hottest," check in with yourself first using a self-empathy practice that leads you to connect with your feelings and needs. Once you're practiced self-empathy and are feeling connected with yourself, then you may wish to direct your empathy outward, toward the person or group you're interacting with. Focusing on the other person does not mean that you're putting aside your own feelings and needs; you're simply "holding" the insight you've gained about yourself through practicing self-empathy until the other person has a chance to be heard and lets off steam. If your self-empathy does not give you the internal space to hear the other person, you may need to take a break, get some empathy from a friend, or engage in other empathy practices before attempting to hear the other party. Those who practice NVC commonly refer to this practice of silent self-care as "emergency self-empathy." You may not get all the empathy you'd like at that moment, and with enough "emergency" self-empathy you can respond to others with choice and discernment.

Even if you're not triggered in a conversation by what another person says, you can repeatedly practice a "short form" of self-empathy whenever speaking with others by checking in with yourself briefly and repeatedly about your own feelings and needs: Do I still have energy for this conversation? Am I engaged? Am I clear about that point? How do I want to continue?

Doing brief, repeated self-check-ins when connecting with others is like monitoring your pulse rate while exercising. It gives you the optimum "workout" and supports flow, depth, and understanding in any conversation, even one that is mundane, not heated at all. In fact, this is one of my favorite NVC practices. I think many people only remember to use NVC during a conflict. Yet it is probably in everyday dialogues with people that NVC has most enriched my life; this is where I have honed my depth of listening, both to myself and others. By checking in with yourself repeatedly in this way, you can support greater connection. Then, if you are triggered at some point, you will notice it sooner and have more choice in how you respond.

I also cherish this practice of continuous self-empathy to support me in staying in the moment—focusing on what is happening *now* in myself, with the other, and in the conversation—rather than thinking about things on my to-do list, what I might cook for dinner, or any other "monkey-mind" thought that can distract me from what's happening. By engaging in this practice, I have developed greater fluency in practicing NVC, become more aware of my body, sensations, and feelings, deepened my level of self-connection, and become more keenly aware of my needs and how to act on them.

The more skilled you become in practicing empathy, the more you will appreciate how related and interconnected different forms of empathy are. In the course of a conversation you will usually make use of every form of empathic connection: self-empathy, empathy, expression, and silent empathy.

Deepening Our Connection With Ourselves Through Our Judgments

Throughout this book, we have talked about how statements of judgment, criticism, blame, or analysis fail to promote connection between people, and frequently stimulate pain. Yet while we don't want to stay with judgments or use them in communicating with others, they can be very helpful as a first step in connecting with feelings and needs. Being aware of our thoughts and evaluations, we can understand the intensity and quality of our feelings and, through the words we use, gain insight and understanding into what we value.

In voicing our judgments, we can share them with a compassionate and supportive listener who can help us translate them into feelings and needs. Or, via self-empathy, we can state our judgments silently to ourselves, aloud, and/or by writing them in a journal. Once your judgments are "out," see if you can connect a feeling and physical sensation to each one. Then see, based on the words you're using, what needs might be underneath your thoughts and emotions.

Let's see how "unpacking" judgment looks in action, practiced via self-empathy.

Early one morning, Mary Beth is in the bathroom at work and overhears Lisa, whom she considers a friend, talking about her to someone Mary Beth doesn't know well at all. Lisa tells this person a number of things about Mary Beth's social life that Mary Beth had told her with the request that she keep them to herself. Lisa also makes a number of statements critical of Mary Beth's maturity and honesty. Mary Beth becomes aware of feeling overwhelmed with anger, rage, pain, and hurt. She decides to explore her feelings and needs further before deciding how to respond.

In private, she writes down all the intense thoughts that come to her mind about what she heard Lisa say. These judgments include:

- I can't believe she's such a two-faced person.
- She said she was my friend, and now she has betrayed me on everything I've said.
- I feel so violated.
- I am disgusted at the thought of people I don't know learning private things about me.
- People are going to look strangely at me now.
- How could I have been such a fool as to trust her?

After writing down her judgments, Mary Beth goes through the list, identifying her feelings and needs for each statement. Here's what a few of her judgments on the list might look like. Note that some of the needs come up more than once:

Statement	Feelings: Wanting (Needed)
1. "I can't believe she's such a two-faced person."	Rage: Wanting trust, integrity Disgust: Wanting caring, consideration Fear: Wanting trust, safety, understanding
2. "She said she was my friend and now she has betrayed me on everything I've said."	Despair: Wanting trust, caring Overwhelmed: Wanting integrity, support Hurt: Wanting caring, understanding

After Mary Beth identifies her feelings and needs and sits with them for a while, she can then make a number of requests of herself or other people to support her in meeting her needs, including Lisa if Mary Beth wishes to discuss her concerns with her.

EXERCISE 12: Composting Judgments Into Live Experience

Based on the situation of Mary Beth and Lisa and the examples above, translate the following judgments into feelings and needs:

Statement	Feelings: Wanting (Needed)
1. "I am disgusted at the thought of people I don't know learning such intimate things about me."	
2. "People are going to look strangely at me now."	
3. "How could I have been such a fool to trust her?"	

Speaking From the Energy of Needs

In a number of the exercises in this chapter, I have invited you to identify the needs that are engaged in a specific situation. The intention, however, is not just for you to be able to name those needs; rather, it is to fully embrace each need or value and be keenly aware of how much it contributes to your life. From that intimate place of self-empathic connection, you can continue your daily activities, potentially including verbal communication. Your goal is to communicate your connection to the needs *as met* in how and what you say and do.

EXERCISE 13: Connecting With and Speaking From the Energy of Needs

A. Think of a situation where some feelings and needs were triggered for you. It could be one in which you experienced your needs as met or unmet. What is your observation about what happened?

B. Identify a key feeling and a key need that are true for you regarding this situation.

C. Formulate a connection request that you might make following an expression of your observation, feeling, and need; for example, "What comes up for you hearing this?"

D. State the expression aloud, without the person the message is intended for being present, including the observation, feeling, need, and request: for example, "When you asked me to move my suitcase, I felt a bit annoyed because I want ease in how we live together and a sense of space for both of us. I'm wondering how it is for you to hear this?" Notice how it sounds. Is it engaging? Matter-of-fact? Inviting open-hearted connection? Is it coming from your head or your heart— from an intention of wanting to connect?

E. Now take a few minutes to connect with the energy of needs. Choose a need that is central for you in the situation you have chosen. Imagine a time, place, or circumstance (actual or hypothetical) in which this need is fully, abundantly, and sweetly met or lived. Picture the whole scene in your mind. What is happening in the scene? Who is involved? What else is present? How is your body responding? What parts of your body are responding the most? In what ways? How do you feel experiencing those feelings? Observe the energy in different parts of your body responding to this scene. Imagine that energy amplified and moving throughout your body. The invitation is for you to completely embrace how much you love that need, how much it contributes to your sense of well-being. Spend several minutes being present with the fullness of your bodily and emotional experience, enjoying how much you treasure that need or value in your life and how much it supports you to know that value.

F. Holding the need and your connection to the energy of that need in your mind, restate aloud the full expression of observation, feeling, need, and request. Does it sound different when you speak with a connection to the energy of the need? Do you feel different about your expression when speaking this time? How do you think it may affect the listener when you speak from this place of connection?

Self-Empathy Through Images, Music, and Movement

Although we often find it helpful to use words to name our feelings and needs, as tools for clarifying for ourselves and others what we are experiencing, the words are not the experience itself. For many people, visual images can be useful tools for recognizing, integrating, and valuing our experience and desires. To explore this practice, I encourage you to make a personal collection of images from magazines, newspapers, and the Internet that speak to your particular feelings and needs. You may wish to browse through them when you reflect on a particular experience, choosing a few that you resonate with. You may wish to place the images where you can gaze at them during the day or week and see if doing so enhances your understanding of feelings and needs for yourself or others.

Just as some people make "vision boards," you can attach these pictures to a piece of paper or a board and note around them the feelings and needs you associate with each picture. You can also focus on feelings or needs you want to experience more of in your life—such as joy, fun, or rest—and pick images that express or represent those needs as met. Regardless of how you work with the images, each time you gaze at them, be sure to notice the response in your body and practice taking in the energy of the need as met.

Similarly, you can develop a collection of musical selections that speak to your inner experience. Is there a particular piece of music that, when you listen to it, meets your need for rest? For play? For excitement or stimulation? You may wish to move your body, arms, legs, or torso when you listen to the music to further explore how you experience it. What happens when you deliberately move in a different way? More intensely? Less intensely? Very slowly? Do you become aware of different feelings or of different needs, met or unmet? This can be a fun exercise, and you can include children, "playing" with feelings and needs and deepening your awareness and experience of them.

Is there a smell or other sensory stimulus that you respond to, one that brings up feelings and needs for you? Is there an animal, plant, object, place, or activity that could be a metaphor for what you feel or value?

We each have many different ways of understanding our experiences. Feel free to use your creative imagination to expand your understanding of your internal terrain; whatever you find there is invaluable information. The needs underlying your experience are all positive and life enhancing. Explore and learn to recognize your feelings and needs in all their richness and diversity. Such awareness and fluency are all forms of practicing self-empathy, which can most broadly be defined as awareness of your feelings and needs in each moment.

Self-Empathy for Celebrating Needs Met

Throughout this book, we have explored how the practice of Nonviolent Communication is about celebrating needs met as well as unmet. Often, if we're focused on resolving conflict, we can forget the beauty and power of naming and appreciating needs met. Putting our focus on needs met when practicing self-empathy, alone or with others, is a profound experience. The next time you're excited, happy, delighted, or relieved, or experiencing some other feeling related to needs met, take a moment and practice self-empathy to further your experience. What positive judgments are you telling yourself about what happened? What feelings and needs are underneath this judgment? What matters most to you (on a needs level) about what you experienced? You can practice self-empathy in this way regarding your own actions and any experience you have related to others or the world.

Moving On

It can take time to develop the skill of self-empathy. As with giving empathy to others, remember to take your time with each step. Allow yourself to be with your feelings and needs, to fully accept and embrace the uniqueness of what you feel. Notice how each feeling and need you experience is a reminder of the vibrant life within you; it is telling you that you are not an inanimate object! Listen to your body. Review the suggestions for increasing your awareness of body sensations as a guide to knowing your feelings and needs, as discussed in chapters 1 and 2. If you get stuck—if you feel unable to fully empathize with yourself or get as clear about your feelings and needs as you would like—you may wish to seek the help of an "empathy buddy," someone who is familiar with the NVC steps and willing to go through them with you.

Self-empathy has broad applications. It can help you respond to others, creating the space within you that enables you to respond with compassion, choice, and awareness. It can also help you create kindness and compassion in how you speak to yourself when you're engaging in self-pity, are in fear of judgment, or are addressing "mistakes" you've made. It can be useful in making choices, especially choosing between strategies where some needs may be met and unmet. It can also help you to celebrate what matters most to you in life, via needs met.

INTEGRATION: Further Questions and Exercises to Explore Chapter 6

A. Consider each of the following questions and then complete the chart that follows:

  1. Imagine that each of the following happened to you. What feelings might you have? What needs might be stimulated? (Use the lists of feelings and needs on pages 367 and 368.)

  2. After completing the chart, take a few minutes to reflect slowly on each need and how much you value and appreciate it, connecting deeply with how much you value that need in your life. You may also wish to find an image or object that speaks to that need for you.

  3. Then consider what intention, course of action, or "self-request" you might make.

Event	Feelings	Needs	"Self-Request"
You receive a letter saying that you are not going to be offered the job you had hoped for.			
You get into an argument about politics with a friend who says that your ideas are "stupid."			

You find out that your afternoon lab class is canceled and you don't have to make it up. (Self-empathy is for when needs are being met as well as for when needs are not being met.)			

4. Having completed the exercise above, did you notice a shift in your understanding or experience of the event that happened? If so, describe this.

B. The daily practice of self-empathy can help you listen and act with compassion. Two to five times during the next week, try taking the following steps when you notice you are reacting to a situation or event. Keep a journal or another kind of log of your self-empathy practice. Remember that empathy can be practiced with "fulfilled" feelings, and needs met as well as unmet. As has been discussed in this chapter, it may also be helpful to start out by looking at your judgments, to unpack what you might be feeling and needing. Here are the four basic steps:

Observation: What is happening (what am I seeing, hearing, thinking about) that is stimulating some response in me?

Feeling: What feelings are being stimulated in me?

Need: What needs and values of mine are not being met at the moment?

Request: What request can I ask of myself (or others) that would meet my needs?

In logging the above, you may also wish to track the following:

- The names of the feeling(s)
- How you are experiencing them in your body—for example, tenseness, heat, restriction, or release.
- Where you're experiencing this sensation—for example, in your head or chest.

As more feelings come up, empathize with what you're needing until you feel "complete." Note in your journal or log any shift you experience, when you feel complete in your empathy, and any strategies you might be considering.

C. Think back on a recent conflict. Out of the four possible empathic and nonempathic ways of responding (blame directed outward, blame directed inward, empathy directed outward, empathy directed inward), how did you choose to respond? What was the result of that choice? How did it meet your needs or not meet them? Looking back, how do you think a different response would have led to different results?

D. Choose someone who is familiar with NVC to be your "empathy buddy" for the week and make an "empathy date." This can be in person or over the phone. At the start of your time together, do a quick check-in (one to three sentences, or about thirty seconds) about what's most "up" for each of you in your life at the moment. Are you angry with someone from work? Annoyed with someone you're friends with? Anxious about bills you've received? Happy about an interaction with your partner? After the two of you check in and get a sense of what's most on your minds, listen empathically to the person whose feelings are most intense first. This will support the first speaker in being more present with the second person when it's their turn to speak during the second half of the session.

As an alternative, either of you can practice using the self-empathy process aloud. The listener provides coaching and support in this process, checking in with the speaker about their observations, feelings, needs, and requests, especially when they get stuck.

7

Stepping Into the Fire: Enjoying and Responding to Anger

Anger is natural. It's part of the force.
You just have to learn to hang out with it.
—TORI AMOS, singer

For me music is a vehicle to bring our pain to the surface,
getting it back to that humble and tender spot where, with luck,
it can lose its anger and become compassion again.
—PAULA COLE, singer and songwriter

In this book, we have discussed a wide range of feelings and needs and how to respond to them. There is a "wild card," however, in the deck of emotions, one that people can find especially challenging to hear and express—anger. Because it involves judgment and can lead quickly to disconnection and even physical violence, anger can feel like fire: dangerous, destructive, and difficult to control. Like all emotions, however, anger can also be seen as a gift. In this chapter, as we come to understand this volatile emotion, we will see how anger can serve us in identifying our values and living authentically.

Only One Person Can Make You Angry

One of the most important things to remember about anger is that no one else can make you angry; only you can. We first encountered the underlying idea in chapter two: our feelings are caused not by other people but by our needs. This concept is pivotal in understanding anger. At first, accepting this may seem like a big leap, because blaming others for our feelings is an integral part of anger. The primary thinking behind this emotion is "I'm upset (scared, hurt, or sad) and it's *your* fault because of what you did—you shouldn't have done that!" Yet while the behavior of other people (or ourselves, in the case of self-judgment) is the *stimulus* or *trigger* for our anger, the way we talk to ourselves about the behavior we see, employing *should thinking* or *right-wrong thinking,* is, in fact, the actual root *cause* of what we're feeling. Anger is feeling mixed with thoughts and judgments.

Let's look at an example. Felicia doesn't want her parents to know she's dating Tony because he's of a different ethnic background and she's sure they won't approve. Tony is angry about that. The stimulus for his anger is Felicia's behavior—her refusing to tell her parents about him. Yet the cause is Tony's thinking. He's telling himself: "She should be happy to tell them about me. She shouldn't be embarrassed or afraid." Other thoughts might be fueling Tony's anger. He may be wondering how committed she is to the relationship, given that she won't let her parents know about it. Regardless, it is his thoughts about the situation—his "should" thinking—not the situation itself that is the cause of his rage.

Taking responsibility for our thoughts and judgments, as well as our needs, is the first step in gaining awareness and control in how we respond to anger. If we fall into cause-and-effect thinking—you *made* me do it, or you *made* me feel this way—we lose full autonomy, responsibility, and choice. This does not mean we always like the actions of others; rather, we take responsibility for our own actions and choices in responding to them. In this way, we can see each situation in our lives simply as a potential stimulus of our emotions, not as an inescapable cause of them.

The table on page 221 shows how the type of thinking we employ can cause us to feel either angry and frustrated or curious and warm.

Our anger is caused by our thinking		
Stimulus: I am about to pull into a parking space in a crowded lot. A small car quickly passes me and turns into the spot.		
Type of thinking	*Examples of thoughts in the situation*	*Feelings stimulated*
Should (right-wrong) thinking	"The driver is aggressive and should respect that I was there first."	Angry, frustrated, discouraged
Should (right-wrong) thinking	"This is disgusting. Incivility and behavior like this are bad for the world. People shouldn't behave this way."	Angry, enraged, despairing, hopeless
Needs-based thinking	"Seeing the driver take the spot I was intending to occupy, I am reminded of how much I love it when people show care for each other's intentions and respect for everyone's needs."	Tender toward myself and my love of care and orderliness, warm because I am connected to my pleasure in respectful living
Needs-based thinking	"I wonder why the driver was so eager to get this spot. Perhaps they are under a lot of time pressure."	Curious, open, aware of my own feelings, concerned for the well-being of the driver

EXERCISE 1: Cause or Trigger?

In everyday conversation and thought, we are continually reinforced in seeing others' behavior as the cause of our anger rather than as the stimulus for it. As we have seen, however, "should thinking" and judgments are the true cause. In this exercise, read each statement and decide whether it describes a stimulus of anger (mark with an "S") or a cause of anger (mark with a "C"). Remember that in NVC, stimuli can be observed; they are events that could be objectively seen through a video camera and experienced in different ways by different observers.

_____ A. "My daughter left food on the counter, and now we have ants in the kitchen."

_____ B. "I overslept and missed my dentist appointment; I should have been more careful."

_____ C. "The clerk at the store should have given me the batteries I asked for; I was clear about what I wanted."

_____ D. "It is the mother's responsibility to see that the child is in the car seat, and she is not fulfilling that responsibility."

_____ E. "I wanted to have sex last night but my partner said, 'I'm tired and want to sleep.'"

_____ F. "If I want to go to medical school, I've got to study more and get better grades."

My responses for this exercise:

A. This is presented as a stimulus for anger because it is an observation of what happened (even if there could be other reasons for ants appearing in the kitchen). If the speaker had said "and she shouldn't have done that" or "she is irresponsible for having done this" after the initial statement, this would be the "cause" of their anger. Conceivably, the response to this stimulus could have been something other than anger: for example, amazement or curiosity—"Isn't it odd that we have ants now and never had ants before? This isn't the first time that we ever left food or dirty dishes out." Note that what the speaker is feeling—irritation, curiosity, or anger—is also indicated via tone of voice.

B. To me, this is presented as a cause of anger. The words "should have been more careful" imply a judgment of wrongdoing. A nonjudgmental description might be "I overslept because I turned the alarm off and then fell back to sleep."

C. This, too, is presented as the cause of anger; the speaker is blaming and judging the clerk, not describing what happened. It would have been a stimulus if the speaker had said, "I asked for AA batteries and the clerk gave me AAA batteries."

D. This statement suggests a cause of anger. The speaker is talking about what the mother should do, because it is her "responsibility." An observation of events without judgment might be "The mother is driving the car, and the child is not in the car seat." "Responsibility" could be named as an unmet need: "Seeing this, I feel concerned; I'm longing for awareness, responsibility, and care regarding safety."

E. This is expressed as a stimulus for anger. There is no judgment. The thought, "Spouses are supposed to please you sexually; that's part of what being in a relationship is about," would be a cause of anger.

F. This is presented as a cause of anger. The speaker is describing what he's "got to do," not describing observations and connecting to needs. A statement describing a stimulus for anger might be "The pre-med advisor said that students with my GPA are not usually accepted to medical school." If I make a "should" thought about the advisor, medical school, or myself (for example, "The advisor should have been more supportive," "Medical schools should be more flexible in admissions," or "I should work harder"), my anger will be directed accordingly to the advisor, the medical schools, or myself.

Watch Those Signals!

The second important thing to know about anger is that it's like opening a floodgate, an intense feeling resulting from an overflow of other feelings. When we become aware of a need or value that is deeply meaningful to us and we notice that we are not experiencing that value in our life, we may experience feelings of sadness, irritation, hurt, or fear. When the stimulation is intense and our response to our unfulfilled needs quickly multiplies, we can go on "overload." Overwhelmed, we may be only minimally aware of what we're feeling; we may even go numb, our feelings of hurt or fear falling beneath our conscious awareness. It is at these moments that we can become aware instead of an intense feeling of anger—perhaps even fury or rage. Like a blaring siren or flashing red light, anger can be seen as an "emergency" signal indicating that something requires attending to: that needs are not being met—and in a big way.

The root meaning of "emergency" is to emerge, or become visible. Anger helps to make visible the needs that are precious to us, and this can be tremendously helpful. Likewise, there is nothing intrinsically "bad" or undesirable about the judgments and "should thinking" that cause anger. Both the judgments and the anger contribute to our well-being by helping us to identify and pay attention to what is really important: valuing our needs.

EXERCISE 2: Getting to the Root of Anger

Part One
Imagine that you are in each of the following situations, and feeling angry.
   A. What judgments, criticisms, or thoughts of blame might you be having?
   B. What feeling might you be experiencing underneath the anger?

C. What need(s) do you imagine might be active in you that
     could be causing these feelings?

Let's begin with an example.

Situation	Judgment	Feelings	Needs
1. Your friend is visiting and asks to borrow your computer. You have left your email window open, and after your friend leaves, based on a comment he makes regarding the content, you are sure he has read one of your emails without asking your permission.	"He is so self-centered, has no concern for my privacy, my rights, my space. Only thinks of himself. Here I was, trying to help him out, and he violated my trust!"	Rage, anger, insecure, hurt, frustration, fear	Care, respect, security, trust, space, choice, consideration
2. You just received notice from your landlord that she is selling the building and you have to vacate your apartment in thirty days; you have just signed a new one-year lease.			
3. You are accused by your supervisor of misplacing an important file at work that you are sure you returned to her the day after you borrowed it.			

Part Two
This week, notice when you become angry. What feelings and needs are beneath the anger? In hindsight, were these feelings and needs "backing up" before you noticed or named them? You may wish to write about this in your journal.

EXERCISE 3: Developing Choice in Responding to the Anger of Others

Part One
Imagine you are in each of these situations and then answer the following questions:

A. Without thinking about it too much, what might your "automatic" response be? Freely express all your judgments; they will assist you in clarifying your needs.
B. What are your feelings and needs beneath your judgments?
C. Once you are connected to your feelings and needs, how might you respond in each situation? Note that you may choose to honesty express your own feelings and needs and/or empathically respond to the speaker.

> *Example:* Your boss says, "You're incompetent and irresponsible. You're fired!"
>
> A. My response might be "You can keep your stupid job! Why would I want it anyway? You have never liked me. You probably want to hire your son."
> B. I'm feeling angry, and underneath my anger I'm feeling scared, hurt, and nervous. I'm wanting security, trust, openness, and honesty.
> C. Connected response: "I'm hearing you say that I'm incompetent and irresponsible. Can you tell me what I've done so I can understand why you're upset with me?"

Now you can try:

1. Your partner says, "You're not doing enough to help out at home. They're your kids too!"

    A.

    B.

    C.

2. Your sister says, "I'm tired of how you take the family for granted—it's always just about you and your work!"

    A.

    B.

    C.

3. When you question a bill at a service station, the attendant says, "If you don't like it, just take your business elsewhere."

    A.

    B.

    C.

4. Your loved one says, "How come we always do what you want to do?"

    A.

    B.

    C.

Part Two

Go back to each situation above and guess the feelings and needs of the other person. Does this impact your feelings and needs about the situation and how you might respond?

The Challenge of Hearing Anger Empathically

How much more grievous are the consequences of anger than the causes of it.

—MARCUS AURELIUS,
second-century Roman emperor

Because anger is an intense emotion, it may stimulate intense feelings and needs in us. If we haven't learned to feel comfortable with such powerful experiences, or even simply be present with them—and many of us have not—we may seek ways to squelch or avoid them. Hearing someone else direct anger toward us can involve hearing judgments of our wrongness, which may stimulate our own self-judgments; this, too, can be difficult to hear. Added to these challenges, the anger of others may stimulate stored memories of earlier experiences with angry people where we feared for our physical or emotional safety. Our responses, therefore, can easily draw from these earlier experiences rather than the reality of what is happening in the present.

With practice, we can learn to respond empathically in nearly every situation where someone is expressing anger, toward another or toward us. We will look at each of these situations in turn.

Facing the Fear of Our Own Judgments

The intoxication of anger, like that of the grape, shows us to others, but hides us from ourselves.

—JOHN DRYDEN, seventeenth-century
English poet and dramatist

If we agree with all or part of the judgment that is mixed up with the anger another person is expressing toward us—if we, too, are bothered about some aspects of the actions we've taken—we can easily move into self-judgment. When we do so, we hear judgment in "stereo"—from both inside and outside ourselves. In such a stimulated state, it can be especially difficult to hear the other person's anger; we're overwhelmed. When we're so distracted by the pain of our own unmet needs (including, perhaps, needs for understanding, acceptance, and shared understanding), it's difficult if not impossible to hear what's going on for the person who's enraged. This phenomenon can occur even when the expression of anger is not particularly intense; screaming or swearing need not be present for the stereo effect to overwhelm us.

At moments such as these, when another person's anger stimulates agreement, self-judgment, or fear within us, it is vital to pause and connect with the feelings and needs that are alive in us so we may speak from this need-connected energy rather than a perspective of *who's right or who's wrong*. We may choose to practice self-empathy and then express what's going on for us, speaking honestly and with transparency, or we may choose to empathize with the other person's needs. Once we have self-connected to our needs, we have the space and capacity to do both.

EXERCISE 4: Unplugging Judgments in Stereo

Think of three recent situations when someone was angry with you. Did you also engage in self-judgment, triggered by their judgments of you? For each situation, write down:
    A. Judgments you heard them express
    B. Judgments that came up for you about them, in response
    C. Judgments that came up about yourself

Now go back to parts B and C and translate each judgment into feelings and needs. If you had been fully connected to the feelings and needs at play, how might you have responded in each situation?

The Carrot and the Stick: Fearing Anger in Others

Great anger is more destructive than the sword.

—INDIAN PROVERB

Sometimes other people's anger can stimulate fear or terror in us. If we have experienced or witnessed physical harm or been punished when people are angry, we may fear this will happen again in the present. We may not remember the trauma, be fully aware of it, or understand cognitively how it relates to current events, yet it can still have an impact. As someone has pointed out, the difference between anger and danger is just one letter. Some of us have experienced this close connection firsthand.

Most of us are accustomed to looking to others for approval or acceptance. If someone is angry with us, we assume we've done something wrong. "It's my fault—again!" Caught up in this kind of thinking, we may do whatever we can to keep the peace, believing, "If they think I'm OK, then I must be OK." We conclude that if anyone feels offended by what we've said or done, we must change. We take responsibility for others' feelings, using their reactions rather than our own internal values and needs as a guide for our behavior. This has been described by the noted therapist Virginia Satir as "people-pleasing."

It's not surprising that many of us become people-pleasers. Most of us grew up with punishments and rewards; we were told that if we did the "right" thing, we would be rewarded and if we didn't, we would be made to suffer. We were rewarded and punished in numerous ways, through grades, treats after dinner, weekly allowances, blame, and corporal punishment (slapping or spanking). When we become adults, this reward-punishment system continues via salaries, promotions, late fees, and traffic violations. Like dogs trained to do tricks, the result is that we look to others to guide our choices. We don't unconditionally hold our own value.

From the start of our lives, we have heard people say things like "I'm angry because you left your toys on the floor!" "He's sad because you won't play with him. Won't you make him happy and share your truck?" "I'm depressed because you always say 'no.'" When people communicate again and again that our behavior has caused their feelings, it's understandable that we're confused.

Most of us like to believe we are acting out of autonomy and choice. So accustomed are we to living in a system of punishment and reward that we rarely, if ever, see how that "system" informs our decisions; it is so pervasive, we don't fully see or recognize it. Almost every day our decisions are motivated by fear or societal norms. We may ask ourselves: "What if I get caught? What will my parents say? Would my friends understand?" In contrast, how often do we reflect on what is important to us—what we truly value and how we want to live and behave? In not reflecting on these questions, and not being fully aware of our values, we may not be living in full integrity . . . or fully living at all.

As a teen, I asked my mother why she'd chosen to have children. She was married just a year when she had my brother at nineteen, and I came along a year later. She answered that she really didn't know—"It's just what everyone did then: got married and had children." It seems getting married and having children was a strategy for acceptance and inclusion (fitting in) and simplicity and ease (not knowing the next step in life). Hearing similar stories from others and reflecting on actions I've taken, I feel sad thinking about how people can make decisions, including what I would consider significant choices, "on automatic pilot," without full awareness or choice.

Seeking and receiving approval seemingly offers acceptance, ease, and peace—yet it comes at a price. It does not support real, honest interactions the way learning how to hear and respond to others' anger can.

EXERCISE 5: Do You Seek the Approval of Others?

Part One
A. Read through the following list. Which behaviors are familiar to you? Do you:
    - Get very anxious when people yell at you?
    - Feel the need to fix things or apologize when people are upset?
    - Try to avoid people when they are upset?
    - Omit information or rely on a "little white lie" in order to avoid scenes?
    - Do things you would rather not in order to avoid saying "no" to people?
    - Sometimes apologize to keep the peace, even when you really don't think you've done anything wrong?
B. Give three examples from your life of when you engaged in people-pleasing. What needs were you trying to meet in your choice to act as you did? You can write about this in your journal.

Part Two
A. Look back on your life, from your earliest years. Think of five examples of punishment and reward that were used in your "education"—at home, at school, and by society at large. We have started you off with an example.
    1. Grades: "failing" or "passing" a test
    2. _____
    3. _____
    4. _____
    5. _____
    6. _____
B. Think about some choices you've made in life, including what you might consider "major" decisions. What informed your choices? Did judgment and/or punishment and reward

influence the choices you made? Or a desire for acceptance or even approval?

C. If you were completely unafraid of censure or judgment, what might you choose to do in your life? In considering this question, check to see that all your needs would be met by this choice (including contributing to life, and care and consideration for others).

Turning the Tables: Expressing Anger to Others

It's safe to say that many people don't enjoy being angry. Physically, it's a stressful and unpleasant sensation, often experienced as tightness, pressure, and restriction. When we're angry, we're probably not experiencing connection, ease of communication, understanding, or trust. We urgently want expression and relief: for most people, these are crucial needs. We intensely desire to be heard, and to see our judgments as "true." (They must be true; why else would we be so enraged?) During such moments, just when we can least express our views in a way that can be heard, we may be especially likely to share our judgments of others. We may do so because we value authenticity and saying what's "real" and "as it is." Yet how will expressing ourselves in this way support our truly being heard, getting our needs met, and living in alignment with our values?

Isn't Anger Ever Justified?

The more intense our feelings and needs, the harder it is to separate them from their stimuli. It also becomes hard to separate the person who stimulated us from the stimulus itself. This is especially true in the case of profound trauma, when it can be hard to imagine that the pain we're experiencing is the result of our own unmet needs. Surely if the driver had not run a red light, you would not be in the hospital now with a broken leg, missing spring break. Surely if your partner had not gotten involved with another person and left you, you would not be distraught and alone. In such cases, it is exceptionally easy to have judgments of others. The stimulus, or trigger, and what you're feeling can seem like cause and effect, clear and simple.

When pain is stimulated in us, especially great and traumatic pain, we may also want someone to take the blame or "pay for" our distress—and have a little taste of it. We may think, "Only if they can hurt the way I've hurt will they understand what I've endured. Then maybe they'll know what it's like, and they'll do things differently in the future." At these moments, we probably want mutuality, understanding, and compassion. We probably also need responsibility and awareness with regard to the impact the other person's actions has had on our lives.

In effect, this way of thinking is a misguided attempt at empathy. We want others to experience pain or retribution as a strategy to create mutuality, shared experience, and accountability. This kind of "deserve" thinking can actually lead people to enjoy the suffering of others. While they may think they're getting empathy, in fact they're simply contributing to more pain and disconnection, continuing the cycle of suffering and loss. Most simply, as Marshall Rosenberg has framed it, "When your concept of justice is based on good and evil, in which people deserve to suffer for what they've done, it makes violence enjoyable." In the interview in the appendix, he explores different examples of this on societal and international levels.

Alternatively, identifying the choices that we and others have made, and showing the inconsistency between these choices and the values we hold, can bring about an understanding far more likely to result in the fulfillment of needs, including needs for restoration, harmony, and justice.

Compassionate Communication is not about idealism, kindness, or generosity to others. It is about creating connection and, in doing so, dramatically increasing the odds that our own needs and concerns will be considered and met.

EXERCISE 6: Restoration or Retribution

Part One

Read the interview with Marshall Rosenberg in the appendix and answer the following questions:

    A. Why is "deserve" the most dangerous word in the English language?

    B. How does the concept of "deserve" motivate and inform retributive justice?

    C. Why did the college students in Texas celebrate capital punishment and have a party when someone on death row was executed?

    D. How is restorative justice different from retribution? What question is it based on?

    E. Why is apology "too cheap and too easy"?

    F. What is the difference between "life-serving" judgments and "moral" judgments?

    G. What "needs" could possibly motivate a person to rape another human being?

Part Two

Think of a situation when you wanted another person to suffer or "pay for" their actions. What were you feeling and needing at that moment? Imagine a dialogue between yourself and the other person, or imagine writing a letter to this person. How might you express your pain and approach restoration, making use of empathic expression?

Moving Through Our Anger

In practicing Nonviolent Communication, we don't avoid or suppress our anger. Rather, we seek to identify what's stimulating us and what values are up in the moment. We seek to share this information and make a request to address our needs and concerns. Perhaps you're afraid to express your anger because the only way you know how to do it is with judgment and blame. Yet beneath that judgment is what really matters most to you. By becoming aware of what you want, you're in the best position to see that you get it—and ask for it in a way you don't regret later.

In responding to your anger, a number of principles, some of which we have already covered, can be especially helpful.

- Take responsibility for your own feelings and needs; distinguish stimulus from cause. Each of us is 50 percent responsible for what happens in an interaction and 100 percent responsible for our experience (the feelings and needs stimulated). I am not responsible for how my behavior lands or is received by others—and they are not responsible for the needs I may experience as unmet by their behavior.
- Be open to different strategies or results. When we believe our needs can only be met in one way or by one person, we are setting ourselves up for frustration, hurt, unhappiness and, perhaps even violence, of some form.
- When tempted to respond with right-wrong energy, also try to remember your goal and purpose: is it to connect with the other person, to address an issue that is stimulating for both of you, or to prove that you are "right"?
- Make use of your judgments. Pay attention to the "judgment show." By listening to the energy and content of your thoughts and opinions, you can more easily connect with your feelings and needs.

- The most vital and frequently missed way to break the chain of judgment and anger is getting the empathy we need to be keenly aware of our feelings and needs so we can share them vulnerably, without any shred of wrongdoing included. Self-empathy is an especially crucial skill in dealing with our own anger and the anger of others.

- Connect deeply with all your feelings, including feelings that may be underneath your anger. Anger is a big feeling that can sometimes have other feelings mixed in, such as sadness, disappointment, or fear. These feelings, especially fear, often drive our rage.

Walking Our Talk

A very useful tool for integrating all the steps we have been talking about is the Anger Floor Map (see Anger Floor Map on page 238), adapted from the work of Raj Gill, Lucy Leu, and Judi Morin in the *NVC Toolkit for Facilitators*. You can examine it and point to the various boxes and steps as you proceed through them. Or, better yet, you can print each box onto an 8½ x 11-inch sheet of paper and lay the papers on the floor in the sequence indicated; leave about a foot of space between each of the boxes. Then you can literally walk back and forth past the boxes as you find yourself addressing the content of each.

Step One

Notice that the words of the map spell "stop." This is to remind you that as soon as you become aware of your anger, it is important to *stop* and *breathe*.

Step Two

Stand by (or point with your finger to) the first box, labeled Sensations.

Anger Floor Map

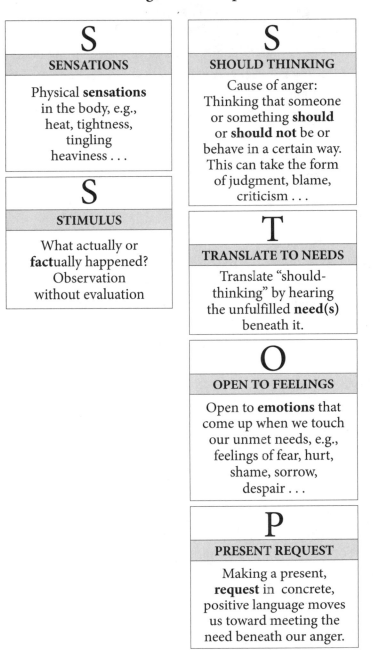

S

SENSATIONS

Physical **sensations** in the body, e.g., heat, tightness, tingling heaviness . . .

S

STIMULUS

What actually or **fact**ually happened? Observation without evaluation

S

SHOULD THINKING

Cause of anger: Thinking that someone or something **should** or **should not** be or behave in a certain way. This can take the form of judgment, blame, criticism . . .

T

TRANSLATE TO NEEDS

Translate "should-thinking" by hearing the unfulfilled **need(s)** beneath it.

O

OPEN TO FEELINGS

Open to **emotions** that come up when we touch our unmet needs, e.g., feelings of fear, hurt, shame, sorrow, despair . . .

P

PRESENT REQUEST

Making a present, **request** in concrete, positive language moves us toward meeting the need beneath our anger.

The best way to develop a sense of having full choice in how you respond to anger is to ground yourself in your awareness of your bodily sensations. Do you notice a throbbing in your chest, a tension in your arms, a shortness of breath, an urge to punch something? Take the time to notice the quality and intensity of your sensations and be present with them without judging or trying to change them.

Step Three

As you become fully present to your sensations, move to the next box, labeled Stimulus.

What was the actual thing that happened, the behavior that anyone could have seen or heard, that stimulated your anger? Who said or did what? Describe it in NVC observational language, as free from judgment and evaluation as possible.

Step Four

This box, labeled Should Thinking, refers to the ideas and judgments in your head, the things that you are telling yourself, that are the cause of your anger. It is our evaluation of what someone should or should not be doing, our blaming them for their behavior, that causes our anger.

Step Five

The box labeled T refers to Translate into needs language.
Listen closely to your judgments in the step above. These are gold mines because they can help you clarify the needs and values that are so important to you that underlie your experience, purpose, and meaning in life. There may be many interconnected and layered needs beneath each judgment. As you delve into this richness and identify each one, a piece of your true self become accessible to you and gives vitality to your self-understanding.

Step Six

The step labeled O refers to being Open to feelings.

As you identify the needs beneath your experience, you will become aware of feelings that may be less familiar to you; these feelings are sitting quietly below the more vocal and visible anger. You may wish to use the feelings list on page 367 to reintroduce yourself to these more nuanced feelings.

Step Seven
The P stands for Present Request.

You are invited here to make a request of yourself or of another consisting of a specific action, one that could reasonably be accomplished, to support a need you have identified or to facilitate the continuation of the dialogue. It can be helpful to generate more than one request so that a sense of relief or movement is not tied to a single strategy.

Step Eight
Walk the talk fully.

Using the Anger Floor Map is *not a linear process*. You will typically move back and forth and skip around boxes multiple times as different components of your experience unfold. For example:

- As you identify one need, you may become aware of more judgments—or more intense ones—than you have expressed so far. In this case, you may choose to move back to the Should Thinking box.
- As you become aware of a less familiar feeling, such as despair, you might choose to move to Translate to needs, such as hope or trust, that underlie that feeling as you experience it.
- Alternatively, you might wish to clarify exactly what happened in the environment (the Stimulus) that was associated with despair for you.
- Another Stimulus may come to mind as you are formulating a request and you may choose to explore that.

Playing Hopscotch With Anger

How does all this look with an example from real life? A few weeks ago, I had a conversation with a young man named Patrick about challenges he was facing completing his course work and dealing with his family. His father was seriously ill and had been told he only had a short time to live; his family was struggling to pay the bills, cope with the emotional intensity of the illness and impending death, and make plans for the future. Patrick sought my input about his seventeen-year-old sister, Samantha, whose behavior was stimulating great anger in him. She was staying out all night, using alcohol and drugs, not helping around the house and, as a result, triggering distress in their parents. He was furious that Samantha was "causing" so many problems when the family was already overwhelmed. He accepted my invitation to walk the floor map, which he had been exposed to in my class, with respect to this situation.

"OK, so first I need to stop and breathe. Whew! In and out. In and out.

"OK, now I'm feeling some Sensations (he moves to the next box), not simply the rage of my anger. My heart is really racing, my legs feel like they are ready to jump. Now I feel myself breathing again and tension is moving out of my arms and hands.

"And when I think of the dumb things Samantha is doing, I really want to punch her (moving to Should Thinking). She's being so inconsiderate, and immature. I've got to get through to her. How can she think it's OK to cause so much trouble?

"I see the next box is Stimulus. Let me see, what exactly has she done? Well, last week she stayed out all night without telling us that she intended to do that, or where she was.

"We were so scared; none of us could relax or sleep all night. It was so thoughtless and unnecessary. (I suggested he move back to Should Thinking at this point.)

"At a time when we're just trying to keep my dad as comfortable as possible, when we have so many worries about finances and being supportive of one another, how could she do that to us?

(He moves to Translate to needs.) "Let me see: what are the needs here? I wanted her to be a support to the family at this time, not add to the problems that are already so overwhelming. That support would mean so much—everyone is hurting bad and it would be good to know that she was caring for the rest of us as we're caring about her.

"I mean, what good could she be up to in the middle of the night? How could she do that to us? (I suggested a movement again to Should Thinking.)

"The people she hangs with don't care about her—they're even more confused and out of it than she is. I am so frustrated, worried, and scared about what might happen to her. I guess those are some different feelings I am aware of now. (Patrick moves to Open to feelings.)

"Yes, I am so scared. I love Samantha. (He pauses and stays with that a bit). I just want her to be safe."

After exploring the different boxes further, back and forth, Patrick moves to Present Request.

"I wonder what I could do to get her to change her behavior."

At this point, I ask Patrick to stay with the feelings (frustration, fear, and worry) as well as the needs he has identified (consideration, support, caring, and safety) as the foundation for formulating requests.

I ask him to consider which of these needs or values he would most like to hold as precious in this moment, including the value of connection: staying in dialogue with each other. After reflecting on these values, all of which are important to him, he indicates that staying in connection is probably the most important. If people in his family are not listening to one another, not trusting that all of their needs matter, they are unlikely to find ways to meet their collective needs.

Patrick then considers what requests he could make of himself to support the connection that he cares about so much. He comes up with some requests: "I could ask Samantha if she would be willing to spend twenty minutes in the next three days to share what has been going on with her. I would also like to use some of that time to tell her how much I love her and how scared I have been for her safety. I don't think I have expressed my feelings in that way. Usually it just comes out as yelling and blaming.

"I also want to make a request of myself to talk with an understanding friend at least twice a week to get empathic support for myself so that I will be more open to listening to Samantha in a nonjudgmental way.

"I also think I'll talk to a local hospice agency to see if they have someone who can support us with specific ideas and guidance for the transition we're facing.

"You know," Patrick continues, "I think it's becoming clearer to me just how much pain Samantha is experiencing now. I sort of knew it intellectually, but now I'm really getting it. The thing is, she tries not to show it, tries to show us she's 'strong.'"

I ask him if he thinks it could be that staying away from home and drinking are Samantha's strategies for getting some relief from the stress of what's happening, and maybe some support from her friends, as well.

"I don't think so," he replies. "I know some of the kids she's hanging with. I really don't think they're doing much for her. And she sure doesn't look happy. Plus, she's always been kind of pig-headed—has to do things her way, especially if someone suggests otherwise."

I reflected that it sounded to me like her need for autonomy—to be the one who decides what she will and won't do—can be pretty strong.

"Yes, and she often says, 'Why can't you just trust me, leave me to make my own mistakes and figure things out for myself?' I guess I do often just tell her what to do, as if she were still a child. I just don't want her to get hurt, to do something really stupid."

And so the conversation continued. By using the Anger Floor Map, Patrick was able to get empathy for his anger and look underneath his judgments, identifying his feelings and needs. He connected with his needs for caring and safety for his sister and came to understand that Samantha had to meet her own needs for autonomy, comfort, and companionship in her choices. Once Patrick was able to connect to the value of his own needs and how meaningful they were to him, he was better able to think of Samantha as also having needs that were important to her. He was able to see her choices in the context of trying to meet her needs, and was more able to hear her effectively. And he was able to release some of the right-wrong energy he had been holding toward her. Together, Samantha, Patrick, and their mother were ultimately able to plan some strategies that were more responsive to everyone's needs.

EXERCISE 7: Hearing the Life in Anger

Translating anger into feelings and needs takes practice. Look at the following situations and see if you can guess what feelings and needs may be involved for both parties: the person who is angry and speaking, and the person with whom they are angry. Once again, we'll begin with an example.

Part One

1. "When I left the store, the security alarm went off because the security device wasn't removed when I paid for the sweater. The guard stopped me and acted like I was a thief. I'm never going back to that store!"

    Speaker's feeling and needs: The speaker is angry, and underneath might be feeling hurt, sad, scared, or embarrassed. The needs might be trust, caring, safety, dignity, and respect.

    Guard's feelings and needs: They might be feeling irritated that they had to question a person who was not shoplifting and who was visibly upset about the inspection. Irritation could be related to values for ease

at work, connection with a customer, and wanting to
be seen for their desire to do their job effectively. They
could also be angry, and wanting understanding that they
are simply doing their job by inspecting the person's bag.

2. "I can't believe the doctor didn't give my sister an X-ray at
her last physical exam! Now the tumor is really large and she
might die from it! Talk about incompetence! Why wasn't he
more careful?"
    Speaker's feelings and needs:
    Doctor's feelings and needs:
    (You could also guess the sister's feelings and needs.)

3. "My friend never calls me. I'm always the one to call her. She
thinks only of herself. It's always a one-way street with her."
    Speaker's feelings and needs:
    Friend's feelings and needs:

4. "I can't believe the partners aren't going to offer me a
partnership in the firm. My work is just as good as that of
the other associate lawyers whom they offered a partnership
to. What do they have that I don't? Why is it that I always get
passed by for opportunities?"
    Speaker's feelings and needs:
    Partners' feelings and needs:

Part Two
Think of a person in your own life toward whom you are feeling some
anger, or use one of the situations below. Use the Anger Floor Map
on page 238 to explore the various facets of your anger experience. Be
sure to move slowly and be patient with the process, allowing yourself
sufficient time to notice fully what arises at each box.
    A. "You told me when I missed work because my dad was
    having surgery that I should just go, and not worry about

anything. Now you tell me that I have to either make up the missed time or lose pay for those days. And I thought you believed in running a compassionate business. That hardly seems compassionate to me!"

B.   "When you said that you wanted to use my car for the evening, it never occurred to me that you would go out when the roads were icy and total it! How could you be so careless?"

C.   "I understand that you told Barbara what I told you in confidence, that I'm attracted to her and would like to go out with her. I really wasn't ready for her to know that, and now I'm feeling very uncomfortable working in the same office with her. And I notice she is pretty distant to me. How could you betray me like that? I thought you were my friend!"

The Connor Compassionate Communication Index

When I first started learning NVC, I was extremely excited about it. More than anything, I wanted to use it with my husband, whom I cherish. But we'd been communicating for years in ways that had become entrenched. Sometimes we were communicating better than ever and were really excited and hopeful about it. Then we'd have a conflict, one or both of us would be emotionally triggered, and we would return to our old patterns. Losing our new-found intimacy, we went through even greater feelings of pain and loss. Because the closeness was greater, losing it was greater too.

At times of conflict, my husband became a huge enemy in my eyes, the person who could wound me most deeply and destroy my happiness. The impact on our communication was devastating. I realized that I needed to slow things down and be patient with myself. After a number of such painful episodes, I developed what

I call the Connor Compassionate Communication Index. During any difficult conversation, I monitor how I'm feeling about the other person, rating my feelings on a scale from one to ten. A rating of ten means this person, in my eyes, is God's gift to humankind. A rating of one means I'm seeing this person as my worst enemy, as Attila the Hun or Hitler.

When my feeling for the person drops below a seven, I stop talking. I may leave the room or the house, or hang up with a quick, "Sorry, gotta go now." I know meaningful connection won't happen until I see the person rating higher on the scale. In the early days, I would just wait: the scale would rise by itself as time passed or after I received empathy from an empathy buddy. Over time, as I became more skilled with self-empathy, I was able to raise my Connor Index quite quickly, sometimes without even leaving the room.

EXERCISE 8: Working the Index

The next time you notice yourself getting angry or annoyed, stop and apply the Connor Compassionate Communication Index. On a scale of one to ten, how much are you seeing the person you're interacting with as an "enemy"? How does this awareness inform the choice you make—to step away or continue to engage?

Angry at the World—and Changing It

Friends and family aren't the only ones who can trigger anger in us. Even interacting with a stranger can be stimulating, especially if the interaction taps into needs that are "up" or have been unmet before. Let's look at a real example, and self-empathy in action.

He who angers you conquers you.

—ELIZABETH KENNY,
twentieth-century Australian nurse

Riding my bike meets a lot of needs for me, including care for the environment, physical movement, and fun. I love stopping on the Manhattan Bridge and watching trains pass by and the movement of barges and tugboats on the East River. I feel fully alive.

Riding my bike has also been a huge source of pain. Almost every day, I experience incidents that do not meet my needs for consideration, care, or safety. People open car doors without looking. Drivers pass me and turn across my path without pausing or signaling. Cars drive within a foot of my bike, coming close to hitting me.

How do I respond to such conflict? For years, I responded in violent ways. I shouted comments back, banging my fist on car windows or hoods. I wanted physical safety, while in fact I was increasing my vulnerability and risk. When I started learning NVC, I decided to put it to the test.

I started by considering the cause of my anger. In this case, it was clear—the drivers were irresponsible and selfish! I was caught up in blame thinking. Yet as we've discussed, no one else can make you angry. I took this principle to heart and decided to look at my own behavior. Rather than turning blame inward or outward, I had another option: empathic connection.

At first, I empathized with the drivers. I guessed they also had needs for movement, spaciousness, safety, and ease. Yet empathizing with people I saw as the "enemy" wasn't working for me; it was intellectual, all in my head, and I was in too much pain myself. This was a clear case of needing "empathy before education." Now aware of this need, I got help from empathy buddies and started practicing "emergency self-empathy" every time I was triggered while cycling.

Empathizing with my own needs, it was clear that I desperately wanted safety, consideration, and ease. I wanted to be seen— literally—on the road. I also wanted appreciation for how I was supporting the environment and the quality of life for everyone in New York by riding my bike, minimizing pollution, noise, and traffic. Each time a stimulating incident happened on the road, I was reminded—in a flash—of larger situations I see in the world that are disturbing for me: those in power (this case, drivers) not having the level of caring I'd like, and all that's happening to the natural world that concerns me. The story in my mind went something like this: "If I can't even be safe riding my bike, what hope is there for the rest of the world? How will we change energy consumption? End global warming—and the war?!" As if activating a volcano, even the smallest "local" incident or event triggered an eruption of larger "global" pain and fear.

I also realized that what I wanted was completely undoable. There was no way that every driver on the road, each and every day, would have the awareness I wanted—or the willingness to act on it. I then felt genuine compassion for all the drivers I'd interacted with. They thought they were passing a cyclist when, in fact, they were passing a loaded stick of dynamite ready to detonate! Without even knowing it, I was making impossible demands.

The more I became aware of my own needs, the more I became aware of doable strategies to meet them. I increasingly found routes that met my needs for safety, including one through a lovely park that I'd never noticed before and some quiet streets in Little Italy. I started using hand signals, which I'd never bothered with and hadn't thought would make a difference. Based on how I've seen drivers respond, I'm convinced that signaling increases visibility, consideration, and safety.

Now I think it's funny that I didn't think of these strategies before. While I was so focused on blaming others, so adamant that the drivers *should* make room for me on the road, I never thought of other options. It was their "fault" and their responsibility. Once I got clear about my needs and mourned those that could not be met, I was able to focus on the needs I *could* meet in this particular situation. I felt excited and empowered. Not only had I gained understanding and movement about what had seemed a hopeless situation, I had also met needs for awareness, responsibility, choice, safety, and ease.

I continue to practice what I call "aggressive" self-empathy. If I get angry on the road, I take the time to really sit with my feelings and empathize deeply with them. Sometimes, if I'm really triggered, I'll pull off the road and take some "time out," sitting with my judgment and the pain motivating it. I check in with my body and notice sensations. When I do choose to engage with drivers, I've learned that before making any comments, human connection is crucial. I start with a question: "Hey, how are you doing?" If I'm not willing to greet a fellow human being, that's a good sign I need some "aggressive" empathy before opening my mouth further.

When I do engage empathically, I find the outcome to be dramatically different from what my hot-headed behavior had led to. Just last week, I used my NVC skills with a driver who'd cut in front of me on the road. On his own, he volunteered, "Next time I'll really look before pulling out." My needs for connection and care were fully met. Self-empathy and choice in how I respond to anger have been lifesavers for me—the best kind of "reflective vest" that this cyclist can have.

EXERCISE 9: Empathy in Action

Think of a situation that's been stimulating for you more than once. This might be a "small" thing—such as your partner or roommate not replacing the toilet paper when it runs out or leaving dirty clothes on the floor. Practice self-empathy and/or get empathy from a friend. What "core" needs and beliefs of yours are being stimulated? How do these needs speak to your vision of the world, and how you desire to live with and interact with others? You may wish to write about this in your journal.

Moving On

For most people, anger—whether they are expressing or receiving it—is a challenging emotion to deal with. In understanding anger, however, and practicing empathy, we can learn to harness the energy of this passionate emotion and better connect with others and ourselves. When we are fully connected to the value of our needs and can begin to explore strategies to better meet those needs, we are stepping into the realm of enjoying anger: finding joy (and insight, self-connection, and learning) where otherwise there may have been only judgment and pain.

INTEGRATION: Further Questions and Exercises to Explore Chapter 7

A. Think of a time when someone was angry with you.
   1. How did you know they were angry? What did they say or do?
   2. What needs were stimulated in you by this anger? Did you feel anxious, afraid, or sad?
   3. What thoughts, judgments, or "shoulds" did you have about this person and/or their anger?
   4. What would you have liked to request of yourself or the other person in relation to their getting angry?
B. Think of someone you are feeling very angry with. Write this person a letter, explaining how you are feeling in OFNR (observations, feelings, needs, and requests). Your first draft may include judgment and blame—that's OK. Let it out, empathize with what you're feeling, and then go back to writing your letter of empathy. You may wish to send this letter or simply write it as an exercise in practicing self-connection and empathy.

8

When Communication Isn't Possible: The Protective Use of Force

We hope that by now you appreciate the value of Nonviolent Communication and can see how it can be applied in diverse situations at work, at home, and in the larger world. As you have thought about how you might practice it, you may also have thought of situations where you cannot imagine how it would be possible to do so, simply because any form of communication may be ineffective. Here are some such scenarios:

- Two drunken students at a party are fighting and refuse to stop
- A toddler is chasing a ball as it moves quickly toward a busy street
- A man approaches you and your friend, pointing a gun, waving it in a way that suggests he intends to use it, and shouting in a language you don't understand
- A person is yelling in an agitated way and threatening to jump off a roof
- Someone holding hostages is threatening to detonate a bomb

In circumstances such as these, you may think that words alone are inadequate and that some kind of physical action is warranted. And we might agree with you.

First, though, we want to be clear that in all cases, behaving in a way that is consistent with the consciousness of Nonviolent Communication is a choice one makes; it is not a demand or an obligation. While we find it meaningful and important to consider choosing to behave in alignment with Nonviolent Communication consciousness, there are many, many times when, for reasons of ease, convenience, habit, or lack of presence or awareness, our actions reflect other choices. We accept our limitations while also seeking to grow the consciousness and habits we value for the ways they enrich the quality of our lives.

Second, there are circumstances under which physical use of force is considered in alignment with the consciousness of Nonviolent Communication. In the case of the two drunken students, for example, we would be unwilling to let them fight it out, risking injury to one or both. Depending upon the circumstances, we might consider intervening to restrain them, tossing water on them to startle and distract them, or asking for assistance, perhaps by calling the police. In a situation where there is not the capacity, time, or willingness to communicate, we might choose to apply what is referred to as *the protective use of force*. As with any use of force, the protective use of force involves the will of one person over another. Yet it is starkly different from a *punitive* or *retributive use of force*.

In this chapter, we will explore four characteristics that distinguish these two types of force. We will then look at ways in which punitive and protective uses of force are sometimes confounded, and follow this with a discussion of cultural and historical contexts that support the punitive use of force. Finally, we will share with you a few stories of the surprising power of dialogue in potentially violent circumstances.

We Are All Motivated by Universal Needs

By now, the idea that all human behavior is an attempt to meet universal human needs is a familiar one. We also understand that individuals can hold one need or value as more significant than another at any given time, and that different individuals will see different strategies as useful or supportive in meeting their needs. In applying these principles to the brawl between the two students, imagine two bystanders, both of whom favor physically restraining the students so as to protect them from each other.

One bystander might be thinking: "These guys are such immature jerks! How dare they behave this way—ruining the party for everyone and risking damage to the house! What idiots!" They might say some variation on these judgments: "Cut it out guys— don't ruin the party and be such idiots!" Directly or implicitly, this person might want to show them that fighting is wrong by punishing them physically, further telling them that their behavior is wrongheaded and self-centered, and refusing to have anything to do with them in the future. In their view, the two students deserve some kind of punishment for behaving "badly" and disrupting the party.

This bystander intends for the students to learn another way to address their conflict by conveying to them the moral judgments others have about them and by administering punishment for their actions. The person probably believes that punishment and suffering are important experiences for learning more acceptable and desirable ways to behave, and they want to ensure that the students experience both. This way of responding to the situation illustrates the characteristics of the *punitive use of force*: its purpose is to punish the person whose behaviors are viewed as wrong, based on the hope and belief that punishment will result in safety, learning, and growth. This bystander may also think, "If we can make them suffer or feel pain as a result of their choice, they'll have a better understanding of how we felt when we saw them doing what they did." Such a thought indicates that the person believes punishment can support the growth of empathic understanding—and indicates that the person thinking it also needs empathy.

The second bystander could respond similarly to the initial situation while coming from a very different belief system. The person might think, "We need to stop these guys from hurting each other right away before someone is badly hurt. They aren't responding to our words—maybe because they're drunk—so let's physically stop them and keep them apart until we can sit down and have a dialogue about this experience. I want to understand why they did what they did, and I want them to understand how their behavior has affected me and everyone else. Together I would like us to figure out ways to deal with the situation so that everyone's needs can be heard and addressed." This bystander, like the first, also wants safety, learning, and growth for everyone as well as empathic understanding. And he believes that dialogue—sharing experiences, feelings, needs, and thoughts—is more likely to accomplish these ends than inflicting punishment and suffering.

How to Distinguish Between Protective and Punitive Use of Force

One can determine whether a person is employing the protective use of force or the punitive use of force by asking the following questions:
- What is the intention behind using force to protect another from harm?
- Is there perceived to be an imminent risk of harm?
- Have all options for dialogue been exhausted?
- Once immediate risk is prevented, is there a willingness to resume dialogue?

What Is the Intention?

Remember, both the person employing the protective use of force and the person employing the punitive use of force are attempting to meet positive, universal needs. The difference is in the belief about the best strategy to accomplish this—the intention associated with the use of force. The first bystander supports an intervention intended to stimulate pain, suffering, or shame and that includes violence—the imposing of one person's will over another through force. This person is also willing to continue the punishment even after the events have passed. The second bystander supports dialogue and the mutual exchange of ideas and experiences as the best way to accomplish a change in behavior. While this person also uses physical force—as a last resort when dialogue is not possible and there is a perceived imminent threat to safety and well-being—after the threat has passed and dialogue becomes possible, the force is withdrawn.

When confronted with a similar situation, the easiest way to assess your intention is to examine the thoughts associated with the behavior that is worrying you. Are you thinking, "How dare they try that!" or "It's an outrage—I won't stand for it" or "I'll show them." Or are you thinking, "How can I best protect everyone in this situation?" "What will be the least harmful way to intervene?" "I really want everyone to be safe, including the one whose actions I find upsetting!"

Is There an Imminent Risk of Harm?
How Dangerous Is Dangerous?

Protective use of force is employed only when circumstances indicate an imminent risk of serious harm, when there is a sense of urgency because there may be consequences that cannot be undone if the situation persists. This feeling of urgency is different from anger. You may not like what a person is saying or doing, and their behavior may stimulate anger in you, yet is there a risk of physical harm right now? Or is there time for connection, dialogue, and an exploration of mutual needs and possible win-win solutions that might bring more effective results in the long term? When you look at your own thoughts about the situation, are you thinking about how terrible the person is who is about to act, or are you thinking about the harmful actions that may occur?

Different people will, of course, assess the potential risk of harm differently, and time permitting, it is useful to ask yourself further questions so your assessment is likelier to be based on the realities of the situation than on personal or cultural biases unrelated to any actual risk. The key is to examine, as objectively as possible, the actual behavior you are encountering. People staffing suicide hotlines, for example, are trained to assess the answers to four sequential questions they pose to the caller:

1. Are you feeling so bad that you're thinking about suicide?
   If the person responds affirmatively,
2. Have you thought about how you would do it?
   If the answer is yes,
3. Do you have what you need to do it?
   If yes,
4. Have you thought about when you would do it?

The answers to these questions provide an assessment of risk that is validated by empirical research. The more affirmative answers there are, the more appropriate it may be to consider protective use of force.

Similarly, we may wish to ask ourselves questions about the facts of the situation and the imminent likelihood of harm. Is a potentially lethal weapon involved? Does the person appear physically capable of harming themselves or another? Am I responding to a realistic feeling of time urgency, or is my sense of urgency the result of my own anger or outrage about what is happening? Am I reflecting on the facts of the situation or my own thoughts about what another person should or should not be doing?

Another reason for examining actual behavior rather than one's evaluation or response to it relates to cultural and historical bias. Experiments show, for example, that white observers are more likely to believe that a threatening action undertaken by an African American will result in harm to another than the same action undertaken by a person of European descent. This bias may contribute to the serious racial disparities that exist in suspensions of teenagers from schools and in shootings of suspects by police officers. Focusing on the action itself (and coming up with a clear observation) can help to distinguish between actual events and biased attitudes.

The Role of Dialogue

It is an axiom of Nonviolent Communication that solutions that enrich the quality of life for all are most likely to be attained when the needs of all parties are fully known and considered and when all people have an active role in formulating the plans to address these needs. This axiom echoes a belief stated by Mahatma Gandhi: that which meets the most human needs comes the closest to truth. For this reason, dialogue that involves all parties as much as possible is essential. Dialogue, however, implies an ability to communicate, the willingness to do so, and resources such as time and space. The toddler running toward the street, for example, may not be able to respond to words as quickly as an adult would judge necessary to prevent harm. If the other person is speaking a language you don't understand, you would need a translator as a resource. If the person can't understand you because of impairment by drugs or cognitive limitations, you may need time for the person to detox or the help of a professional trained in communicating with those who have such a disability.

In all these instances, dialogue is not feasible in the moment, and you might choose to use force protectively. When circumstances change, however, dialogue can resume. And in the meantime, our actions can be informed by our caring and our intention of serving everyone's well-being. Concerning the toddler, for example, as you pick the child up—exerting your will over them—and take them to safety, you can say, "Because I care about you and your well-being, I'm putting you inside this fenced yard where I'm confident you'll be safe." This is a very different response from picking the child up and saying, "Bad boy! You never listen to me! I told you not to run into the road!" and hitting him in punishment.

Let's examine some other situations. Imagine you witness someone who is about to take a dangerous action, such as driving while intoxicated or even committing suicide. Given the available time and the obstacles to communication, taking physical action— restraining the suicidal person or taking away the car keys of the person who is too drunk to drive—would be life serving. If someone is about to swallow pills or jump from a bridge, it is probably not the time to empathize and find out why they are contemplating such an act. There will be time for such connecting when they are safe. As with the toddler, when you are acting with force before dialogue is feasible, you can let the person know your intention: for example, "I'm taking these pills from you (or retraining you) because I care about you and want you to be safe." Making an empathic connection with a person who's inebriated is difficult if not impossible; you can connect with them later when the immediate danger has passed. Still, you may wish to tell the person why you're undertaking the physical action: "Tom, I'm concerned about your safety. Knowing how much you've drunk tonight, I'm driving you home."

Mixing Oil With Water

Even when people take action to protect others, such action is often tainted with judgment and condemnation; other needs and core, judgment-based beliefs can get mixed in with the desire for a person's safety and well-being. Although a protective act may start with life-serving intent, as soon as judgment or blame enters in, it can no longer be considered life serving and protective.

Let's say a mother sees a young child approaching a hot stove, and she's afraid the child will get burned. She may say, "Jimmy, don't be such a bad boy! Mommy told you to stay away from the stove! I told you to stay away from it and I mean it!" Surely she has genuine concern for the child's safety. At the same time, there may also be other needs at play besides a desire for protection and preserving life. She may want ease, consideration, and to be "respected" and heard. Such needs can sometimes be found behind statements such as "Don't be a bad boy. You listen to me, or else!"

Fear often manifests as aggression, or can be perceived by others in this way. When we're afraid, our tone and words can sound especially forceful, even more so than we sometimes realize. When someone goes into moral judgment—"Don't be so stupid!" or "Don't misbehave," it is often their fear (again, connected to a life-serving need) that is driving their judgment. To practice protective use of force in full integrity, it is key to be grounded in self-connection and to practice self-empathy—including emergency self-empathy—when triggered. It is crucial to pay attention to apprehension and fear: these strong feelings alert us to vital needs that are up for us. When we are fully connected to our feelings and the underlying needs (for safety, protection, peace, well-being), we can act from greater choice and from a place of discernment and compassion.

Isn't Violence Sometimes Necessary?

Many people believe that violence is a "necessary evil" that can sometimes be used for good. When parents hit their children, for example, they may say, "This is for your own good" and "This hurts me more than it hurts you." When governments lead nations to war, citizens are told it is a necessary "sacrifice" to "keep the peace." The vast majority of statues and monuments in our public parks celebrate past wars, all supposedly fought for high and noble purposes such as freedom, security, peace, and democracy. Many religions tell us to "turn the other cheek," yet some of the same traditions tell us, "an eye for an eye and a tooth for a tooth." Vengeance and retribution are seen as fair, acceptable, and even desirable. It is only then that the other side "will learn a lesson" and "wrongs can be righted." It's safe to say that every war has involved enemy images of other human beings and right-wrong thinking. Key to this thinking is the belief that "good" ultimately prevails, that God is on the "right" side: ours.

Educated so completely in this belief, some people maintain that punishment is sometimes justified and more effective than other methods in teaching people to behave differently. Teachers, parents, and others in positions of authority especially hold this view. This longstanding and pervasive belief drives much in our society, from corporal punishment to prison sentences and fines. In many cultures, force, obedience, and punishment are held in great esteem; to *not* use them is seen as detrimental or dangerous, especially with children. "Spare the rod, spoil the child" is an old saying that supports this view.

Research, however, has consistently shown that the punitive use of force is not effective in changing human behavior. It may seem to work in the moment (in terms of meeting some needs, such as for protection) and it backfires in the long term. It has negative side effects, such as resentment, retaliation, and revenge, and has a very poor record of success for actually meeting needs. Certainly cases exist where if not for physical punishment applied by a parent, an offspring might have gone down a different, less desirable path. Yet for many people, the application of punitive force leads to resentment, hostility, and ultimately, aggression against others.

If you are considering use of force, especially violent force, you may wish to revisit the two questions we considered earlier in this book: *What do we want people to do? And why do we want them to do it?* Do you want others to act in a manner consistent with their values? Or do you want them to act (or not act) out of fear, judgment, or punishment? And if fear or punishment is the primary motivator, what can you expect of their behavior when they aren't being watched? We know of instances, for example, where parents have told their children not to smoke, and most definitely not to smoke in the house. There are usually consequences for breaking these rules. And what do the children do? They simply smoke when the parents aren't around. Is this what their parents were hoping to achieve?

In the end, when parents and others use punishment to teach children "right" from "wrong," the children's attention focuses on the external consequences of behavior—the rewards and punishments—not the intrinsic value of the behavior. The results can be very different from what is desired, and not necessarily healthy or life serving. Kelly Bryson in *Don't Be Nice, Be Real* gives an example where Pizza Hut offered children coupons for free pizza every time they finished reading a book. As a result of this incentive, the children searched for the thinnest books they could find. Reading was only motivated by the reward of the pizza, not by the pleasure or benefit of reading itself. He suggests that the long-term consequence of this "reward" system will be a bunch of kids who are overweight and hate to read.

Similarly, if a child's reason to refrain from hitting another child is that a bigger person might hurt or punish them to "teach them a lesson," the smart-thinking child (and all children are smart thinkers) would conclude that the thing to do is fight when others can't see them. The child will also learn that it's OK to hit other children as long as you're stronger or bigger or as long as you have words to justify what you've done: "I was teaching him a lesson." "I was showing him who was right!" Is this the outcome you want?

More Protective Than a Gun: Protective Use of Force in Action

Suppose you're walking down the street and someone attacks you. Should you try to talk with them compassionately, or should you physically protect yourself? There are numerous real stories of compassionate connection being more effective than a black belt or a gun. The Quakers, who do not believe in carrying weapons, share many such stories. A woman in one of our workshops described the following experience.

One day Lauren, who was nineteen years old and of limited means, was walking through a wealthy neighborhood. An unshaven young man dressed in tattered clothing grabbed her and said, "Give me your money or I'll kill you." Instead of freezing or panicking, she was able to focus intently on what was happening. She looked the man calmly in the eye. "I don't have any money," she said. "And why would you want to kill me?" He didn't answer. "Why would you want to kill me?" she asked again, with evident curiosity. The man, unable to respond to this question and clearly surprised by it, simply turned and left.

In a similar true story, an elderly woman was walking home with her groceries. She became aware that a man was following closely behind her, and sensed that he might intend to rob her. Rather than trying to run away or confront him, she turned around and greeted him warmly. "I'm so glad you came along!" she said. "I really need help with these bags." With that, she handed him one and they proceeded to walk to her apartment. At the door, she took the bag from the man and thanked him, offering him some money for his help. The man refused and went on his way.

As these stories illustrate, empathic connection can be highly effective in the face of violence or the threat of it. Acting from compassion even when their own safety was perceived as threatened, the two women were able to respond as full human beings, inspiring their potential assailants to act from their own, fullest humanity. Consistent with this anecdotal evidence, studies have shown that those using nonviolent means in response to violence have a much higher success rate in surviving than those resorting to violence.

Many of us might find it difficult to respond with as much equanimity as the people in these stories, especially if we are new to practicing empathy. You will need to judge for yourself what will best meet your needs, including self-care and care and concern for others.

No Contact, No Violence

A final Compassionate Communication alternative we can consider involves withdrawal, silence, or noncommunication. Sometimes a relationship may be so deteriorated, trust may be so low, and hope for improved relationship so minimal that the best alternative may be to conserve energy and resources by breaking contact. This option, too, can be undertaken in the interest of preserving and protecting life, health, and well-being and can be considered a different form of protective use of force. Hanging the phone up on someone or not answering the door can certainly seem like aggressive acts. Yet if the person you're severing contact with is stalking you or threatening physical violence, such actions may in fact be life serving. If done compassionately and without judgment, they may meet your needs for safety and care.

The criteria we explored earlier in this chapter—such as "Is dialogue possible?" and "Is my heart open and compassionate?"— are key here. Internal resources (what we are able to handle at the present time) also impact what is possible. For example, after extensive dialogue, I decided it would be life serving for me to limit contact with a person I know because of the impact on my life of being in a relationship with them. I expressed this choice with care and compassion: "I care about you and I also care about my own well-being. Given the conversations we've had, where you've expressed unwillingness to change behaviors that I find harmful, I'm unwilling for us to be in a relationship for now."

Acting Out of Empathy, Not Punishment

One of the foundational tenets of nonviolence, as described by Gandhi, is that the means we employ are in integrity with our objectives. This is in bold contrast to a belief that has informed much of world history: that the ends justify the means. Some people believe, for example, that it is justifiable to use armed force to remove dictators and untenable forms of government that they consider "wrong" or "evil." Yet history shows us, again and again, how much suffering, loss of life, and violence ensues. In South Africa, where Nelson Mandela, Desmond Tutu, and others insisted on nonviolence and civil disobedience (inspired by Gandhian practices and the Civil Rights movement in the United States), the social and spiritual impact was truly transformative. A similar "social revolution" occurred in Egypt recently, where organizers based their campaign on nonviolent social action.

We can bring this spirit of nonviolence into everyday interactions by holding an awareness of protective use of force. Are you feeling angry, indignant, or scared? Is criticism or judgment passing through your mind? How does your body feel? If you're not feeling centered or fully present in the moment, use the judgments that are coming up to help you focus and explore the feelings and needs connected to them. Attempt to connect with the other person on an empathic level, then choose the course of action that will best meet your needs, including care and protection of others. Again, the simplest way to check your motivation in using force is to ask yourself: "Is my heart open at the moment? Am I acting out of compassion?" If you perceive danger, determine that dialogue is not possible, and feel that you're acting "from the heart," you are most likely acting in alignment with the protective use of force.

INTEGRATION: Questions and Exercises to Explore Chapter 8

A. Choose a war or international conflict that you're familiar with, either from studying history or from your own experience or knowledge of current affairs. Then answer the following questions:

1. Would this incident, or some aspect of it, qualify as a protective use of force?

2. Why or why not? What other needs or intentions might have been at play other than serving life?
3. What, if anything, could the protective use of force have looked like in this situation, and how may the results have been different?

B. Read the interview with Marshall Rosenberg, "Beyond Good and Evil: Creating a Nonviolent World" that appears in the appendix of this book. Then answer the following questions:
1. How would you describe "restorative justice" based on Marshall's description of it?
2. Why is Marshall less concerned with physical acts of violence?
3. Why does Marshall oppose capital punishment? What protective use of force does he suggest instead?
4. How was the protective use of force used by people demonstrating? How did they change their message, and how was it ultimately effective?
5. According to Marshall, what was the cause of the 9/11 attacks? How could they have been avoided? How does a lack of empathy lead to increasingly violent acts?
6. Did the United States attack on Iraq qualify as a protective use of force? Why or why not?
7. Marshall comments, "We are getting to a point where our best protection is to communicate with the people we're most afraid of. Nothing else will work." Based on the context for this statement in the interview, why does Marshall think this is the case? Do you agree with him? Why or why not?

C. Consider the following situations. What could the protective use of force look like in each context? (Remember that the protective use of force is also about the intention of our actions—this cannot necessarily be seen.) The first item serves as an example:
1. Situation: A child is playing near a hot stove.
   Protective Force: Ask the child, "Would you like to play with me in the other room using some blocks?"

2. Situation: A child is running out of a yard and onto a busy street.
   Protective Force:

3. Situation: One person is threatening to hit another.
   Protective Force:

4. Situation: You are a passenger in a car that is being driven at a speed you consider unsafe. You have already made two requests for the driver to slow down.
   Protective Force:

9

Thanks, But No Thanks

Your gift was great! Perfect—and so thoughtful!

You're the best ever. No one tops you as a friend.

You're such a good boy when you pick up your toys.
I love you so much when you're being good.

You did a great job with that client.

I magine someone saying these kinds of things to you. How would you feel? Many people would say "super" or "great." Who wouldn't? After all, these are words of gratitude and respect. What could be more delightful?

Yet such statements, while they express or imply pleasure with respect to something the other person has done, are all judgments: they evaluate the listener and their behavior. While most of us prefer praise to blame, judgments—whether approving or disapproving— are all forms of "right-wrong" thinking on the "good-bad" continuum. Such thinking, "positive" or not, supports our valuing others' opinions in assessing our own behavior. And such statements provide little or no information about what we've actually done (or not) to contribute to another's well-being.

Look at the first example: "Your gift was great! Perfect—and so thoughtful!" What does "great" mean? While it's stronger in degree than "nice" or "good," it doesn't tell us exactly what pleased the speaker. Did the receiver of the gift feel seen because the gift related to an interest that was especially meaningful to them? Will the gift support ease in the life of the recipient because it decreases the effort they expend regularly to complete a certain chore? Without hearing a clear observation and the needs that are satisfied by the gift, it's impossible to know why it was experienced as so wonderful; thus, our ability as the gift giver to connect fully to the joyful experience of the recipient is limited. In contrast, full connection to the recipient's joy nourishes our own joy because it gives us complete information about how we've contributed.

In this chapter, we explore how to express gratitude in a way that is judgment free and relates to the values that are meaningful to us. When we use gratitude in this way—rather than as a strategy for other ends such as acceptance or approval—it becomes the "power-fuel" of life, and giving itself becomes the greatest reward. We also explore how, when necessary, to say "no, thanks" with integrity.

EXERCISE 1: Grateful for Judgment?

Part One
Think of three expressions of gratitude you recently heard or spoke:

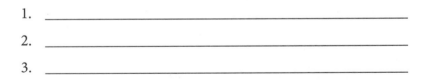

1. _____
2. _____
3. _____

In each case, were you completely clear about what actions you'd taken that pleased the speaker, or vice versa? In each expression, what judgment was stated and/or implicit? You can write about this in your journal if you like.

Part Two
Think back on your life to times when you received positive feedback or compliments. Did these judgment(s) influence you in any way? Did you make choices and/or change your behavior in ways that were not in full integrity with your values?

Example:
My high school science teacher gave me a lot of compliments, so I took more science classes, including advanced courses on anatomy, dissection, and histology. The teacher continued his praise. After about two years, though, I realized I wasn't even that interested in science! I'd been taking all these classes because I was hungry for appreciation and for being seen, and because someone was telling me I was "good" at it. When I shared this with my science teacher, I could tell he was hurt and disappointed because his intention was to support my development in a way that was meaningful to *me*, not to get me to do something that *he* valued. He enjoyed my participation in class, and he valued teaching students whom he experienced as interested and engaged; this was also part of his motivation to encourage me to take more science electives. In hindsight, I wish he'd given me a different kind of feedback; and I know he didn't know how. If I'd better understood his needs and mine, I think I would have made different choices that would have supported me more in actually focusing on what I truly had the greatest interest in.

The Power Juice of Gratitude

As we've explored throughout this book, needs are the compelling motivators of all life. When we contribute to another's well-being, we're contributing to meeting their needs, and doing so, in turn, meets one of the greatest needs we all have—to enrich the lives of others. When we do things to enrich our own lives, we have an immediate feedback system—our feelings—that tells us whether or not we have succeeded in meeting our needs. Yet when we take actions to contribute to others, we don't have direct access to their feelings and needs. As a result, we may not know whether we have succeeded—unless they tell us what their feelings and needs are. Receiving gratitude is an important way in which we find out whether our behavior (intentional or not) has been valuable.

Sometimes, especially when people know each other well or where the context is clear, a simple "thank you" or a smile will suffice. Still, through receiving "needs-based" gratitude, we can better understand a person and what they most desire. We can know how our choices meet needs, and have clarity for decision making, now and in the future. Most gratitude leaves us in the dark. Giving "empathic gratitude"—including observations, needs met, and feelings—is a way to turn on the lights.

EXERCISE 2: The Pleasure Principle

Think of something you did recently that you're confident contributed to the well-being of another.

Part One
Thinking about this action, how do you feel? What sensations do you notice in your body? How does this sensation feel different from sensations you have when you're angry or sad?

Part Two
   A. What action did you take? Describe it in one or two sentences.
   B. What needs were you hoping to meet and what values were you trying to support in taking this action?
   C. Were these needs met and these values supported? How do you know?

D. What observations do you have from the other person that confirms that you contributed to their well-being?

E. What in their response leaves you unclear about whether their needs were fully met or not?

Part Three

Have you ever taken an action that you were sure would contribute to another, only to find it wasn't being received as such? This can especially be true for gifts. One time, for example, I cooked up a treat for a friend, only to find out that she was allergic to some of the ingredients. Think of an action that you took to help or contribute to another that did not, in fact, meet needs, all or in part. How did you know needs were not being met?

Use ONF Often

In giving life-enriching gratitude and making clear how an action has contributed to ourselves or another, we simply use the first three steps of the NVC model—Observations, Needs, and Feelings (ONF). Note that I am suggesting we look at needs before feelings in expressing gratitude, and I will explain that shortly. For now, here's how these steps look when expressing gratitude:

(O for Observation)

What, specifically, did you *observe* that you appreciated?

(N for Needs)

Which *needs* did this behavior meet or support? What values do you hold that are consistent with this behavior?

(F for Feelings)

What *feelings* did this behavior stimulate in you?

These steps are familiar to you by now. Yet in expressing gratitude, there are a couple of additional points to keep in mind. Often with gratitude, if we look at the *feelings* the other person's behavior has stimulated without considering the *related needs and values* first, we are primarily aware of feelings of gratitude and pleasure—feelings that are quite general. After connecting with our needs and values, we are likely to become aware of more subtle, specific feelings that convey aspects of our experience that are more tender and personal.

Let's look now at a few examples of "low-octane" gratitude (simply thanking someone) and then the same appreciation translated into high-impact ONF:

> *Thanks*: Thanks for always being there for me. You're the best friend ever.
> *ONF*: When you picked me up at 3 a.m. at the bus station last night, your care and support really meant a lot to me, especially given how ill my mom is. I felt so relieved to have you there and to not have the anxiety of trying to find a taxi and worrying about the expense.

> *Thanks*: Your present was terrific. I can't thank you enough.
> *ONF*: The gift certificate you gave me for that new restaurant is just what I needed! I wanted to celebrate finishing my thesis, and my boyfriend and I are low on funds. Now we can celebrate in style! I'm so excited.

> *Thanks*: You are the best boy ever. I love you so much when you're being good.
> *ONF*: I love how you put your toys back on the shelf today. Because the room is in order now, I feel safe walking around and can easily find things.

In looking at these examples, you may notice they don't follow very closely the "formal" NVC model. The word "needs" is not used, and only in some cases will you find universal needs explicitly mentioned. Yet in each of these expressions of gratitude, there is a clear observation given—whether about a gift certificate for dinner or being picked up at the bus station at 3 a.m. A feeling is mentioned—for example, safe or excited. And, even when it's not named directly, a need is clearly alluded to and met—be it for celebration, care, safety, ease, or support.

Try reading these aloud. Do you find the ONF gratitude more satisfying and meaningful? How do you experience each kind in your body? In the ONF versions, you may have enjoyed greater understanding and connection (as well as physical openness and relaxation) since you could clearly see the impact on the experience of the receiver, connect with what they're feeling, and appreciate the needs met. This gives a full picture and shared understanding. You may also have been surprised by what you learned, since our actions can contribute to others in unexpected ways. Regarding the gift certificate, for example, a student on a limited budget is certain to enjoy it. Hearing that the student just completed her thesis and wanted to celebrate the event in a special way adds a whole new level of richness and value to the gift.

Perhaps most important, ONF gratitude is always stated in the positive. When giving gratitude, of course, we're talking about fulfillment and "up" experiences. Yet ironically, when giving thanks in a traditional way, people often use negatives. In the case of the boy picking up his toys, for example, the parent might say, "It's great you picked up your toys—it was so messy in here!" Or if someone turns down the music they were listening to, the person who'd requested it might say, "Thanks. That was really giving me a headache." Referring to what was wrong with the situation—"messy" and "headache"— lacks the same clarity, satisfaction, or connection as describing the needs met, so the statement could easily be heard as an indirect criticism of the gift giver. Stating our needs in the positive—such as for order, safety, or peace—increases the chances that they will be understood, acted upon, and celebrated with us. It also increases the chances of their being met in the future, since those around us now know what we *want* (rather than what we don't).

EXERCISE 3: Guessing the Need

Part One
Imagine someone making each of the following statements to you. What needs do you think might have been met for the speaker in each expression?

Statement	Possible Needs Met
A. "Thanks so much for your work on the carnival."	Support, creativity, caring
B. "Your presence at my birthday party meant a lot to me."	
C. "You've been a good friend."	
D. "I've always loved your spirit."	
E. "You do so much for me. Thanks a lot."	

Part Two
Think of three expressions of gratitude you recently made that were judgment based. Then translate them into ONF:

    A. Judgment based: _____

         ONF gratitude: _____

    B. Judgment based: _____

         ONF gratitude: _____

    C. Judgment based: _____

         ONF gratitude: _____

Part Three

Take the following "negative" praise and put it in ONF "positive."

    A. Negative praise: "I'm so glad you cut your hair. It really didn't suit you before."

        ONF positive celebration: _____

    B. Negative praise: "My mom's really relieved that you left that dead-end job."

        ONF positive celebration: _____

    C. Negative praise: "This room looks a lot better since you painted it. It was really dreary before."

        ONF positive celebration: _____

What About Compliments and Praise? Aren't They Good?

The way you played the piano was incredible! You're a fantastic musician.

You are so smart. You can do anything.

You're the best athlete in the whole school. I wish I could score the way you do.

Many people think that compliments such as these help others feel appreciated and can boost confidence and self-esteem. Yet if someone feels good hearing positive judgments, how are they supposed to feel when they hear—and they inevitably will—negative judgments? Should we determine what we think of ourselves and our choices by relying on the judgment of others? Often in giving compliments, we want connection and shared understanding. Judgment-based compliments, like appreciation of the same ilk, focus attention on the *speaker*'s opinions, not on what the recipient did or did not do. They provide little or no information about exactly what happened that impressed the speaker. For example, what does "perfectly" mean? "Perfect," like any judgment, can mean different things to different people.

As judgments, such appreciation also places the recipient in a no-man's-land of static, immovable permanence. No one plays the piano "perfectly" at all times. No one knows everything. Often judgment-based compliments can leave us feeling uncomfortable because we suspect the speaker's opinion might be different if we'd been seen at another time. We don't want the responsibility of trying to live up to a global statement of praise. We are much more comfortable when we know specifically what we did, in the moment, that left a positive impression on the speaker.

As with gratitude, we can use the ONF model to create judgment-free compliments. What did we see or hear that was consistent with our values? What action allowed us to experience our values as supported, embraced, or exemplified? Again, the request step will probably not be necessary unless we're curious about how it is for the other person to hear our appreciation and praise.

In giving ONF gratitude and compliments, you may wish to refer to them simply as "feedback" since you're consciously not engaging in evaluation or judgment. Rather, you're giving "back" about how others' words and actions have contributed to your life. It is in this exchange (giving and receiving—and letting others know what you've received) that you experience the real delight of contributing to others.

EXERCISE 4: Live Feedback—in ONF

Part One
Look again at the examples above of judgment-based compliments and translate them into ONF. Here's the first one, done for you as an example:

Judgment: "The way you played the piano was incredible! You're a fantastic musician."

ONF feedback: "Hearing the speed with which you played the notes in the middle section and the slow meditative way you played the last section was inspiring to me. I didn't think the same person could play the instrument in such different ways. I feel intrigued to consider experimenting with some contrasts in my own artistic expressions. Bravo!"

A. Judgment: "You are *so* smart. You can do anything."
    ONF feedback: _____

B. Judgment: "You're the best athlete in the whole school. I wish I could score the way you do."
    ONF feedback: _____

Part Two

Think of three compliments that you've given or might have given recently that involved judgment. Use ONF to translate each of these judgments into live feedback. Note that for gratitude, the order we're suggesting is Observations, Needs, and Feelings (ONF)—a different order than the usual, classical model.

A. Judgment-based compliment: _____
    ONF feedback: _____

B. Judgment-based compliment: _____
    ONF feedback: _____

C. Judgment-based compliment: _____
    ONF feedback: _____

Twice Judged—Not Praised?

There's another thing to watch out for with judgment-based compliments: the judgment can go both ways. Consider an earlier example: "You're the best athlete in the whole school. I wish I could score the way you do." The speaker is complimenting you, and they're also judging themselves, directly or indirectly, via comparison. By saying, "I wish I were just like you . . ." or "I wish I had done that . . ."
they're speaking about their *own* behavior and about needs that have been unmet by the choices they made. The speaker is using your performance (or at least their interpretation of it) as a mirror for what they see as their own deficiency. In such cases, how have your actions contributed to another? Is it really enjoyable to hear "inverted" compliments of this kind? Rather than being a celebration, such "compliments" are in fact coded messages about unmet needs. They bring attention back to the person who's giving them, rather than keeping the focus on the person being celebrated.

When you hear an inverted compliment, you can use your empathic listening skills to support the speaker in connecting to values that are important to them and to how much those values enrich their life. Here's an example:

Speaker: You are the fastest runner ever. I wish I could do that.
Listener: Sounds like you're discouraged. You'd like to be a fast runner too?
Speaker: Not really. It's just frustrating that I practice so much and still never win a race.
Listener: So what you really want is for your effort to pay off?
Speaker: Yeah, maybe this just isn't my sport. But I'd like to think that if I really work at something, it will show.
Listener: What you really want, then, is effectiveness?
Speaker: Yes, exactly. And for there to be some balance between

the effort and energy I put into something and what I achieve. It doesn't actually matter if I win—I just want to see clear improvement.

Listener: Right—I get it. A sense of achievement.

Speaker: Exactly. Hey, how do you practice anyway? Maybe there are some tips you could give me so I could train better?

Listener: Sure! Why don't you run with me tomorrow when I practice—I could show you some tips then.

Speaker: Great! And thanks for listening. I really appreciate it. I'm much clearer now about what I really want.

Compliments as Strategy

In addition to being a form of self-criticism, compliments can also serve as a way of simultaneously not being present and attempting to influence the mood of another. Have you ever noticed that if you're feeling sad or discouraged, some people will try to cheer you up with compliments? They might say, for example, "Don't let one low grade get you down—everyone knows how smart you are, that you're the best in the class!" How satisfying or consoling is a compliment like this? While you may hear the intention behind such a statement, potentially meeting your needs for understanding and support, such "compliments" can negate how you feel and try to "fix" it; they are rarely effective in building confidence. Rather than hearing that your feelings are unfounded (which indicates that the listener is not fully present to hearing your feelings), it is far more satisfying to have the gift of another person's presence and care—for example: "I see that you're feeling really low about the grade you received. Are you worried about mastering the material and reaching your goals?"

Compliments—or Coercion?

As we've discussed, contributing to the well-being of others is one of the most primary of human needs. When met, it leads to the development of connection, trust, and meaning. At the same time, there is a subtle and crucial distinction between doing something because we are responding to our own inner need to contribute to another's well-being and doing it because we want reward, approval, or payoff. Judgment-based compliments and appreciation can easily blur the lines.

In the example about the little boy picking up his toys, does he pick them up because he wants to please his mother and be considered "good"? Perhaps he knows from experience that if he's not "good," he might be screamed at or punished. This is far different from picking up his things out of care for his mother, because he understands how it contributes to her enjoying order, ease, consideration, and safety. This goes back to the questions we've considered before: *What do we want people to do? And why do we want them to do it?* When we give judgment-based compliments and appreciation, the motivation for people's actions can easily come from fear or a desire for approval or reward—not from contributing to others and enjoying shared values, both motivations that support loving connection and openhearted giving.

De-strategizing Praise

What can you do if you suspect praise is being used for a purpose other than appreciation and celebration? Regardless of the strategy— be it punishment and reward, comparison (negative self-judgment), or attempting to influence your feelings, you can go back to OFNR. In the case of negative self-judgment, you can offer empathy for needs unmet. You can check what needs the speaker is attempting to meet by asking, for example, "Are you wanting to show your care for me by trying to cheer me up?" Or you may wish to guess, as a form of silent empathy, what those needs might be. In doing so, you can gain clarity and understanding about what might be motivating the use of gratitude for other aims in the moment.

EXERCISE 5: Praise as Celebration, Not Strategy

For each of the following statements where praise is used as a strategy for something other than celebration, give an empathy guess to foster understanding and connection. Let's begin with an example.

Example:
    A. "I can never get things right. I wish I were good at things, the way you are."
        Empathy: "So hearing that you didn't get the job you wanted, you're feeling discouraged? You'd like to have the security of a regular income and to trust that you'll be seen for your talents?"
    B. "You did your homework—you're such a good girl. And now you can go out and play."
        Empathy: _____
    C. "I wouldn't worry about losing that game. Everyone knows you're the best on the team, and that our school is number one."
        Empathy: _____
    D. "You look so beautiful in that outfit. I wish I could wear dresses like that—they just don't suit me."
        Empathy: _____

ONF Feedback in Action: Enriching Lives, Empowering Choices

Let's look at a real example of these principles in action. About a month ago, I was observing a teacher and a teacher's aide in a small class for students who were having difficulties at school. I noticed both teachers frequently praising the students, saying, for example, "great job," "super," "fine work." The head teacher told me the children were used to receiving a lot of criticism and very little praise. She wanted to build their self-confidence. I valued her intention and was moved by what I saw as her caring and dedication. I was also concerned that the way she was praising the students encouraged them to rely on her judgments rather than developing their own internal sense of what they valued.

At one point the teacher's aide was telling a boy, John, that his poster showing how lungs work was "great, just great." I asked him, "Is there something you like about your drawing?" He said, "No." I told him that I liked the symmetry—the pair of lungs was balanced—and then I asked the aide what she liked about the drawing. She shared what she liked, and soon John was pointing out what he appreciated about it too. If we had not had this conversation, it's likely John would have had no idea what he had done that was so "great." Now he could see for himself, and he was in a position to believe it and act on it again in the future. This was also far more effective in building up his self-confidence and trust than the unclear, nonspecific praise.

"Uh, Thanks!"

The Power of the Observation—A Story of Two Great Cellists

"My great wish was to hear Pablo Casals. One day, my desire was almost fulfilled and I met him. But ironically, it was I who had to play. It was in the home of the Von Mendelssohns, a house filled with

El Grecos, Rembrandts, and Stradivaris. Francesco von Mendelssohn, the son of the banker, who was a talented cellist, telephoned and asked if he could call for me; they had a guest in the house who would like to hear me play.

"'Mr. Casals.' I was introduced to a little bald man with a pipe. He said that he was pleased to meet young musicians such as Serkin and me. Rudolf Serkin, who stood stiffly next to me, seemed, like myself, to be fighting his diffidence. Rudi had played before my arrival, and Casals now wanted to hear us together. Beethoven's D-Major Sonata was on the piano. 'Why don't you play it?' asked Casals. Both nervous and barely knowing each other, we gave a poor performance that terminated somewhere in the middle.

"'Bravo! Bravo! Wonderful!' Casals applauded. Francesco brought the Schumann Cello Concerto, which Casals wanted to hear. I never played worse. Casals asked for Bach. Exasperated, I obliged with a performance matching the Beethoven and Schumann.

"'Splendid! Magnifique!' said Casals, embracing me.

"Bewildered, I left the house. I knew how badly I had played, but why did he, the master, have to praise and embrace me? This apparent insincerity pained me more than anything else.

"The greater was my shame and delight when, a few years later, I met Casals in Paris. We had dinner together and played duets for two cellos, and I played for him until late at night. Spurred by his great warmth, and happy, I confessed what I had thought of his praising me in Berlin. He reacted with sudden anger. He rushed to the cello, 'Listen!' He played a phrase from the Beethoven sonata. 'Didn't you play this fingering? Ah, you did! It was novel to me . . . it was good . . . and here, didn't you attack that passage with up-bow, like this?' he demonstrated. He went through Schumann and Bach, always emphasizing all he liked that I had done. 'And for the rest,' he said passionately, 'leave it to the ignorant and stupid who judge by counting only the faults. I can be grateful, and so must you be, for even one note, one wonderful phrase.' I left with the feeling of having been with a great artist and a friend." [7]

—GREGOR PIATIGORSKY, author of *Cellist*

Uh, Thanks!

Another way we can express gratitude without clarity is through our learned tendency to say "thank you" when we don't really mean it. From an early age, we're admonished, "Say thank you!" when we receive a gift, whether we like the gift or not. When I was young, I don't think I was asked even once whether a gift or action had in fact met my needs. Instead, I was supposed to be "polite" and grateful for what I'd been given. I'm sure that demanding such "gratitude" was an effort to create connection between others and me, and to foster appreciation. Yet how can we feel connected with another if honesty and authenticity are lacking? How can we appreciate gifts and contributions if there is not integrity in how they have in fact contributed to us and our lives?

Even as adults, we sometimes receive gifts that are not consistent with our taste and values. Sometimes a person does something that was intended to meet a need, but it doesn't have the result that was intended. How do we respond in such a situation? This topic generated a lively discussion in one of my classes: Should you lie and pretend to like the gift, return it, or pass it on to someone else? Should you refrain from letting someone know that their "help" was not helpful? Could you just express your appreciation for the beauty of the intention behind the gift? Each of these strategies, of course, could meet different needs—including for consideration and ease. Yet if we share with honesty and care how we're truly feeling and how our needs have been met or not, this in itself can be a contribution, fostering intimacy, connection, trust, and understanding.

An incident several years ago illustrated this for me. I came across a doll that I thought my brother's daughter would love. While I don't see them often because we live far apart, I know he's a specialist in Russian studies, and this doll was dressed in a traditional Russian outfit. Also, my niece was of an age that I associated with liking dolls, and I thought this one was adorable. With eagerness and excitement, I bought the gift and sent it to her. Some time later I spoke to my brother. "Did Monica get the doll? Did she like it?" "Well, yes, she did get it. We appreciate the thought that went into it and why you thought of us. But actually Monica has never liked dolls. We gave it to someone who does. I hope you don't mind." I felt sad and disappointed that my "perfect" present, which I had purchased and sent with the intent of providing pleasure, had not reached its mark. In the discussion that ensued, though, I learned some new things about my niece, such as what kinds of things interested her and what didn't. I also appreciated my brother's honesty and trust, and as a result of this conversation, our relationship was strengthened as we got to know each other better. My disappointment shifted to feelings of connection and appreciation.

Polite or Real?

When people talk about being "polite" when receiving a gift or assistance, it's often in the context of wanting to avoid hurting others' feelings. In my experience, though, when authenticity, understanding, and connection are present, the feelings associated with unmet needs, such as hurt or anxiety, quickly shift. Regardless, do we want to "fake" our responses to people? Do we want to smile when disappointed, or say "yes" when we mean "no"? Or do we want authenticity and realness, including genuine connection and gratitude? If we're not fully aware of needs met and how our actions have contributed to others, how satisfying is it to hear words of appreciation? It's almost like getting a huge box wrapped up with a bow and finding it empty inside.

Of course, we also desire to have care and consideration for others. When you're concerned about others' feelings or how your honesty may be received, it's helpful to be aware of all your feelings and needs at the moment and perhaps share them with others in all their complexity. If you're feeling hesitation and concern because you care about someone's feelings, for example, you can name these feelings. You can then also share that you value honesty and integrity, and that you want authentic connection. You may also wish to mention all the needs met and unmet by their gift or helpful act, such as care and consideration, and honor what you see as their intention. You can honor needs met while, at the same time, being honest and authentic.

EXERCISE 6: "No, Thanks" as a Gift

Part One
Think about a gift you received that you did not enjoy. What needs did the gift not meet for you? Did you tell the person how you felt? Why or why not?

Part Two
Imagine saying "No, thanks" in ONF for each of the following situations. As part of your response, try expressing gratitude for needs met and/or what you see as the other's intention in giving:

  A. A friend offers to help you straighten up your house before a party, yet that is a chore that you find relaxing to do in solitude as a meditative experience.
      No: _____

  B. Your supervisor is leaving to join a start-up company and invites you to join him. You have concerns about the financial riskiness of such a move and prefer to stay with your current position.
      No: _____

  C. A friend asks you to join her and her husband for an evening playing bridge, but you don't like playing bridge with them because they argue about how they play their hands.
      No: _____

The Appreciation Shortage

Appreciation, when genuine and needs based, is like liquid gold. It energizes the whole giving and receiving system, facilitating needs being identified, celebrated, and met. Yet if gratitude is so energizing and satisfying, why is there not more of it in our lives? As the old saying goes, why is it that most people focus on the glass being half empty rather than half full? Perhaps that's because when our needs are met, we feel contented, satisfied, and fulfilled. In contrast, when our needs are not met, the experience is so unpleasant that we're more expressive and proactive. This can lead to not celebrating what we enjoy in life and instead focusing on what we're lacking. How unfortunate!

Perhaps this explains the lack of appreciation most people seem to feel. Ask yourself: Do you feel appreciated for what you do at work, school, and home? Do you feel that your efforts to contribute to the well-being of others are seen and recognized? Do you know whether your contributions have hit the mark and been experienced as the contributions you intended them to be? Sadly, most people do not feel that their actions are seen, acknowledged, or appreciated. What a missed opportunity!

Enjoying Praise

Many of us have been told that we shouldn't let compliments "go to our head," or become too impressed with ourselves. Some people find it very difficult to accept appreciation or a compliment and will try to deny or minimize the speaker's words by saying things like "Oh, it's not really anything" or "I really did a terrible job—it's not good at all" or "I was just lucky." There can be various reasons why we find compliments difficult to hear. Many of them are probably related to compliments usually occurring as judgments. Being judged, even "positively," can lead us to also judge ourselves and/or compare ourselves to others, often negatively. As discussed earlier, when we hear an affirming judgment from another, we can experience "performance anxiety," as well as the prospect of later disappointing the same critic.

For years, I struggled with receiving compliments, and I still do if they're judgment based. I also enjoy knowing, of course, how my actions have contributed. I've now learned to ask people for more information, and I very much enjoy the results. Not only do I receive more appreciation, I've also come to recognize how many needs a single act can meet! After a poetry reading recently, I tried this experiment. Each time a person thanked me for reading my work, I asked them to name one need it met for them. Repeatedly, both the speakers and I were surprised by the results. No one named the same need and, after reflecting a moment, all seemed satisfied and surprised by what they'd identified. Thinking in this way gave them a whole new appreciation of the reading and what it meant to them. Translating "judgment-based" compliments into needs was like opening a fortune cookie!

In teaching and giving workshop presentations, I often ask the same question: "Would you be willing to tell me one thing that you found helpful about the talk?" The answer helps me to translate a general statement of appreciation into a more useful ONF statement. Like my poetry reading experiment, it gives me numerous "fortune cookies" to open and learn from. I also learn more about others— what they value most and what makes them "tick." In a similar way, when I hear others praising someone, I like to ask, "What does this person do that leads you to say they're 'awesome'? This would help me to see what's most important to you!" In doing so, I learn a great deal about the speaker: what they see and appreciate and, often, want to emulate themselves.

I try to respond similarly when people tell me they don't like my presentations, although they are usually more specific in those instances anyway. The assumption seems to be that if we're giving people "positive" feedback, no further details are necessary.

The reality is that whatever another person has done, feedback with clear observations and an account of needs met or unmet is extremely helpful. Often people talk about "constructive criticism" as the kind that is given with details and care. Similarly, ONF feedback can be seen as a "constructive compliment"—information that aids and supports you in further meeting your own needs and contributing to others. Hearing such "praise," you will find yourself wanting to give and receive more gratitude, since it actually has content and is "positive" and "constructive" in a truly meaningful and impactful way.

EXERCISE 7: Naming the One Thing

Think about three things that you're really excited about and/or enjoy. This could be a person you admire, a work of art or music you love, or an activity you like. For each thing, think of one aspect, in ONF, that is satisfying about it.

1. _____

2. _____

3. _____

Exploring the Appreciation Shortage

In order to understand more deeply the feelings and needs underlying the scarcity most of us experience regarding appreciation, I asked some of my students to write an expression of appreciation—using O, N, and F—that they would love to have received from a particular person.

One student wrote that she would have loved to hear her father give her this appreciation:

When I saw that you had scored more goals than any other
girl on the soccer team this year, I was very, very happy. I value
you developing your skills to the best of your ability, and I am
grateful to have been a part of it by our practicing together.
More than anything else, I want you to develop and grow into
a strong and healthy person. It also gave me hope that you
might get a college soccer scholarship, which I also desperately
want for you because I believe college will enrich your life,
and I don't earn enough to pay your college expenses. I am so
relieved and joyful to have the trust now that you will be able to
follow your dreams.

Another student wrote that he would have loved his former
girlfriend to have said this:

When I think about the times you have held me in your arms
and listened to me talk about my problems with my family and
with school, I want you to know how much it meant to me to
experience your caring and love. Even though we have chosen
not to be together because of different visions we have of the life
we want to live, I feel tears of appreciation forming in my eyes
when I think of your kindness and support of me.

I then asked them each to guess the needs the person wanted to
meet by *not* expressing appreciation in this way. The first student
wrote:

I think he was afraid that if he told me how he felt, I wouldn't
work so hard and do so well. I also know that talking about
feelings is difficult for him. He might have been afraid that I
wouldn't think he was strong and a "real man." I also know he
had a lot of shame about not earning more money, and perhaps
he thought that talking about this would make him feel worse
and make us think less of him.

The second student wrote the following:

I'm thinking that my girlfriend didn't want to let me know
how much my love meant to her because she was afraid it
would threaten her independence and autonomy, which
she also valued highly. Breaking up has been hard for us,
even though it feels like the right thing, and maybe she
wants to protect herself and me from feeling the pain of the
breakup again.

In these and other similar stories I hear, fear is the most common
thief of appreciation. Fears of being vulnerable or being judged by
others can keep people from expressing how they're truly feeling.
They fear speaking about their feelings, or how the person receiving
their gratitude will hear it. Many of us simply are not accustomed to
talking about gratitude; instead we're used to "tough love"—showing
how we "care" through criticism and demands. At other times when
we receive positive feedback, it comes with a disclaimer: "You're
doing X better now, so now you need to do Y."

In addition to fear and lack of gratitude "fluency," another
barrier to the expression of appreciation is that people often think
their needs are in competition. How can the father earning low
wages express his appreciation of his daughter without revealing
his sadness and regret about not earning the money he'd like?
How can the girlfriend express her gratitude while also meeting
her needs for dignity and autonomy? When we really understand
them, however, needs are never in conflict; there is never a
scarcity in expressing what we most value in life. The strategies
we choose to meet one set of needs can sometimes conflict with
strategies to meet other needs; the needs themselves, though, are
not in competition. The need for encouraging a child's athletic
development, for example, is not in conflict with the need for
seeing and valuing one's own contributions and integrity. The need
for autonomy is not in conflict with the need for connection; you

can't be connected to someone in a meaningful way if you are not given the space to be a separate person.

How do we navigate between seemingly competing feelings and needs and name our gratitude, even if we're fearful? One way is to connect with all that we feel and need in the moment and, if we wish, be transparent about the complexity of our needs. Before expressing our gratitude, we might want to mention other "layers" of feelings that are also alive within us. In the case of the soccer-playing daughter, for example, the father might have said:

> I feel sad thinking about how little I earn and my ability to pay for your education. And I'm also really proud of how well you play soccer, and how I've supported you in learning to play. I'm so happy and relieved to know this might help you financially to get through college.

The girlfriend might have said:

> You know I really value my autonomy, so I feel a bit self-conscious and even nervous saying this . . . I want you to know how much I appreciate all your support. I don't think I've ever enjoyed so much tenderness and caring.

When you're being transparent in this way, you will probably want to make a connection request, asking how your words are landing or being heard. Connection and shared understanding are especially crucial when we're feeling vulnerable.

When people give us value-based appreciation or compliments without judgment, it is much easier to hear and digest what they are sharing with us. Rather than resorting to false humility or denial, we can join in their celebration of needs met, both for ourselves and for them. Ultimately, this becomes a celebration of shared values and mutual care.

EXERCISE 8: Appreciation You Would Love to Have Received

A. Write down an expression of appreciation that you would love to have received from a particular person. Be sure to include:
1. What specific appreciated behavior of yours did the person *observe?*
2. What *needs* in them did your behavior meet or support? Which values did they hold that this behavior was consistent with?
3. What *feelings* did this behavior stimulate in them?

B. Stop now and write the appreciation.
Observation: _____

Needs: _____

Feelings: _____

C. Now that you have written your appreciation, consider what feelings and needs stopped or prevented this person from giving you this appreciation. Try to put yourself in their shoes. Review the list of needs on page 368, if that would be helpful. You may wish to write about this in your journal.

EXERCISE 9: Living With Gratitude

Try practicing empathic gratitude every day for a week. Each day, in the morning or evening, make a list of five things you are grateful for (observations) and then what you are needing and feeling. Be sure to include gratitude you have for yourself!

Example:
 Observation: "Last night you drove us fifty miles to see a play
      that I wanted to see."
 Needs: Support, fun, companionship, connection
 Feelings: Warm, tender, thankful

Now you try it.
 Observation: Needs: Feelings:
 1. _____

 2. _____

 3. _____

 4. _____

 5. _____

Appreciating Ourselves—and Our Choices

It's safe to say that most of us don't get the appreciation we'd like
from others. It's also likely that we don't give much appreciation to
ourselves. Because we're the ones contributing to meeting our *own*
needs, it can be easy to take our *own* efforts for granted. Yet only by
expressing self-gratitude can we become fully aware of what we're
doing that's effective (or not) in meeting our needs. In this way, self-
gratitude offers a highly enjoyable and stress-free way to engage in
"behavior modification"—focusing on and reinforcing the actions we
find most life serving and valuable.

 Of course, we're not always happy with the choices we make. I
have found, though, that choices I regret in some ways (due to unmet
needs) I now celebrate in other ways (due to needs met). Awareness
of both helps me fully celebrate and act on my values; the gratitude
really helps with self-acceptance, ease, and balance.

For example, I am still sad that I left Ireland, where I lived for years. In leaving, I did not meet needs for clarity, understanding, self-care, awareness, self-connection, discernment, and choice (in how I made the decision to leave). No longer living there, I've often had needs that are "up" for beauty, meaning, connection with nature, and shared values (among many others). As a result of leaving, however, I have, over time, met needs for learning, self-development, and self-acceptance; I also learned about NVC, which may not have happened if I'd not returned to the United States.

I can now express gratitude to myself about this once painful choice I made. When I think about how I coped with leaving Ireland, a place I loved so much and that met so many needs for me, I am amazed by my passion for life, determination, and resiliency. Having survived that, I am confident I can survive anything! Expressing gratitude to myself in this way is very satisfying. It gives me appreciation, confidence, self-acceptance, and peace. Ultimately, both mourning needs unmet and celebrating needs met are about celebration: honoring what we most value in life and what contributes to our well-being.

EXERCISE 10: Celebration and Mourning

Choose a situation or decision that you regret in some ways and that you also now celebrate in some ways. Make two lists, one of needs unmet and the other of needs met. If the needs unmet are "up" for you, empathize first with those. Then write how you are grateful to yourself for the needs you have met in response to the same situation. How does it feel to express gratitude to yourself in this way?

Situation (observation): _____

Needs not met: _____

Needs met: _____

Gratitude to yourself: _____

Inviting Gratitude From Others

Just as we're reluctant to engage in self-praise, society has taught us that it's unacceptable (judged as self-serving, arrogant, or perhaps insecure) to request or invite gratitude from others. Yet I hear regularly, especially from couples and members of organizations, about how infrequently individuals' contributions are seen and appreciated to the extent they would like. In the spirit of making requests to meet needs, I like to celebrate when I've taken an action that meets my own needs. And if I want feedback and/or to be seen by another for what I've done, I like to speak up and request it. I find this empowering and connecting, and I also get information about how the other person experienced my actions—which is not always how I imagined! While at first this practice can be a little scary, especially if you're concerned with how the other person may judge you for asking, I have found it consistently worth the risk in terms of the overall connection and understanding that I experience. Sometimes requests for recognition and gratitude can actually resolve misunderstanding and disconnection.

Recently, for example, I was working at a large company to support a team that was in conflict. An employee was complaining about his immediate supervisor, who, in his judgment, was demanding and never happy. Further, he was unreasonable. He did not follow corporate policy regarding life-work balance; the weekend overtime hours this employee had been putting in were, he believed, expected of him. As I listened empathically to his concerns, the core needs that came up were appreciation and recognition. The worker cared about the project and his team, and was more than willing to continue working extra hours, including some weekends. He'd never had a sense, though, that his boss fully appreciated this effort. After some NVC-based coaching, he approached his boss and shared the following:

I'm a little concerned how this may sound to you because I've never done this before. And I'm wondering if you have a sense of how many hours I've worked, including on weekends, over the last two months on this project? I'm pleased about what I see as my level of commitment. And I'm wondering what you see—and if there is anything in particular that you appreciate about how you see me working on this project? I'd really appreciate that feedback.

In response, the worker got information beyond what he was expecting: his boss saw something in his performance that even he had not seen—his ability to collaborate with others on the team. After the supervisor shared this feedback, the employee thanked him and explained that while he was personally motivated to perform on the project, when working the amount of overtime that he was racking up, it was helpful to get some input from his boss, as well. They then made a plan to check in monthly about the various ways needs were being met on the project, rather than focusing simply on what was wrong and needed to be changed.

I find the same dynamics in working with couples, families, and in my own life: gratitude, when observation based and authentic, is connecting and energizing. Many couples and parents focus solely on what's wrong, and after a while, others in the relationship can start to think that nothing is right. Studies have shown that couples who express gratitude to each other regularly have much more success in creating happiness in their relationship and in staying together in the long run.

Inspired by the power of gratitude, I keep a regular gratitude journal, writing in it for ten minutes each day. I continue to be amazed by how much I learn and how deep I can go in self-understanding by focusing on needs met. I've also become what I call an urban gratitude bandit. When I see or hear something I like on the subway or the street, I go up to complete strangers and tell them how I feel. For example, I might say, "I just overheard how you were speaking to your child, and I'm filled with happiness and appreciation—hearing how you were with her when she was crying gives me hope about how all of us can parent our children!" Or I might say, "I really love the outfit you're wearing, with so many colors. It really brightens my day!" Each time I've delivered a gratitude "valentine" of this kind, the person's face lights up. And I enjoy a brief moment of connection with a passing stranger. I know I've contributed to making their day by noticing and naming something they have said or done that, in my view, has contributed to life being more satisfying and delightful.

EXERCISE 11: Filling Your Gratitude Well

A. This week, try at least once to play gratitude bandit. If you're too nervous to try it with a complete stranger, try it out first with family members or friends. Remember to give the observation, needs met, and how you genuinely feel.

B. Is there a place in your life where you'd like recognition and appreciation? If so, think of what actions you've taken that you appreciate and identify the needs this met. What request could you make of another to both celebrate what you've done and invite their appreciation?

C. Try this week to keep a gratitude journal. Focus on needs met in every area of your life. What impact does keeping this journal have for you?

D. If you have an empathy buddy, or the next time you have an opportunity to receive empathy, choose to celebrate needs met.

Living in Gratitude

Marianne Williamson sums up well the spirit of value-based compliments and appreciation, and how they involve being fully ourselves, honoring others, and serving life:

Our deepest fear is not that we are inadequate. Our deepest fear is that we are powerful beyond measure. It is our light, not our darkness, that most frightens us. We ask ourselves, "Who am I to be brilliant, gorgeous, talented, fabulous?" Actually, who are you *not* to be? You are a child of God. Your playing small does not serve the world. There is nothing enlightened about shrinking so that other people won't feel insecure around you. We are all meant to shine, as children do. We were born to make manifest the glory of God that is within us. It is not just in some of us; it is in everyone. And as we let our own light shine, we unconsciously give other people permission to do the same. As we are liberated from our own fear, our presence automatically liberates others.[8]

It is difficult, if not impossible, to express too much appreciation—as long as it is genuine. We hope you will practice expressing appreciation every day, both of yourself and others. It is one of the best ways to foster compassionate relationships and to become fully aware of what you most value, desire, and want to experience more of in life.

INTEGRATION: Questions and Exercises to Further Explore Chapter 9

A fundamental assumption of NVC is that there is joy in giving. The following exercise is designed to help you explore the part of yourself that is nourished by giving to yourself and others.

A. During the next week, deliberately and consciously choose to do one thing for yourself that meets your needs, be it for fun, stimulation, rest, or self-care. It could be a material gift, such as an article of clothing, a concert ticket to see your favorite band, a special food item, or something else that you find pleasurable. Or it could be a nonmaterial present, such as a leisurely bath, meeting up with a friend you've not seen for a while, taking time to read a book, or going for a jog, walk, or swim—anything you would enjoy.

Before deciding on your "gift," you may wish to do a "needs inventory." Make a list of all the needs that are most "up" for you now. After empathizing with those needs, see what gift comes to mind to meet those needs. Then, after giving yourself this gift, see how you're feeling. Are you feeling gratitude and appreciation? What needs have you met, such as for self-care?

B.   Now do something for someone else that you are confident would give them pleasure. Choose something you would genuinely enjoy doing and/or giving and that would meet your needs, as well, such as for expression, meaning, authenticity, and integrity. This action could be as simple as calling a friend or family member you've not connected with recently to let them know that you're thinking about them. Or it could involve helping a friend prepare for a test, assisting your parents with some yard work, or helping out at a local food bank. How did you feel during and after taking this action? What needs did it meet? If you experienced negative feelings, what needs, including your own, seemed to be unmet?

C.   How did the two experiences compare? In what ways were the stimulated feelings similar or different? Which stimulated stronger feelings? Were the needs, met or unmet, similar or different?

10

Integrating NVC in Your Life—and on the Streets

I f you've read the preceding chapters, you've learned about ways to powerfully transform how you relate to yourself, others, and the world. You've learned about the three major choices available to you every moment you wish to live in NVC consciousness: self-empathy, empathy, and honest expression. And you're learned about various "supports" in practicing NVC, such as pacing conversations. We're hoping you've already tried some of these steps and seen for yourself the impact and power of empathic connection.

If you have experimented with these tools, you may also have found times when practicing NVC did *not* foster the connection and understanding you'd hoped for. Perhaps these experiences were disappointing, frustrating, or disheartening and you are not quite sure what to make of them. It sounds so good in theory. Why doesn't it always work?

I experienced this myself at my first major immersion in NVC, a nine-day International Intensive Training (IIT) in 2003 organized by the Center for Nonviolent Communication. Those were nine life-changing days; I became aware of NVC's enormous potential to bring greater understanding and connection into my life. I also saw firsthand the possibility of stimulating significant pain in others while practicing NVC, especially if our relationship history was such that our needs had gone unmet.

For several years, I'd been having a major conflict with my teenage daughter regarding the hours she was keeping, the friends with whom she was spending her time, and her use of alcohol. At the IIT, I was thrilled by the possibility that incorporating NVC into my life would provide a clear road map for our relating more easefully with each other. I was excited and called her a few days before the end of the training; I was eager to try out my new skills, drawing on the concepts I was learning and the dialogues I had been practicing. Ever the optimist, I was sure that now we'd have a warm, fuzzy "kumbaya" conversation that would touch both our hearts.

We talked for a while about small things, events of the day, and so forth. And then the dialogue shifted.

> *Me:* So what plans do you have for the weekend?
> *Daughter:* Oh, I'm going to spend Saturday night at Barbara's house.

I immediately thought: "Wonderful! Now I can apply all the great tools I've been learning." Thinking about her plans and practicing self-empathy silently to myself, I connected with how I was feeling: nervous and scared, needing her safety and security. I also wanted to be heard about my concerns and to be seen for my caring. Connecting with these desires, I decided to opt for honest expression—to tell her in a heartfelt and honest way what my concerns were by expressing my feelings and needs. Then I would make a connection request to see if she understood where I was coming from. I had a plan! I took a deep breath and began:

> *Me:* Hearing you say you're planning to spend Saturday night at Barbara's, I feel nervous and worried because I value your safety. Can you tell me what you're hearing from me? I want to be heard for my concern and care for you.

This did not get the reaction I had envisioned:

Daughter: Mom, why don't you just quit with all the words!
If you're going to forbid me to go, just come out with
it and quit being manipulative. I don't need all this
bullshit stuff!

Me: I don't know why I even bother to try anymore. Why can't
you just cooperate for a change?

As you can imagine, the conversation only went downhill
from there, and I hung up feeling heartbroken and immensely
discouraged. What had happened to all my NVC training? Why
hadn't it worked as well as what we'd practiced in the workshops I'd
attended? It had seemed so easy there!

I learned from this interchange a lesson oft-quoted in NVC
circles. "NVC's simple—but not easy." What we mean by this is
that getting the concepts of NVC on a head level can be fairly
straightforward. When practicing in real-life situations, however—
especially where there are painful histories with others or
circumstances that can trigger old pain or hurt—it can be far more
challenging to stay present in NVC consciousness. In the situation I
just described, for example, I came to it with the best of intentions;
practiced self-empathy live, in real time; and shared my concerns in
a heartfelt way. Even so, hearing my daughter's response—which was
so far off from what I was hoping for—led me to fall back into old
patterns, stories, and despair. I would come to learn that when we're
triggered, we're all beginners.

In this chapter, we will explore how to further deepen your
practice of NVC so as to support a natural integration of it in your
life. We will then consider aspects of NVC as a language tool and
how that tool can be used in a colloquial ("street") NVC way that
more fully and easily supports practicing NVC consciousness in
a range of cultures and subcultures. Finally, we will review how to
revisit a conversation where there may not have been the level of

connection you'd wanted: practicing a kind of "NVC first aid."
With all these topics, much of what we will be covering is a review
or further application of the practices we've already considered
earlier in the book. In reading this chapter, understand that what
matters most in practicing NVC is your mind-set: a consciousness of
compassion—seeing the full humanity of each person, even at their
worst moments—and a desire to hold everyone's needs as valuable.
The tools and the model support you in maintaining that mind-set
and spirit.

It's an "Inside Job"

Integrating NVC into your life entails a major change in how you
view yourself and others. For many years of my adult life, I blamed
others, especially those closest to me, when I experienced feelings
of upset stimulated by something they had said or done. Since their
behavior was the stimulus for my upset, I assumed it was the cause.
"What you did *makes me* furious," I would say or think, certain that
my anger was caused by their words or actions. I was also certain
that as the instigator, *they* were the ones who had to change to make
things "right." I had no clue that my upset was caused by my needs
or values being unmet. Either they had done something "wrong,"
or I had, or perhaps we both had been "partly at fault." It was then
a question of how much was their fault and how much was my
fault: a fault/blame way of looking at the situation and seeing the
world. It was beyond my thinking to consider that perhaps *neither*
of us had done anything wrong. It was hard for me to move from a
view of conflict— based heavily on blaming, labeling, and statically
classifying people as being one type of person or another— to a view
that both parties were attempting to meet valuable and life-serving
needs. And when my view was coming from that blaming and
labeling perspective, it was hard for the listener to hear my words as
nonjudgmental or to imagine that I could be genuinely interested in

them and their well-being. Their most likely response was to become defensive or to attack in return.

How do we get out of the vicious cycle of spiraling disconnection? The most important task for living a greater proportion of our lives in NVC consciousness is to work on our own awareness and presence. Yet how do we increase our awareness of things we are not presently aware of? As the punch line of the old joke "How do I get to Carnegie Hall?" tells us, "Practice, practice, practice!"

As when learning any new skill or way of being, there are different ways to practice: to integrate the new concepts, to remind ourselves of what we already know, and to integrate this knowing in our lives. We can engage in these practices on our own, with an NVC buddy, with NVC trainers, and with the larger NVC community. We can also engage in practices that foster mind-body connection and self-awareness; this provides the best possible "soil" to "plant" your NVC practice in each day.

Following are suggestions (divided into practices you can engage in on your own and with others) for practicing on a regular basis and/or supporting an awareness and consciousness consistent with practicing NVC. These items are not listed in order of priority and are just a few examples. You may wish to consider which will best support your practice and then make an agreement with yourself about what you would like to do on a daily, weekly, monthly, and/ or semi-annual or annual basis to support your learning. Regardless of the form it takes, what most supports integration is sustained and regular practice.

Ways to Practice NVC on Your Own

- Read and/or listen to NVC books to reinforce the NVC model and consciousness and to hear examples from other practitioners (see the CNVC bookstore for a full range of materials).

- Do written exercises (from this or other NVC books). Remember, you can do the same exercise multiple times, on different days and applied to different situations, to further your practice.

- Journal. Many NVCers like to keep a daily empathy journal. You can use the journal to practice self-empathy, guess the needs of others, celebrate needs met, support yourself in making decisions (assessing the needs that will be met and unmet through different strategies), as a gratitude journal, or to practice NVC dialogues before or after a conversation. You can also use your journal for "state of the self" explorations (what you are feeling and needing in this moment or point in your life), reviewing recent events in your life, or celebrating milestones. Another use of the journal is to set NVC practice goals for yourself and check in on your progress.

- Keep a judgment journal. As described earlier in this book, you can get a small notebook and record your judgments during the day and then translate them into feelings and needs.

- Watch videos of NVC being practiced, via YouTube (search for NVC, or individual trainers' names) or by purchasing CDs (from cnvc.org).

- Check in with yourself during the day. While doing tasks that don't require your full attention (showering, washing dishes, cooking, doing laundry, gardening, driving, etc.), check in with yourself every few minutes to practice and build fluency with the model. Ask yourself: What am I feeling in this moment? What am I needing? See if you can track the thoughts your feelings and needs are connected to (the observations), and see how often your feelings and needs change. You can also check in with yourself during the day in conjunction with a specific activity, such as any time you check your email, hear the phone ring, or eat a meal. Regular check-ins both support the practice of the NVC model and support self-awareness and connection—both are key in holding NVC consciousness.

- Join NVC Listservs. See the resources section for Listservs on NVC and parenting, social change, and other topics. In addition to sharing information about NVC, upcoming events, and related topics, some lists include members sharing their experiences in practicing NVC.

- Get a set of "GROK" (feelings and needs) magnets and put them on your fridge at home or on a magnetic bulletin board at work. Use the magnets to practice and check in with yourself. (GROK cards and magnets can be ordered from www.collaborative-communication.org)

Ways to Practice NVC With Others—Virtually and in Person

- Find someone to be your empathy buddy. You can meet weekly or biweekly via phone. Take turns (a half-hour each) listening to the other empathically, practicing the four steps of the model and reflection skills. You can also have an agreement about being available to each other for "emergency empathy," calling each other when needed. Be sure to check in first when you are seeking emergency empathy to see if the other person is willing to listen empathically at that time and, if so, how much time they're willing to spend.

- Attend NVC trainings, classes, workshops, residential intensives (IITs), family camps, or retreats with a CNVC Certified Trainer and/or other experienced practitioners. See cnvc.org for upcoming trainings and Certified Trainers and supporters. If you'd like to organize a training or retreat in your area, contact individual trainers listed at cnvc.org or request CNVC to post your request on the Certified Trainers list.

- Participate in a teleclass or webinar. Many are offered by the NVC Academy; see the resources section for more details.
- Join an empathy or practice group in person or by phone, ideally one led by a Certified Trainer or experienced practitioner for support. You can also join or organize "leaderful" groups that are self-led by participants; if so, you may especially wish to use Lucy Leu's book (see resources) for guidance and support and/or receive support from a trainer. You may wish to use NVC lists or meetup.com to organize such groups.
- Join a study group. Invite your friends and others who practice NVC to read, watch, or listen to NVC materials and then practice together; again, such gatherings can be in person or via virtual technology (phone, Skype, webinars).
- Practice through email. Each time you send or receive an email, it's an opportunity to practice self-empathy, empathy for others, and honest expression.
- Make use of social media (Facebook, Twitter, LinkedIn, and the like) to connect with others and practice.
- Work with a Certified Trainer or experienced practitioner. During these coaching sessions, you can be heard empathically, practice NVC skills, do role-plays (rehearsing or reviewing conversations or situations in your life), and set and assess goals regarding the development of your NVC practice, and your life (personal and professional) in general. Some NVC trainers are also professional life coaches; see the list of trainers and their bios at cnvc.org
- Join a world-wide virtual NVC community that promotes NVC consciousness, such as ctc.learnnvc.com
- Practice at home, at work, and on the street (at the post office, when shopping, or wherever you may be) with everyone you meet, at each moment you remember and are willing to do so. Remember that practicing silently can be as effective as, and sometimes even more connecting than, practicing

NVC aloud. For inspiration on practicing NVC in everyday situations, you may wish to see the book *Urban Empathy*, a collection of verbatim examples of practicing NVC.

Ways to Support Self-Connection and Mindfulness

The following activities support the consciousness that supports the practice of NVC.

- Meditation, such as that taught by Inessa Love (see the resources section) or another form of meditation, sitting in silence, or chanting.
- Focusing and inner relationship focusing (www.focusing. org). This practice is highly consistent with NVC and supports mind-body awareness and self-connection.
- Prayer, intentions, or affirmations (about your intentions for the day or a particular situation or conversation).
- Inspirational readings, poems, or "rememberings" that invite a return to your values in alignment with NVC consciousness. Some authors you may wish to explore could include the Sufi poets Rumi and Hafiz or contemporary poets such as David White or Mary Oliver.
- Yoga, aikido, or tai chi. I find that the stretching and deep breathwork of yoga can be very grounding. Aikido, a nonviolent martial art, offers a physical practice that is highly consistent with NVC principles. You may wish to consider other forms of exercise that help ground and "center" you.
- Connect with nature, walks outdoors, or find other ways to explore the natural world.
- Engage in a spiritual practice. Any practice that supports your sense of interdependence with others or communion with the world fosters a sense of what Martin Luther King Jr. called the "beloved community" and supports the sustaining

of NVC consciousness. This beloved community can include human beings and all life.

Again, it is the consciousness itself—our focus on connection and the value of holding everyone's needs with care—that truly informs and supports the practice of NVC. In your regular practices, remember to check whether you are indeed holding this awareness and way of being.

EXERCISE 1: Planning to Practice

Review these lists of suggestions again. Which ones resonate with you? Can you think of other ways to practice? What will support your intention and help you remember to practice?

In your journal or on a piece of paper, make a plan for the next week, month and/or year. This could include, for example, writing in your journal each day or several times this week, finding an empathy buddy in the next month, or attending at least one residential training this year.

To make your requests doable, remember to set clear goals and timelines and check in with yourself to see how your practice is working for you. For example, you could decide to meet with your empathy buddy once a week for the next month. At the end of the month, you can check in with yourself and your buddy about how that's working for both of you. No plan or commitment has to last a lifetime!

If you're creating daily or weekly practices, see if you can "link" to other regular activities in your life—such as doing laundry, food shopping, going to the gym, cooking, and the like—as a way to remind you to practice NVC. For example, you could decide that each time you hear the phone ring, you'll take a moment to check in with yourself about your feelings and needs. You could also decide to do a regular check-in about your practice each time you get your hair cut or when you get your car's oil changed. The idea is to use another activity in your life as a mnemonic device to help you remember your NVC practice.

Empathy From Hell

In being empathically present to ourselves and others, our consciousness and intention—not the form, method, or words we use—has the greatest impact. Remember that old paradox: which comes first—the chicken or the egg? When it comes to NVC practice, it's clear that consciousness comes first! The model supports this consciousness; it does not replace or "fake" it! If you use one of the empathy templates in the model ("Are you feeling ____because you're needing___?"), this is intended to guide where you direct your attention; it is not intended to be a formula for speaking. If your heart isn't in the expression and you're doing the form by rote, this can become what we in NVC call "empathy from hell." "Hollow," heartless empathy is so unpleasant to receive that it's worse than getting no empathy at all. If you offer this kind of "faux" empathy, don't be surprised if you get a strong response: "Just quit that psychology crap!" or "Why can't you talk like a normal person?" or "I don't need you to tell me what I'm feeling!"

If you find yourself practicing "empathy from hell," take a moment to check in with yourself. Are you practicing the NVC form mindlessly, as a habit? Are you using the form as a strategy to meet some other need besides connection? One time, my former partner was telling me about something distressing that had happened during her workday. I was focused on something else. I also wanted to have some light, easy time together after my busy day and was longing to be together in the present moment. I didn't really have the "bandwidth" to take in the intensity of what she was sharing. On automatic, I made an empathy guess—and it landed like concrete hitting the pavement from a ten-story building. She responded with an edge in her voice, "Don't pull that NVC stuff on me!"

At that particular moment, I *was* "pulling" NVC stuff on her! My heart and my presence were not with her. Honest expression would have been a greater contribution than empathy: "I'm getting that you're stressed about your day, and I notice I'm wanting some space and peace right now—my day was full too. Would you be OK with our just taking a walk silently for a few minutes? I think after dinner I'd be willing to hear about your boss."

If you are engaging in hollow empathy, it could be because your own needs are not being satisfied in the moment. Perhaps you're going through the motions of empathy because you think you "should" be compassionate or you think it will defuse the situation, while what you're really wanting are peace, ease, and relief. Whatever the reason, you've chosen to empathize with another without first attending to yourself, when in fact you may be the one most in need. You can be attempting to focus on the needs of another, yet if you have feelings and needs that are up for you, you may be distracted and unable to be fully present.

In these situations you need to fill your empathy cup. Take a moment to check in with your own feelings and needs and give yourself emergency self-empathy. If you can't get the self-connection and presence you're wanting, you may wish to postpone your conversation until you can get the empathy you need. You can practice honest expression—as I modeled in the preceding example.

Sometimes, of course, when you're fully connected to your intention to be empathically present and genuinely wanting to connect, you still get "NVC pushback." Just because we're in a place of being present and caring, this does not necessarily mean that it will be heard or received by the other person. At such moments, the response we're receiving can offer a further opportunity for empathic connection: "Are you having trouble trusting my intention?" or "Do my words sound odd to you?" or "Does this sound weird because you've never heard me talk like this before?"

Regardless of the "negative" response to your practice of NVC, the pushback can offer a reminder and further opportunity for connection with yourself and others. Whatever the judgment or reaction is, there are feelings and needs underneath it that you can connect with. Once the other person has been heard, you can then share the needs you're meeting by practicing NVC and attempting to empathically hear them: "This is something new I've been learning that I hope will help us hear each other. I'm hoping, even though it may sound a bit odd at first, that you'll be open to my trying it!"

EXERCISE 2: Moving From Hell to Heaven

Part One
With your journal in hand, think back to a moment when someone responded to you as if you were offering "empathy from hell." Recreate the dialogue, this time responding empathically (either with honest expression or with a further empathy guess). You may also wish to practice self-empathy, considering what you were feeling and needing at that moment and whether you were in fact focused on empathic connection.

Part Two
Role-play with someone who is familiar with NVC, such as your empathy buddy. Here are the steps to take:

Offer an empathy guess to your partner. "Are you feeling _____ because you're needing _____?"
- Your partner responds as if you've just given "empathy from hell." "What's that jargon you're using?"
- Take a breath and self-connect, practicing self-empathy. What are you feeling and needing at this moment?
- Respond to your partner with honest self-expression and/ or further empathy. For example, "Are you confused because you've never heard me speak like this before?" See how your partner responds now, and restore connection through the role-play if you can. Once connection is made, share with

your role-play partner what needs you're seeking to meet in practicing NVC with them.

- Switch roles.
- When both of you have had a turn playing each role, discuss the experience. How was it for your partner to get "empathy from hell"? How was it for you to practice self-empathy and respond with empathy and honest expression? What did you learn from this exercise?

Being Honest: You're a Newbie!

When you're new to NVC and first learning to be a more empathic listener, you can easily elicit cries of "fake empathy." Here you are, working your hardest to communicate more effectively, and what does it get you? More grief! You have your empathy "antennae" on; they are not yet strong or sturdy enough, though, to get the connection you're wanting or to help you to be as relaxed or authentic with the model as you'd like. You're trying so hard to listen and care, and all you're getting in return are dissatisfaction and static. Others are experiencing your speech as strange: "What's happened to you? You talk strange" or "Are you trying to pull something over on me? Why are you talking that way?" or even "That sounds manipulative to me—telling me how I feel!"

At such times, being proactive up front, using honest expression, is very helpful. Be transparent about your learning something new, and tell the person why it matters to you. When you do, you already have an opportunity for connection and to practice NVC, including requests. "I really want to improve the quality of our communication and am trying out different ways of talking and listening. Could you bear with me for the moment, even though it's a bit awkward?" Or "I know I can come down a bit hard sometimes and be judgmental. I'm trying to learn some new ways to communicate. Are you open to my trying it? I'm new to it, so I know it may sound a bit stilted."

Here's an example of what this can sound like real time in a conversation:

George is a noncustodial parent of a twelve-year-old son, Jeremy, with whom he has been having a lot of conflict. Part of George's motivation for studying NVC is to improve that relationship, which has not been a close one for a number of years and has become significantly worse since George and his wife separated a year ago. In preparation for this conversation, George spent time over two sessions exploring with his empathy buddy what his relationship with Jeremy means to him and how important empathic connection and mutual respect are to George. He identified feelings of sadness, fear, and hurt within himself, related to times when he was living in ways that were not aligned with values that are important to him. He realized that in talking with Jeremy, he wanted to build on the connection they already have, express his openness, and desire to know Jeremy better, and use connection requests to keep the dialogue going. He did some practice role-plays with his buddy so he would be more fluent in translating his feelings and needs in the moment into words. He was not trying to memorize a script; rather, he practiced connecting to his values and expressing what was true for him about these values.

The dialogue ultimately went like this:

George: Jeremy, I want to tell you about this course I'm taking on something called Nonviolent Communication. I want to let you know about it because I'm learning a lot of things about myself, how I express myself and how I listen, and that sometimes I don't listen very well. Are you open to hearing about it?

Jeremy: Well, OK. I was going to go over to Tim's house—he rented a movie.

George: Would you be OK with our talking for about ten minutes before you go?

Jeremy: I guess that would be OK. Tim was still eating dinner.

George: Great. I really appreciate this chance to tell you about something important to me. This course I'm taking, I think it can help me be a better listener, to put more effort into understanding your view of things. How does that strike you?

Jeremy: Sounds good, I guess.

George: I'm happy to hear that. I know we don't always think alike, and I honestly do want to learn more about your point of view. And there is another important piece too. I want to express myself honestly without blaming you or me—to tell you how I feel about certain things that happen between us. When I don't tell you what's going on with me, it just builds up, and eventually it comes out in an outburst that I think is hard for both of us. Do you know what I mean?

Jeremy: Sure I do. I hate when you yell at me.

George: Me too. And because I'm trying a new way to talk, it may sound strange at times. I want you to be honest about how you feel about the changes in me, and I also want you to have some patience with me. Does this make sense?

Jeremy: You're going to talk differently?

George: Yes. I want to talk respectfully, not just yell. And it may sound awkward at first. But neither of us likes the yelling. I want you to hang in there with me, and together we both may figure out a new way to talk about our disagreements.

Jeremy: OK. Whatever. Can I do my stuff now?

George: OK. So you've had enough talking for now?

Jeremy: Yep.

George: You're OK, though, with my trying this new thing I'm learning?

Jeremy: Yeah. It can't be any worse than when you yell at me!

(They both smile and high-five each other.)

In this dialogue, George clearly identifies a number of values that are very important to him: learning about himself, listening, understanding, self-expression, honesty, and respect. He doesn't directly name his feelings of hurt, loss, and sadness; he implicitly refers to them when he says that he, too, does not like his yelling. George specifically asks Jeremy about how he's reacting to what he has to say, showing appreciation of and openness to Jeremy's perspective.

In some situations it is helpful to first name how one is feeling about even raising an issue because unstated feelings, especially fear, can often be experienced by the other party as aggressive. Naturally, the way you express yourself will be informed by the nature of the current relationship.

Here's another extended example of putting this into practice:

Natasha is bothered by her friend Sophia's habit of leaving her personal belongings in Natasha's living room, hall, and kitchen rather than the guest bedroom when she comes to visit for the weekend. Sophia visits fairly regularly because she does business in the city where Natasha lives. Natasha knows that her own value for orderliness in the home is higher than Natasha's because she has seen Natasha's apartment, and she has been hesitant to tell Natasha that her behavior is bothersome because she doesn't want to damage the friendship. She has been thinking of coming up with an excuse for not hosting Natasha in the future, such as saying she's busy that weekend as a way to avoid the issue, which could potentially make things worse. After studying NVC, she decides instead to address the issue directly, as well as her own feelings of apprehension.

> *Natasha:* Sophia, I'd like to tell you about something you do that bothers me, something I've been afraid to bring up because I really value our friendship and I don't want it to suffer. And yet I am also afraid that not talking about it would be worse—it would mean that we couldn't be real with each other, and grudges and resentments might build up. Is now an OK time to talk about this?

Sophia: Sure. I don't want secrets between us either—or you talking to someone else about what's bothering you and not telling me. I wouldn't like that. What's going on?

Natasha: Well, when you stay with me, I often find your umbrella, coat, books, and other things in the hall, the kitchen, or the living room, not in your guest room. For me, having things around the house like that is uncomfortable and disorienting. I need a certain level of order to find things easily, and to move around the apartment. I'm wondering how this sounds to you?

Sophia: Sure, not a problem. I get it. I might forget sometimes. I know I am just not as neat as you are. But I'm happy to be reminded if need be. I'm surprised this was such a big deal for you. Why didn't you tell me sooner?

Natasha: I guess I'm just not used to making waves. Sometimes when I've spoken up in the past, people got defensive and things were uncomfortable between us. I didn't want to negatively impact our friendship.

Sophia: Yeah, I can understand that. Sometimes I do the same thing—I just don't say anything about what's bugging me. I'm glad we could talk about it. I'd rather be honest with each other and work it out.

Natasha: Me too. I think it will be easier next time if there's a concern I want to share with you. This conversation gives me more confidence about being honest with you.

Sophia: Cool. I really appreciate staying at your house, and I like hanging out together, so I'm glad we could talk about this too!

Given that the whole intention of NVC language is to direct our attention toward understanding other people and their experience, words, and actions, the way in which you express yourself will be informed by the nature of your current relationship with the person. And you may want to get some empathy for your attempts to communicate in a new way. Changing long-established communication patterns is not a piece of cake. Understand that you may need to get recognition and the "Purple Heart" for all your efforts from someone else, at least at first.

EXERCISE 3: Naming Change

Think of a person you'd like to practice NVC with whom you've known for some time; this could be a friend, family member, or co-worker. After practicing with an empathy buddy or in your journal, honestly express with this person about your learning NVC and why you are doing so. Check whether they are open to your practicing NVC with them, and name what you'd like—such as patience and understanding—as you try something new.

Talking Like a "Regular Person": Street NVC

In Nonviolent Communication, we place the highest priority on connection between people (and with ourselves). We have spent a substantial amount of time in this book elaborating upon the components of *observations* (free of evaluations), *feelings* (free of thoughts), *needs* (free of strategies), and *requests* (free of demands) because being aware of observations, feelings, needs, and requests supports establishing and maintaining openhearted connection. However, as we have mentioned before, there are many times in real-life dialogue when we do not use strict OFNR format; instead, we use more colloquial expressions. Remember, the goal is *connection*, not a specific way of speaking. We hold an awareness of OFNR in our minds—like having a road map in our back pocket—while our speech can take a wide range of forms that may support connection. When you have a destination to get to, there are usually numerous routes available.

Street NVC refers to language that may not fit an OFNR model and is expressed with an NVC consciousness of caring about the needs of all. For example, suppose I have a friend who is feeling grief and outrage because her boyfriend said that he was dating only her and she found out he was also seeing someone else. I might guess that her intense distress is related to a value for more trust and honesty in her life. If she's talking about how she can't trust this specific person, I might initially empathize with how much she wants trust in this particular relationship rather than trust in general. Compare these two types of responses:

> *Virginia:* I can't believe what a liar he is! He swore he was only
> seeing me, and now I know that was all a lie!
> *Classical Response:* Thinking about his dating other people, are
> you furious because you value trust and honesty?
> *Street Response:* Are you furious because you wanted to trust he
> was being honest with you?

The classical response refers to the general universal values of trust and honesty. The street response refers to the specific situation of wanting *him* to be honest. In the beginning, a guess that references the specifics of the situation (i.e., the person, location, action, time, or object—PLATO) can feel more connecting to the speaker because it includes aspects of the situation that the speaker is attending to. The specifics, by definition, identify a particular strategy for addressing a general need. Assisting the speaker in ultimately connecting to the general values and needs that are important to them frees and empowers them because there are many, many ways to experience the general values that enrich the quality of our lives. While she realizes that her need for trust can be met in a variety of ways and in a variety of relationships (including her relationship with herself!), she doesn't need to hold this particular relationship as the only way to meet her need for trust, and this opens her to a fuller range of possibilities.

In addition to referencing particular aspects of a strategy with the need, it can be helpful when practicing street NVC to leave out formal words in the model such as "feel" or "need" and instead simply state *what* the person is feeling and needing: "Are you *tired* because you're wanting *support?*" Even while you're inquiring, with openness, about what the person is actually experiencing, in the colloquial practice of NVC you can also make a statement that communicates a question using intonation (your voice going up at the end of the sentence) or using word choices that indicate you're checking about the other person's experience. "So you really want some understanding now . . . is that accurate?"

It's also helpful to think of synonyms for the formal aspects of the model that more closely match how you speak every day. You may note that the way you speak at work, for example, will be different from how you speak with a loved one at home or a stranger on the street, or that you speak differently depending on the age of the person you're talking to. For example, in a work environment I would be unlikely to say, "Let me reflect that back to you." Instead, using words more familiar in a work setting, I might say, "Let me recap that" or "Let's review what we just discussed." I might couple this with the need in a colloquial form: "I want to make sure we're on the same page" (clarity, shared reality) or "The details matter here, for accuracy and moving this forward" (accuracy, movement, effectiveness). Again, feelings and needs can often be implied. What matters is your intention—for understanding and collaboration. You also can include modifiers that are colloquial—such as "a little" or "a lot"—to add naturalness to your NVC speech.

On the next page is a chart that reviews some of these concepts—omitting key words from the model, using synonyms, and using adverbs to make your expression sound more natural.

Street NVC

Street Observations
Leave out "hear, see, think" and put the action in a verb form (direct observation):
"So when Tom *asked* her out for dinner . . ."
"When you *forgot* your wallet . . ."
"So *knowing* that Sue said X . . ."

Street Expression of Feelings
Here, as with the needs section below, where you see an ellipsis (. . .) you add subject and verb (predicate) and where you see an underscore, you insert a word from the feelings list. For example: "*Are you* sitting with *some sadness* thinking about your work situation?" or "*I'm* tapping in to *some real delight* learning to play the piano." Note that in these colloquial examples the observation step follows the verb—in this case, "your work situation" and "learning to play the piano."

Being With	Touching On	Experiencing
. . . sitting with ____	. . . sitting with ____	. . . not feeling fully ____
. . . holding ____	. . . holding ____	. . . exploring _____
. . . having ____	. . . having ____	. . . going through ___
. . . carrying ____	. . . carrying ____	. . . experiencing ____
. . . aware of ____	. . . aware of ____	

Street Expression of Needs
In the following examples, where you see an ellipsis (. . .) you can insert different phrases and subjects with the appropriate verb and tense; where you see an underscore, you can insert a need. For example, before the words "grateful for," you could add, "*I'm*

grateful for" or "*You're* grateful for" or "*They're* grateful for." For the need (where the underscore occurs) you could give any need met (or object) that you're experiencing gratitude for. For example, "I'm grateful for having *a sense of completion* with this issue." To take another example, from the well-being group, "*A sense of companionship* supports me in my work."

Meaning/Value	Well-Being	Gratitude
You/I value _____ ____ is important to you/me ____ matters to you/me ____ helps you/me feel ____ You/I care about ____ ____ gives you/me	You/I thrive on _____ ____ helps you/me feel settled ____ nourishes you/me ____ supports you/me ____ sustains you/me ____ keeps you/me going ____ gives you/me hope	You/I appreciate ___ . . . love ____ . . . cherish ____ . . . treasure ____ . . . grateful for ____ . . . really floats your/ my boat
Longing	Pained Longing	Hope/Future
You/I . . . desire _____ . . . yearn for ____ . . . crave ____ . . . thirst for ____ . . . long for ____ . . . wanting ____ . . . long to experience _____	You/I . . . ache for _____ . . . starved for ____ . . . hunger for ____ . . . dream of having ____	. . . desire _____ . . . wish for ____ . . . hope for ____ . . . aspire to experience ____ . . . want to cultivate/ create/manifest/ develop/envision/ support/maintain __

Street Requests
Willing: would like to . . . hoping that . . . imagining it'd be helpful if . . . enjoying the idea of . . .

Examples
   "Would you like to go to dinner now?"
   "Are you hoping that we'll talk about this today?"

"I'm imagining it would be helpful if we reread the report
    before responding."
"Are you enjoying the idea of staying home tonight?"

Confirming: "Are you OK with that?" "Is that something you'd
    do?" "What do you think about ...?" "Does that match
    your understanding?" "Does that work for you?"

Note: With all steps, you can add modifiers or modal verbs (might,
could, can) to match intensity, expression, or accuracy, such as the
following:

    Observation: "So you're *really sure* you heard/saw ... "
    Feeling: "You're feeling *a little* ... "
    Need: "You *might* like ... "
    Request: "I have a *strong* desire ... "

EXERCISE 4: Colloquial NVC

What differences do you notice between colloquial and classical
NVC? Come up with two more examples for each category that *you*
could imagine saying.

    A. Offering reflection (Observations about what was heard):
- "So what I get from this is ... "
- "What you're saying is ... ?"
- "What I'm hearing in this is ... "
- "What matters most to you is ... ?"
- "Based on what I've heard/read, it sounds like ... "

    B. Requesting reflection:
- "Could you tell me back what you heard me say to make
  sure we're on the same page?"
- "Can you recap what I just covered so I know I made it
  clear?"

- "I'm really excited about this and want to fully take it in ... can you say it back to me so I can hear it a second time?"
C. Observations:
  - "So you heard/saw ... "
  - "What you saw/heard is ... "
  - "When you think about ... "
  - "From your point of view, you saw/heard/read ... "
D. Feelings (leave out the word "feeling" and use a feeling word from list):
  - "In my gut, I'm ..."
  - "I'm noticing I'm ... "
  - "I'm a little ... "
  - "Are you ... ?"
E. Needs (use a synonym for "need"):
  - "What I'm/you're wanting is ... "
  - "I'm/you're hoping/looking for ... *or* I'm/you're desiring/ longing for ... "
F. Connection requests:
  - "How is it for you to hear this?"
  - "I'm wondering what's going on for you, knowing this?"
  - "I'm curious what thoughts you have about this."

Choosing the "Right" Frequency

In addition to omitting some key words in the model, using synonyms, and adding colloquial expressions to "naturalize" your practice of NVC, it can also be helpful to consider what intensity of feeling and need you're using and modify this, depending on the environment and whom you're speaking to. In a work environment, for example, I would probably be hesitant to ask someone if they were scared. This might not meet other needs, such as comfort, trust, and ease. Instead I'd probably use a word more commonly used in a work environment, such as "concerned," even though it's toned down from what might be the actual intensity of the person's feeling. Similarly, when speaking with a five-year-old, I'd probably not say, "Are you bored and wanting stimulation and aliveness?" Instead, I'd use familiar vocabulary at their language level: "Do you want to have some fun and play?"

In thinking about these ranges, it's also helpful to think of how formal the word is. In English, words from Latin (usually polysyllabic) are the most formal and academic. Words from German that came into English tend to be more slang-like and informal. For example, "depressed" and "down" have similar meanings in English; the first is more formal and the second more informal. Often the informal, German-based words make use of a preposition: "*up*set," "shut *down*," "opened *up*." Making use of everyday, colloquial language (the German-based words in English rather than the Latinate ones) can also help your "NVC speak" sound more street. Making use of a range of words can also support your comfort and ease in honest expression, balancing your own needs for authenticity, honesty, and transparency with ease, comfort, confidence, and trust—and creativity and choice! Regardless of the level of formality or intensity, making use of a range of feelings and needs freshens your practice of NVC.

Following are some sample ranges of feelings, addressing formality and intensity:

Intense/Formal	Medium	Low Intensity/Informal
Furious	Mad	Irritated
Despair	Discouraged	Bummed
Euphoric	Happy	Upbeat
Panicked	Afraid	On edge
Shocked	Surprised	Freaked out

Now here are some sample ranges of needs. Note that these words are not exact synonyms; rather, they are in similar "families" of needs. Further, the words that you consider low or informal will depend on your own cultural and social background:

Intense/Formal	Medium	Low/Informal
Harmony	Peace	Ease
Affection	Warmth	Connection
Gratitude	Appreciation	Thanks
Mutuality	Equality	Balance

Also see how you can bring fun, humor, and aliveness into your practice of street NVC by using synonyms, colloquial expressions, and metaphors. For example, you could ask, "Sounds like this news hit you like a ton of bricks?" as a way of referring to surprise or shock. Or you could ask, "At this point you're wanting a détente regarding this situation at work?" as a way of naming the person's desire for ease, peace, and reconciliation.

Exercise 5: Speaking Street

Part One
Choose three feeling words not used in the example above that you consider formal or intense and come up with medium and low/ informal versions of the same words. Include colloquial expressions, metaphor, and prepositional phrases (verb and preposition combinations).

Part Two
Look at the needs list on page 368. What needs words would you feel comfortable using at work? At home? With friends?

Part Three
Look at the feelings and needs list. Come up with five metaphors to
describe these experiences.

Silence is Golden: The Value of Silent Empathy

If your NVC "wings" are still new, or if you have tried practicing NVC
with someone and experienced NVC pushback, remember the value of
silent empathy. While the person is speaking, silently guess to yourself
what they are feeling and needing. Also practice self-empathy silently:
what are you feeling and needing? Thinking about the model, you may
notice it's helpful to check in silently about what observation (stimulus) the person is responding to; similarly, you can silently consider
what strategy (request) might serve at this point. If you continue to
practice the model silently, eventually it will begin to influence the way
you speak to yourself and others. This is probably the most natural
and easily accessed form of street NVC: be clear about your intention
(for connection) and practice silent empathy with yourself and others.
What comes out of your mouth—and how situations unfold—will
already be completely different from what you would have said or
done before as a result of this inner connection work.

EXERCISE 6: Silence Speaking

Think of a person or situation you consistently find challenging.
Make a conscious choice to practice silent empathy the next time
you interact with this person. Without making an effort to change
how you speak, notice after the conversation how practicing silent
empathy made a difference in the quality of your understanding and
connection.

The Golden Rule: Practice What You Seek

Like many people, when I first started to learn NVC, I had a whole list of people I wanted to "try it out on" and who I was certain "needed" NVC—more than I did! I couldn't wait to use NVC with them and tell them about it. I wanted *them* to change—and fast! If only my mother knew NVC, and my boss, and my dad, and my brother, and some of my friends. It was a pretty long list! If only they learned NVC, life would be so much easier. This was a strategy, of course, for many needs I had: for movement, ease, connection, and relief.

Of course, the person who needed NVC most of all was me. It's like that old expression: Physician, heal thyself. I was the one being triggered, and I was longing for change in my life. I was the one responding to situations in ways I was not enjoying. I was the one suffering in these interactions. Ultimately, NVC is about taking supreme responsibility for our own experiences, our own feelings and needs, how our needs are held with care, and how they are met. No one else can do that for you—or for me. We can all contribute to one another's well-being. In the end, though, it was *my* job to learn NVC.

Ironically, by changing my own thoughts and expressions, I started to interact with others differently. And they, in turn, interacted differently with me. While this was not my plan—I know I have no control over how others act, believe, speak, or think—it was the eventual outcome. As the saying goes, it takes two to tango; once I changed my own dance steps, the whole dance changed.

Also, once I modeled NVC in my own life, others became interested in what I was doing differently. One of my favorite stories about this concerns my family. One holiday a few years ago, I was sitting at the dinner table with my mother and brother. My mom said something that clearly irritated my brother, and he turned and said to me, "How do you take her? She's impossible!" Before I could even reply, my mom piped up, "She can handle me because she knows NVC." Since then, my mom has also started to learn NVC. Our practicing it together has tremendously supported our relationship and mutual understanding. I'm convinced this would not have happened if I'd suggested she learn NVC, especially if I'd had any expectation or demand around it. She saw the difference it was making in my life and in our relationship; that's what motivated her to want to learn more.

I believe that practicing NVC yourself, on yourself, is the fastest and most efficient way to learn it. After all, you're with yourself 24/7. I'm also convinced that the vast majority of violence that goes on every day is in our own heads: in how we speak to ourselves. By holding NVC consciousness with yourself, via self-empathy, you can develop your practice of NVC *and* deepen self-connection, mindfulness, and compassion. All of this further supports your practice of NVC with others.

EXERCISE 7: Practicing What You Preach

Take a moment to reflect on how you will practice NVC on yourself this week. What times in your day and week are conducive to practice? When showering, driving, riding the subway, first waking up, or before going to sleep? Will you journal? Will you practice checking in with yourself? Or will you decide to practice self-empathy the next time you're triggered by a particular event?

Charging Your Empathy Batteries; Uncovering Core Beliefs

Throughout this book we've revisited the value of practicing self-empathy. This is especially helpful when you want to be empathic to others and you're triggered by what's happening, when you want to get clear about your own feelings and needs (such as when making decisions), when you're celebrating needs met (when you're happy with choices you've made), and when you're exploring regret (when your actions have left your own needs unmet). A regular practice of self-empathy is crucial to the overall practice of NVC. We cannot be compassionate with others if we are not practicing compassion with ourselves.

On a meta level, when we're triggered it's usually because some core need comes up: a need that's often unmet in relation to a certain person or situation, or unmet in a significant way since our early years. In addition to practicing self-empathy in the moment, it can be helpful to look at the core beliefs we have that inform these triggers. Many of these we have learned from others (such as parents, siblings, teachers, or society). Many are based on core beliefs in our society as a whole, and these are usually related to separation and scarcity. They are usually "globalized" in some way and, as such, are expressed using adverbs such as "never" and "always." Some versions of core beliefs might include: "I'll never get it right." "No one will ever love me." "There's no point in trying—it never works out." "I always miss the boat."

Because they are so intrinsic to how we see and move through the world, core beliefs can at first be difficult to see. They're like the air we breathe or fish moving through dark water. If you practice self-empathy regularly, though, including connecting with sensations in your body (where old triggers are often held), over time you will begin to notice patterns, both around what kinds of words and situations trigger you and the feelings and core needs that consistently come up for you. This gradually increasing awareness also helps in your self-empathy practice. It's like meeting an old friend on the street—"Oh, there you are again!"—which makes it easier and faster to practice self-empathy. Self-empathy can also offer insight into the core beliefs that are motivating or driving a trigger in the present moment. This is the first step toward liberating our core beliefs and deciding, from a level of full awareness, whether they are truly serving us and our lives or are instead baggage we now wish to let go of.

In this practice of surfacing core beliefs, it can be helpful to receive what's often referred to as "deep empathy" and to do this work with a skilled trainer. Your empathy buddy may also be willing and able to support you in noticing core belief patterns and connecting with the deeper feelings and needs living underneath them. While the language used may be different, some people also find they can do this kind of deep, healing core belief work with a therapist or coach. I also find I can explore this terrain by journaling and locate more of what I call the "Loch Ness monsters": the triggers that are lurking beneath the surface of everyday life and consciousness.

EXERCISE 8: Liberating Core Beliefs

Part One

Core beliefs involve heavy doses of self-judgment and judgments about the world. Many of these beliefs in our culture are expressed via idiomatic expressions, such as "The early bird gets the worm" or "You have to watch out for number one." Take a moment and reflect on idiomatic expressions you heard in your family while growing up, from teachers or among your friends. Then reflect on how these ideas turn up in your own core beliefs. Consider how these beliefs impact triggers you may experience on a regular basis—turning up in a judgment or reaction—and examine what your core needs are. After connecting with your core needs, take a moment to hold them with care and appreciate how much these qualities matter to you. In this step, speak to yourself gently and with compassion, as if to a young child for whom you have complete love and caring. Here's an example of this process:

> *Idiom:* Everyone's out for number one.
> *Core belief:* People walk all over me. They just care about
>   themselves.
> *Trigger:* Someone steps in my way, bumps into me, or moves in
>   front of me in line.

Judgment/reaction: What am I, invisible? Chopped chicken liver?
Needs: To matter, to be seen, caring, for my needs to matter.
Self-compassion/integration practice: Take a moment to speak
    with yourself tenderly, as if to a young child: "You really
    want to be seen and your needs to matter? You really
    want caring in the world—and for your needs."

By repeatedly practicing this process of deep self-empathy you
can, over time, transform core beliefs into awareness, openness, and
choice.

Part Two

Another way in which core beliefs become part of how we see the
world is when they are the result of repeated experiences or trauma
early in our lives. Sometimes these experiences are connected to
things we heard again and again from our parents, influential family
members, or others, or connected to their repeated actions or
behaviors.

In my family, for example, I was often criticized and blamed for
doing something "wrong"—and this could be followed by physical
punishment. So I became determined at an early age to "get things
right." No matter how hard I tried, though, at some point my parents
would inevitably become angry again. My hope and excitement
during periods of "reprieve" (when there were relative harmony and
safety) collapsed once again into discouragement, apprehension,
and fear. The core beliefs I adopted during this time (as a strategy to
protect myself from further disappointment and self-blame) was "It's
no use—I'll never get it right!" and "It's never good enough." I also
internalized comments I heard my parents say, such as "You just have
to pay attention!"

As an adult, I realized that I was giving "free rent" to these
beliefs and that often my emotional responses in the present (such as
deep and sudden disappointment and discouragement) were being
triggered by my early experiences. This also impacted my choices

and responses in the present; because these were rooted in core beliefs, I often didn't see this clearly at first, and they were so familiar to me that they seemed "natural."

Through the regular practice of empathy, self-empathy, and other mindfulness practices, I've become aware of many of my core beliefs and have learned to befriend them. I can now recognize them more easily and respond with compassion for myself (and my parents). I even chuckle sometimes when I see them surface once again—"Oh, there you are!" As a result, I am enjoying more choice in the present moment.

Take a few minutes and brainstorm a list of the statements you heard in your family when you were growing up. You may notice that these relate in some way to beliefs in scarcity or isolation. For example, in the context of sharing with others you may remember, "Don't be such a pig!" or "You expect too much." You may also wish to reflect on repeated painful experiences from your childhood (such as a parent being absent from the home) that led to your adopting certain core beliefs. Next, take some time to explore how these beliefs manifest today in your life, both in what you tell yourself and in the actions you take.

As a bonus, you may wish to guess your family members' feelings and needs when they spoke as they did or acted in these ways, as well as the needs you were meeting or seeking to meet by adopting your core beliefs. (In my own example, a need beneath my adopting the belief that "It's never good enough!" was to protect myself from further disappointment.)

Finally, you may wish to create a new "story," some feeling- and needs-based affirmations for yourself, and practice deep self-empathy and compassion around these early experiences and how your core beliefs have continued to play out in your life. A sample affirmation might be, "There's sufficient space for everyone, and I can fully meet my needs." You can gently remind yourself of this new story throughout the day and when you notice one of your familiar friends, a core belief, popping up. You can also return to the deep self-empathy and compassion practice in part one above. Most simply, this is a practice of holding gentleness, loving kindness, and compassion for yourself as well as any history of sadness and loss around unmet needs. Ultimately, this kind of "mourning" becomes a celebration of all that you most value in life and wish to see fully manifest in yourself and in the world.

Profound Moments of Compassion

However you go about liberating your core beliefs, unearthing them into the light of day, this kind of deep empathy is hugely helpful in freeing up internal space for greater compassion and living in NVC consciousness. The more you practice NVC and the more self-empathy and deep empathy you do, the more you will find that old triggers fall away. You will become better and better able to turn up fully in each moment with authenticity, connection, and power. In those moments, it doesn't matter what words or formal model you are using. Through your consistent practice with it, the NVC road map has already brought you to the place you desire to be.

I recently experienced a profound moment of such trigger-free response. I was running late to teach a class and hit more traffic than expected. I had just put on my turn signal and was backing into a parking space (with one minute to spare!) when someone else pulled into the spot I had chosen. Given the time I had and the time of day (and the number of spots available in midtown Manhattan), I didn't want to continue looking for parking. Before my NVC training, if an incident like this had happened I would have cursed, given up the spot, and kept looking—even though I would have been aggravated and even later for my class. It was the first night, and I really wanted to be on time! I would have been in a "bad" mood for hours.

This time, though, I experienced what I would consider an NVC "miracle." I put on the hazard lights, turned off the car, left it double-parked where it was, and went to speak with the driver of the other car. I could tell he was reluctant to roll down his window—or even speak with me. When he did lower it, I said, "Hi! I had my turn signal and backup lights on and was planning to take this spot—I'm late to teach a class. I'd really appreciate it if you'd pull out and let me take it." At first he protested: "No, you did not have your signal on—and you were pulled too far ahead!" Of course, he didn't want to give up the spot and continue looking any more than I did—I could understand that! I repeated my request, this time with a dose of empathy: "I know you're already parked here, and I really am late. I'd so appreciate it if you'd let me have this spot! It would really help me out."

The man rolled up his window without replying. I assumed this meant he wasn't going to listen to me anymore—or budge from the spot. Before learning NVC, looking at my core beliefs, and practicing self-empathy numerous times, I know how I would have responded: I would have been triggered and "lost it" at this point, and probably shouted some choice words at him. Instead—and it is this moment that I consider the true miracle—I simply went back to my car. I was practicing self-empathy (sitting with my disappointment and imagining my choices at this point, such as paying $20 to park) when I looked in my rearview mirror: the man was leaving the spot so I could take it! I waved thanks to him, parked, and made my class on time.

For me, this was a powerful example of "dogging" for my own needs, making a true request (while being open to hearing no), making a powerful request (clear, concrete, and doable), and holding compassion for myself and for the other person. This is a golden reminder for me of a certain paradox: we have no control over others *and* the choices we make infinitely impact what happens and the choices others make. I could have just driven away, given up, and spent the evening cursing the other driver. Even more compelling for me, if I'd shouted at him or cursed him out when he rolled his window up, he may have decided to simply turn off his car, lock his doors, and leave. I didn't know that he was planning to give me the spot at that point. While I cannot prove this, I believe it was my response in the moment that supported him in following through on his decision to offer me the parking place.

While I was practicing a colloquial form of NVC, what really made a difference were my consciousness and energy. I was completely neutral and calm when speaking to the man and making my request and even when he rolled his window up. Of course, it was the four steps of the NVC model that supported me in holding this consciousness, as well as years of developing ease in practicing the model. The model feeds the consciousness, and it is the consciousness that matters most.

I could offer many, many other examples of what I consider to be NVC miracles. Many have happened while I was receiving deep empathy from others ("a-ha" moments when I experienced a shift and insight), while journaling or practicing self-empathy (furthering self-awareness and compassion), and while practicing NVC consciousness face to face with others. It has happened in more challenging situations than conflict over a parking space; I have truly experienced nonviolence, collaboration, and compassion in action. I consider these moments miracles because the outcomes were radically different from what I would otherwise have expected and from what I have experienced in similar situations before. I have also repeatedly experienced levels of internal resources, peace, and choice within myself that I continue to find inspiring.

⁚⁖⁚

Our wish for you is that soon you will experience these kinds of miracles yourself. We trust that the practices in this chapter for integrating NVC in your daily life and practicing a colloquial form of the model will support your ease in practicing NVC, living in NVC consciousness, and generating miracles every day.

AFTERWORD

Creating a Nonviolent World

In this book, we have focused on communication. Yet what is the link between the words we use and physical acts of violence? Where does violence begin and end?

Violence, from an NVC perspective, is a tragic expression of unmet needs. The more human needs are experienced as unmet, the greater the chance that violence will occur. When we express unmet needs in the form of violence, we often imagine urgency and consider such actions "necessary" and even unavoidable. The use of violence is for the person's "own good" or for a "greater" good, such as ensuring justice or peace. Such thinking occurs in the paradigm of right and wrong and good and evil. It assumes that people need to be reformed and, in order to have care and consideration for others, must be punished and rewarded.

In this book, we have considered the possibility of a very different world. This world, based on compassion, recognizes that human beings act out of wanting to meet positive needs, and that at every moment we have choices about how we will meet these needs. This awareness is crucial in choosing how we relate to others and ourselves; it is key in creating a world where the needs of all people can be met.

A rock has no choice. We, as human beings, have arguably more choice than any other living, breathing creature. As Viktor

E. Frankl observed, "The last of human freedoms [is] the ability to choose one's attitude in a given set of circumstances." We hope that from reading this book and practicing the exercises, you now feel a greater sense of choice in what you think and feel, how you respond to events in your life, and what strategies you choose to meet your needs. Remember, the less choice we have—that is, *the less choice we see or perceive ourselves as having*—the less alive we are.

Violence can be seen as leading to a kind of death—in the most extreme form, physical death and destruction; in more transmuted forms, a narrowing and diminishment of life and its expansiveness. When we don't fully connect with others, when we don't have full awareness and choice, when we confuse strategies for primary, life-expressing needs, we are, in effect, closing the aperture—even if only slightly—on the fullness of life and all that we can experience and receive.

Is hitting a child necessary to serve life? Is killing another human being, bombing another nation, or seeing that another suffers when we have suffered ourselves necessary to meet our needs for fairness, hope, safety, and justice? These are the questions we hope you will consider. Why? Because we believe the world depends on it. Given our current circumstances, as Marshall Rosenberg concludes in the interview in this book, "We are getting to a point where our best protection is to communicate with the people we're most afraid of. Nothing else will work."

Carl Sandburg also expresses this eloquently in his short poem "Choose."

> *The single clenched fist lifted and ready,*
> *Or the open asking hand held out and waiting.*
> *Choose:*
> *For we meet by one or the other.*

What would a nonviolent world look like? It would be a world where each person has the resources to feel compassion for another. It would be a world where the needs of all people are held with care—not just for themselves, their friends, family, town, state, country, or continent. Thinking in such a global and interconnected way may feel overwhelming, discouraging, and even impossible. How can you ensure the needs of people on the next street over or in the next town are met, never mind on the other side of the world? And indeed, As Inbal Kashtan, coordinator of the Parenting Project for the Center for Nonviolent Communication, observes:

> As powerful and effective as it can be for addressing problems in the social and political arenas, the language of NVC by itself does not remedy the enormous challenges humans face when they don't have the financial or social resources to meet their own or their children's needs. NVC does not eliminate social inequalities that relate to race, gender, class, sexual orientation, physical ability, and the like.[9]

Yet the method you have just learned is powerful. Think of the number of people you communicate with every day. Imagine what would happen if you and ten others began to communicate in a more compassionate way. What if those ten people inspired ten others to do the same? Compassion, just like violence, can easily spread across the world. Like any great change, it begins with one person making a start and groups of people working together. You can choose to contribute to that change. It is a choice you can freely make, again and again, every day.

GRATITUDE

We would like to express our appreciation to Dr. Marshall B. Rosenberg for creating the tool of Nonviolent Communication, his lifetime commitment to finding ways to meet the needs of all people, and his continuous sharing of this material all around the globe. We are grateful for what we see as both his creativity and passion in bringing this life-changing practice to the world.

We would also like to thank the many trainers who have contributed so much to our growth, learning, and sense of NVC community, including Walter Armstrong, Jeff Brown, Duke Duchscherer, Robert Gonzales, Dow Gordon, Sylvia Haskvitz, Rita Herzog, Arnina Kashtan, Christine King, Barbara Larson, Gina Lawrie, Lucy Leu, Kristin Masters, Kit Miller, Ruby Phillips, Susan Skye, Wes Taylor, and Towe Widstrand.

We would like to especially thank NVC trainers Miki Kashtan, Inbal Kashtan, and the late Julie Greene, the founders of the BayNVC North America NVC Leadership Program, for their vision, clarity, and passion in sharing NVC and for their tremendous contribution to our learning and development. We would also like to thank Meganwind Eoyang and Nancy Kahn, current BayNVC trainers, for their openhearted courage and support in living and modeling NVC consciousness, as well as the 2004 and 2005 Leadership Program support teams and all the participants. All of you have contributed profoundly to our integrating NVC and learning to balance compassion for ourselves and others.

We would like to thank those who created graphics or gave feedback to the earlier editions of this book, including Andrew Jung, Sam Zavieh, Meredith Woitach, Michelle Russo, Jonathan Crimes, Peter Przeradzki, Inbal Kashtan, and Jet and Martha. Much appreciation also goes to the editor of this current edition, Sheridan McCarthy, for her gracious and helpful contributions and "go team!" support and also to Hadassah Hill and Jenna Peters-Golden for illustrations.

❖

Jane is also appreciative of the support and contributions of Roxanne Manning, who has always been available to listen and assisted with the development and editing of the graphic model of Compassionate Communication in this book. Roxy has also brought passion to organizing both the New York Intensive and the NVC and Diversity retreats, which have contributed so much to the meaningful presence and growth of NVC as a process that supports people from all walks of life.

Jane is also grateful to the many students who were enthusiastic and eager to contribute their experiences for this book. She gives special thanks to her "empathy buddies," Meganwind Eoyang, Martha Lasley, Kanya Likanasudh, and Eileen McAvoy, whose support has meant so much to her in becoming more compassionate with herself and with others, and who have supported her during the protracted revising of this latest edition. And she is thankful for the learning and challenges offered by Gar Young, which assisted in connecting her more fully to the joy behind the writing and the fun of challenging herself. She wishes to thank her coauthor, Dian Killian, who has shared and supported the vision of this book so ably with her talents and provided an *in vivo* laboratory for working out our differences with grace and compassion.

Jane would like to express her thanks to her family—Bill, Justin, Jolien, Jill, Jordan, Jessicca, and Paul—for supporting and encouraging her to grow and learn in ways that are meaningful to her. She regrets that her parents, Sam and Rhoda Marantz, are not here to see this book, since they modeled caring for the needs of all people on this planet their entire lives.

Dian Killian is grateful to her former partner, Martha Grevatt, for all her companionship, tenderness, laughter, and support over nearly fifteen years of sharing life together, and is glad for their continued friendship. Dian would also like to thank the many friends who have been with her over many years, through thick and thin and numerous deadlines, life changes and challenges, including Grainne Carty, Katharina and Michael Heinrich, Sean Broe, Maria Ortigosa, and Sara Baum. She would also like to thank her NVC buddies, many of whom she "grew up" with as an NVC trainer: Jeff Brown, Jude Lardner, Lynda Smith, Sue Holper, Gina Cenciose, Kanya Likanasudh, Martha Lasley, Jean-Phillipe (JP) Bouchard, Gail Epstein, Eliane Geren, Kristin Masters, Simone Anliker, Curtis Watkins, Valérie Lanctôt-Bédard, and Jean Morrisson. (A special thanks to Simone for her generous gift of *shree Ganesh murti*, which continues to remove obstacles, including to meeting book deadlines.) Gratitude also to all those who have participated in NVC training at, and/or have been supportive of, The Center for Collaborative Communication and now Work Collaboratively, especially Nellie Todd Bright, Paul Merrill, Kit Miller, and all past and current board members. A warm shout-out to her writing friends who continue to inspire: Sarah Falkner, Nina Karacosta, and her writing buddy, Lisa Freedman, and to Laurie Twilight Jetter, who movingly reminds her of how compelling and vital NVC is in the world.

Warm appreciation also goes to her coauthor, Jane Connor, who has been so delightful to work with, offering companionship, learning, fun, inspiration, humor, and, not least important, focus and support in meeting deadlines.

Finally, Dian would like to thank all those in her family who have been her greatest teachers of NVC, especially her grandmother, Lillian Sophia Endress Seelen, who brought compassion and beauty into the world each day both with the quality of her presence and the lilt of her voice.

APPENDIX 1

Beyond Good and Evil: Creating a Nonviolent World— An Interview With Marshall Rosenberg

I first met Marshall Rosenberg when I was assigned by a local paper to cover one of his "Nonviolent Communication" training seminars. Disturbed by the inequalities in the world and impatient for change, I couldn't imagine what use a communication technique could be in solving problems such as global warming or the debt of developing nations. But I was surprised by the visible effect Rosenberg's work had on individuals and families caught in conflict.

Nonviolent Communication, or NVC, has four steps: observing what is happening in a given situation; identifying what one is feeling; identifying what one is needing; and then making a request for what one would like to see occur. It sounds simple, yet it's more than a technique for resolving conflict. It's a way of understanding human motivation and behavior.

Rosenberg learned about violence at an early age. Growing up in Detroit in the thirties and forties, he was beaten up for being a Jew and witnessed some of the city's worst race riots, which resulted in more than forty deaths in a matter of days. These experiences drove him to study psychology in an attempt to understand, as he puts it, "what happens to disconnect us from our compassionate nature, and what allows some people to stay connected to their compassionate nature under even the most trying circumstances."

Rosenberg completed his Ph.D. in clinical psychology at the University of Wisconsin in 1961 and afterward went to work with youths in reform schools. The experience led him to conclude that, rather than help people to be more compassionate, clinical psychology actually contributed to the conditions that cause violence because it categorized people and thus distanced them from one another; doctors were trained to see the diagnosis, not the person. He decided that violence did not arise from pathology, as psychology taught, but from the ways in which we communicate.

Humanistic psychotherapist Carl Rogers, creator of "client-centered therapy," was an early influence on Rosenberg's theories, and Rosenberg worked with Rogers for several years before setting out on his own to teach others how to interact in nonaggressive ways. His method became known as Nonviolent Communication.

No longer a practicing psychologist, Rosenberg admits that he has struggled at times with his own method, resorting to familiar behavior or fearing the risks involved in a nonviolent approach. Yet each time he has followed through with Nonviolent Communication, he has been surprised by the results. At times, it has literally saved his life.

On one occasion in the late 1980s, he was asked to teach his method to Palestinian refugees in Bethlehem. He met with about 170 Muslim men at a mosque in the Deheisha Camp. On the way into the camp, he saw several empty tear gas canisters along the road, each clearly marked: "Made in U.S.A." When the men realized their would-be instructor was from the United States, they became angry. Some jumped to their feet and began shouting: "Assassin! Murderer!" One man confronted Rosenberg, screaming in his face, "Child killer!"

Although tempted to make a quick exit, Rosenberg instead focused his questions on what the man was feeling, and a dialogue ensued. By the end of the day, the man who had called Rosenberg a murderer had invited him home to Ramadan dinner.

Rosenberg is founder and director of the nonprofit Center for Nonviolent Communication (www.cnvc.org). He is the author of *Nonviolent Communication: A Language of Life* (PuddleDancer Press) and has just completed a new book, to be released by PuddleDancer in fall 2003, on the application of NVC in education: *When Students Love to Learn and Teachers Love to Teach*. He is currently working on a third book addressing the social implications of Nonviolent Communication. [Editor's note: this article was originally published in *The Sun* magazine (www.thesunmagazine. org) in 2002. The second two titles mentioned were eventually released as *Life-Enriching Education* and *Speak Peace in a World of Conflict*.]

A tall, gaunt man, Rosenberg is soft-spoken but becomes animated when describing how Nonviolent Communication has worked for him and others. He has three children and currently lives in Wasserfallenof, Switzerland. Rosenberg is in great demand as a speaker and educator and maintains a relentless schedule. The day we spoke was his first free day in months. Afterward, he would be traveling to Israel, Brazil, Slovenia, Argentina, Poland, and Rwanda.

Killian: Your method aims to teach compassion, but compassion seems more a way of being than a skill or technique. Can it really be taught?

Rosenberg: I would say it's a natural human trait. Our survival as a species depends on our ability to recognize that our well-being and the well-being of others are, in fact, one and the same. The problem is that we are taught behaviors that disconnect us from this natural awareness. It's not that we have to learn how to be compassionate; we have to unlearn what we've been taught and get back to compassion.

Killian: If violence is learned, when did it start? It seems to have always been a part of human existence.

Rosenberg: Theologian Walter Wink estimates that violence has been the social norm for about eight thousand years. That's when a myth evolved that the world was created by a heroic, virtuous male god who defeated an evil female goddess. From that point on, we've had the image of the good guys killing the bad guys. And that has evolved into "retributive justice," which says that there are those who deserve to be punished and those who deserve to be rewarded. That belief has penetrated deep into our societies. Not every culture has been exposed to it, but, unfortunately, most have.

Killian: You've said that deserve is the most dangerous word in the language. Why?

Rosenberg: It's at the basis of retributive justice. For thousands of years, we've been operating under this system that says that people who do bad deeds are evil; indeed, that human beings are basically evil. According to this way of thinking, a few good people have evolved, and it's up to them to be the authorities and control the others. And the way you control people, given that our nature is evil and selfish, is through a system of justice in which people who behave in a good manner get rewarded, while those who are evil are made to suffer. In order to see such a system as fair, one has to believe that both sides deserve what they get.

I used to live in Texas, and when they would execute somebody there, the good Baptist students from the local college would gather outside the prison and have a party. When it came over the loudspeaker that the convict had been killed, there was loud cheering and so forth—the same kind cheering that went on in some parts of Palestine when they found out about the September 11 terrorist attacks. When your concept of justice is based on good and evil, in which people deserve to suffer for what they've done, it makes violence enjoyable.

Killian: But you're not opposed to judgments.

Rosenberg: I'm all for judgments. I don't think we could survive very long without them. We judge which foods will give what our bodies need. We judge which actions are going to meet our needs. But I differentiate between life-serving judgments, which are about our needs, and moralistic judgments that imply rightness or wrongness.

Killian: You've called instead for "restorative justice." How is that different?

Rosenberg: Restorative justice is based on the question: how do we restore peace? In other words, how do we restore a state in which people care about one another's well-being? Research indicates that perpetrators who go through restorative justice are less likely to repeat the behaviors that led to their incarceration. And it's far more healing for the victim to have peace restored than simply to see the other person punished.

The idea is spreading. I was in England about a year ago to present a keynote speech at the international conference on restorative justice. I expected thirty people might show up. I was delighted to see more than six hundred people at this conference.

Killian: How does restorative justice work?

Rosenberg: I have seen it work, for example, with women who have been raped and the men who raped them. The first step is for the woman to express whatever it is that she wants her attacker to understand. Now, this woman has suffered almost every day for years since the attack, so what comes out is pretty brutal: "You monster! I'd like to kill you!" and so forth.

What I do then is help the prisoner to connect with the pain that is alive in this woman as a result of his actions. Usually what he wants to do is apologize. But I tell him apology is too cheap, too easy. I want him to repeat back what he hears her saying. How has her life been affected? When he can't repeat it, I play his role. I tell her I hear the pain behind all the screams and shouting. I get him to see that the rage is on the surface, but beneath that lies the despair about whether her life will ever be the same again. And then I get the man to repeat what I've said. It may take three, or four, or five tries, but finally he hears the other person. Already at this point, you can see the healing starting to take place—when the victim gets empathy.

Then I ask the man to tell me what's going on inside of him. How does he feel? Usually, again, he wants to apologize. He wants to say, "I'm a rat. I'm dirt." And again I get him to dig deeper. And it's very scary for these men. They're not used to dealing with feelings, let alone experiencing the horror of what it feels like to have stimulated in another human being such pain.

When we've gotten past these first two steps, very often the victim screams, "How could you?" She's hungry to understand what would cause another person to do such a thing. Unfortunately, most of the victims I've worked with have been encouraged from the very beginning by well-meaning people to forgive their attackers. These people explain that the rapist must have been suffering and probably had a bad childhood. And the victim does try to forgive, but this doesn't help much. Forgiveness reached without first taking these other steps is just superficial. It suppresses the pain.

Once the woman has received some empathy, however, she wants to know what was going on in this man when he committed this act. I help the perpetrator go back to the moment of the act and identify what he was feeling, what needs were contributing to his actions.

The last step is to ask whether there is something more the victim would like the perpetrator to do, to bring things back to a state of peace. For example, she may want medical bills to be paid, or she may want some emotional restitution. But once there's empathy on both sides, it's amazing how quickly they start to care about one another's well-being.

Killian: What kinds of "needs" would cause a person to rape another human being?

Rosenberg: It has nothing to do with sex, of course. It has to do with the tenderness that people don't know how to get and often confuse with sex. In almost every case, the rapists themselves have been victims of some sort of sexual aggression or physical abuse, and they want someone else to understand how horrible it feels to be in this passive, weak role. They need empathy, and they've employed a distorted means of getting it: by inflicting similar pain on someone else. But the need is universal. All human beings have the same needs. Thankfully, most of us meet them in ways that are not destructive to other people and ourselves.

Killian: We've long believed in the West that needs must be regulated and denied, but you're suggesting the opposite: that needs must be recognized and fulfilled.

Rosenberg: I'd say we teach people to misrepresent their needs. Rather than educating people to be conscious of their needs, we teach them to become addicted to ineffective strategies for meeting them. Consumerism makes people think that their needs will be met by owning a certain item. We teach people that revenge is a need, when in fact it's a flawed strategy. Retributive justice itself is a poor strategy. Mixed in with all that is a belief in competition, that we can get our needs met only at other people's expense. Not only that, but that it's heroic and joyful to win, to defeat someone else.

So it's very important to differentiate needs from strategies and to get people to see that any strategy that meets your needs at someone else's expense is not meeting all your needs. Because anytime you behave in a way that's harmful to others, you end up hurting yourself. As philosopher Elbert Hubbard once said, "We're not punished for our sins, but by them."

Whether I'm working with drug addicts in Bogota,

Colombia, or with alcoholics in the United States, or with sex offenders in prisons, I always start by making it clear to them that I'm not there to make them stop what they're doing. "Others have tried," I say. "You've probably tried yourself, and it hasn't worked." I tell them I'm there to help them get clear about what needs are being met by this behavior. And once we have gotten clear on what their needs are, I teach them to find more effective and less costly ways of meeting those needs.

Killian: Nonviolent Communication seems to focus a lot on feelings. What about the logical, analytic side of things? Does it have a place here?

Rosenberg: Nonviolent Communication focuses on what's alive in us and what would make life more wonderful. What's alive in us are our needs, and I'm talking about the universal needs, the ones all living creatures have. Our feelings are simply a manifestation of what is happening with our needs. If our needs are being fulfilled, we feel pleasure. If our needs are not being fulfilled, we feel pain.

Now, this does not exclude the analytic. We simply differentiate between life-serving analysis and life-alienated analysis. If I say to you, "I'm in a lot of pain over my relationship to my child. I really want him to be healthy, and I see him not eating well and smoking," then you might ask, "Why do you think he's doing this?" You'd be encouraging me to analyze the situation and uncover his needs.

Analysis is a problem only when it gets disconnected from serving life. For example, if I said to you, "I think George Bush is a monster," we could have a long discussion, and we might think it was an interesting discussion, but it wouldn't be connected to life. We wouldn't realize this, though, because maybe neither of us has ever had a conversation that was life-connecting. We get so used to speaking at the analytic level that we can go through life with our needs unmet and not even know it. The comedian

Buddy Hackett used to say that it wasn't until he joined the army that he found out you could get up from a meal without having heartburn; he had gotten so used to his mother's cooking, heartburn had become a way of life. And in middle-class, educated culture in the United States, I think that disconnection is a way of life. When people have needs that they don't know how to deal with directly, they approach them indirectly through intellectual discussions. As a result, the conversation is lifeless.

Killian: If we do agree that Bush is a monster, though, at least we'll connect on the level of values.

Rosenberg: And that's going to meet some needs—certainly more than if I disagree with you or if I ignore what you're saying. But imagine what the conversation could be like if we learned to hear what's alive behind the words and ideas, and to connect at that level. Central to NVC training is that all moralistic judgments, whether positive or negative, are tragic expressions of needs. Criticism, analysis, and insults are tragic expressions of unmet needs. Compliments and praise, for their part, are tragic expressions of fulfilled needs.

So why do we get caught up in this dead, violence-provoking language? Why not learn how to live at the level where life is really going on? NVC is not looking at the world through rose-colored glasses. We come closer to the truth when we connect with what's alive in people than when we just listen to what they think.

Killian: How do you discuss world affairs in the language of feelings?

Rosenberg: Somebody reasonably proficient in NVC might say, "I am scared to death when I see what Bush is doing in an attempt to protect us. I don't feel any safer." And then somebody who disagrees might say, "Well, I share your desire for safety, but I'm scared of doing nothing." Already we're not just talking about George Bush, but about the feelings that are alive in both of us.

Killian: And coming closer to thinking about solutions?

Rosenberg: Yes, because we've acknowledged that we both have the same needs. It's only at the level of strategy that we disagree. Remember, all human beings have the same needs. When our consciousness is focused on what's alive in us, we never see an alien being in front of us. Other people may have different strategies for meeting their needs, but they are not aliens.

Killian: In the United States right now, there are some people who would have a lot of trouble hearing this. During a memorial for September 11, I heard a policeman say all he wanted was "payback."

Rosenberg: One rule of our training is: empathy before education. I wouldn't expect someone who's been injured to hear what I'm saying until they felt that I had fully understood the depth of their pain. Once they felt empathy from me, then I would introduce my fear that our plan to exact retribution isn't going to make us safer.

Killian: Have you always been a nonviolent revolutionary?

Rosenberg: For many years I wasn't, and I was scaring more people than I was helping. When I was working against racism in the United States, I must confess, I confronted more than a few people with accusations like "That was a racist thing to say!" I said this with deep anger, because I was dehumanizing the other person in my mind. And I was not seeing any of the changes I wanted.

An Iowa feminist group called HERA helped me with that. They asked, "Doesn't it bother you that your work is against violence rather than for life?" And I realized that I was trying to get people to see the mess around them by telling them how they were contributing to it. In doing so, I was just creating more resistance and more hostility. HERA helped me to get past just talking about not judging others, and to move on to what can enrich life and make it more wonderful.

Killian: You have criticized clinical psychology for its focus on
pathology. Have you trained any psychotherapists or other
mental health practitioners in NVC?

Rosenberg: Lots of them, but most of the people I train are not
doctors or therapists. I agree with theologian Martin
Buber, who said that you cannot do psychotherapy as a
psychotherapist. People heal from their pain when they have
an authentic connection with another human being, and I
don't think you can have an authentic connection when one
person thinks of him- or herself as the therapist, diagnosing
the other. And if patients come in thinking of themselves as
sick people who are there to get treatment, then it starts with
the assumption that there's something wrong with them,
which gets in the way of the healing. So, yes, I teach this to
psychotherapists, but I teach it mostly to regular human
beings, because we can all engage in an authentic connection
with others, and it's out of this authentic connection that
healing takes place.

Killian: It seems all religious traditions have some basis in empathy
and compassion—the bleeding heart of Christ and the life
of Saint Francis are two examples from Christianity. Yet
horrible acts of violence have been committed in the name of
religion.

Rosenberg: Social psychologist Milton Rokeach did some research
on religious practitioners in the seven major religions. He
looked at people who very seriously followed their religion
and compared them to people in the same population who
had no religious orientation at all. He wanted to find out
which group was more compassionate. The results were
the same in all the major religions: the nonreligious were
more compassionate. Rokeach warned readers to be careful
how they interpreted his research, however, because within
each religious group, there were two radically different
populations: a mainstream group and a mystical minority.

If you looked at just the mystical group, you found that they were more compassionate than the general population.

In mainline religion, you have to sacrifice and go through many different procedures to demonstrate your holiness, but the mystical minority see compassion and empathy as part of human nature. We *are* this divine energy, they say. It's not something we have to attain. We just have to realize it, be present to it. Unfortunately, such believers are in the minority and often persecuted by fundamentalists within their own religions. Chris Rajendrum, a Jesuit priest in Sri Lanka, and Archbishop Simon in Burundi are two men who risk their lives daily in the service of bringing warring parties together. They see Christ's message not as an injunction to tame yourself or to be above this world, but as a confirmation that we *are* this energy of compassion. Nafez Assailez, a Muslim I work with, says it's painful for him to see anyone killing in the name of Islam. It's inconceivable to him.

Killian: The idea that we're evil and must become holy implies moralistic judgment.

Rosenberg: Oh, amazing judgment! Rokeach calls that judgmental group the salvationists. For them, the goal is to be rewarded by going to heaven. So you try to follow your religion's teachings not because you've internalized an awareness of your own divinity and relate to others in a compassionate way, but because these things are "right" and if you do them, you'll be rewarded, and if you don't, you'll be punished.

Killian: And those in the minority, they've had a taste of the divine presence and recognize it in themselves and others?

Rosenberg: Exactly. And they're often the ones who invite me to teach Nonviolent Communication, because they see that our training is helping to bring people back to that consciousness.

Killian: You've written about "domination culture." Is that the same as "salvationism"?

Rosenberg: I started using the term "domination culture" after reading Walter Wink's works, especially his book *Engaging the Powers*. His concept is that we are living under structures in which the few dominate the many. Look at how families are structured here in the United States: the parents claim always to know what's right and set the rules for everybody else's benefit. Look at our schools. Look at our workplaces. Look at our government, our religions. At all levels, you have authorities who impose their will on other people, claiming that it's for everybody's well-being. They use punishment and reward as the basic strategy for getting what they want. That's what I mean by domination culture.

Killian: It seems movements and institutions often start out as transformative but end up as systems of domination.

Rosenberg: Yes, people come along with beautiful messages about how to return to life, but the people they're speaking to have been living with domination for so long that they interpret the message in a way that supports the domination structures. When I was in Israel, one of the men on our team was an Orthodox rabbi. One evening, I read him a couple of passages from the Bible, which I had been perusing in his house after the Sabbath dinner. I read him a passage that said something like "Dear God, give us the power to pluck out the eyes of our enemies," and I said, "David, really, how do you find beauty in a passage like this?" And he said, "Well, Marshall, if you hear just what's on the face of it, of course it's as ugly as can be. What you have to do is try to hear what is behind that message."

So I sat down with those passages to try to hear what the speaker might have said, had he known how to put it in terms of feelings and needs. It was fascinating, because what was ugly on the surface could be quite different if you sensed the feelings and needs of the speaker. I think the author of that passage was really saying "Dear God, please protect us from people who might hurt us, and give us a way of making sure that this doesn't happen."

Killian: You've commented that among the different forms of violence—physical, psychological, and institutional—physical violence is the least destructive. Why?

Rosenberg: Physical violence is always a secondary result. I've talked to people in prison who've committed violent crimes, and they say, "He deserved it. The guy was an asshole." It's their thinking that frightens me, how they dehumanize their victims, saying that they deserved to suffer. The fact that the man went out and shot another person scares me too, but I'm more scared by the thinking that led to it, because it's so deeply ingrained in such a large portion of humanity.

When I worked with the Israeli police, for example, they would ask, "What do you do when someone is shooting at you already?" And I'd say, "Let's look at the last five times somebody shot at you. In these five situations, when you arrived on the scene, was the other person already shooting?" No. Not in one of the five. In each case, there were at least three verbal exchanges before any shooting started. The police recreated the dialogue for me, and I could have predicted there would be violence after the first couple of exchanges.

Killian: You have said, though, that physical force is sometimes necessary. Would you include capital punishment?

Rosenberg: No. When we do restorative justice, I want the perpetrators to stay in prison until we are finished. And I am for using whatever physical force is necessary to get them off the streets. But I don't see prison as a punitive place. I see it as a place to keep dangerous individuals until we can do the necessary restoration work. I've worked with some pretty scary folks, even serial killers. But when I stayed with it and forgot about the psychiatric point of view that some people are too damaged ever to change, I saw improvement.

Once, when I was working with prisoners in Sweden, the administrator told me about a man who'd killed five people, maybe more. "You'll know him right away," he said. "He's a monster." When I walked into the room, there he was a big man, tattoos all over his arms. The first day, he just stared at me, didn't say a word. The second day, he just stared at me. I was growing annoyed at this administrator: *Why the hell did he put this psychopath in my group?* Already, I'd started falling back on clinical diagnosis.

Then, on the third morning, one of my colleagues said, "Marshall, I notice you haven't talked to him." And I realized that I hadn't approached that frightening inmate, because just the thought of opening up to him scared me to death. So I went in and said to the killer, "I've heard some of the things that you did to get into this prison, and when you just sit there and stare at me each day and don't say anything, I feel scared. I would like to know what's going on for you."

And he said, "What do you want to hear?" And he started to talk.

If I just sit back and diagnose people, thinking that they can't be reached, I won't reach them. But when I put in the time and energy and take a risk, I always get somewhere. Depending on the damage that's been done to somebody, it may take three, four, five *years* of daily investment of energy to restore peace. And most systems are not set up to do that. If we're not in a position to give somebody what he or she needs to change, then my second choice would be for that person to be in prison. But I wouldn't kill anyone.

Killian: For horrendous acts, don't we need strong consequences? Just making restitution might seem a light sentence for some.

Rosenberg: Well, it depends on what we want. We know from our correctional system that if two people commit the same violent crime, and one goes to prison while the other, for whatever reason, does not, there is a much higher likelihood of continued violence on the part of the person who goes to prison. The last time I was in Twin Rivers Prison in Washington State, there was a young man who had been in three times for sexually molesting children. Clearly, attempts to change his behavior by punishing him hadn't worked. Our present system does not work. In contrast, research done in Minnesota and Canada shows that if you go through a process of restorative justice, a perpetrator is much less likely to act violently again.

As I've said, prisoners just want to apologize—which they know how to do all too well. But when I pull them by the ears and make them really look at the enormity of the suffering this other person has experienced as a result of their actions, and when I require the criminals to go inside themselves and tell me what *they* were feeling when they did it, it's a very frightening experience for them. Many say, "Please, beat me, kill me, but don't make me do this."

Killian: You speak about a protective use of force. Would you consider strikes or boycotts a protective use of force?

Rosenberg: They could be. The person who has really spent a lot of time on this is Gene Sharp. He's written books on the subject and has a wonderful article on the Internet called "168 Applications of Nonviolent Force." He shows how, throughout history, nonviolence has been used to prevent violence and to protect, not to punish.

I was working in San Francisco with a group of minority parents who were very concerned about the principal at their children's school. They said he was destroying the students' spirit. So I trained the parents in how to communicate with the principal. They tried to talk to him, but he said, "Get out of here. Nobody is going to tell me how to run my school." Next I explained to them the concept of protective use of force, and one of them came up with the idea of a strike: they would keep their kids out of school and picket with signs that let everyone know what kind of man this principal was. I told them they were getting protective use of force mixed up with punitive force: it sounded like they wanted to punish this man. The only way protective use of force could work, I said, was if they communicated clearly that their intent was to protect their children and not to bad-mouth or dehumanize the principal. I suggested signs that stated their needs: "We want to communicate. We want our children in school."

And the strike was very successful, but not in the way we'd imagined. When the school board heard about some of the things this principal was doing, they fired him.

Killian: But demonstrations, strikes, and rallies are often presented as aggressive by the media.

Rosenberg: Yes, we've seen protesters cross the line in some of the antiglobalization demonstrations. Some people, while trying to show how terrible corporations are, take some pretty violent actions under the guise of protective use of force.

There are two things that distinguish truly nonviolent actions from violent actions. First, there is no enemy in the nonviolent point of view. You don't see an enemy. Your thinking is clearly focused on protecting your needs. And second, your intention is not to make the other side suffer.

Killian: It seems the U.S. government has trouble differentiating between the two. It tries to make war sound acceptable by appealing to our need for safety, and then it acts aggressively.

Rosenberg: Well, we do need to protect ourselves. But you're right, there is so much else mixed up with that. When the population has been educated in retributive justice, there is nothing they want more than to see someone suffer. Most of the time, when we end up using force, it could have been prevented by using different ways of negotiating. I have no doubt this could have been the case if we'd been listening to the messages coming to us from the Arab world for so many years. This was not a new situation. This pain of theirs had been expressed over and over in many ways, and we hadn't responded with any empathy or understanding. And when we don't hear people's pain, it keeps coming out in ways that make empathy even harder.

Now, when I say this, people often think I'm justifying what the terrorists did on September 11. And of course I'm not. I'm saying that the real answer is to look at how we could have prevented it to begin with.

Killian: Some in the United States think that bombing Iraq is a protective use of force.

Rosenberg: I would ask them, What is your objective? Is it protection? Certain kinds of negotiations, which have never been attempted, would be more protective than any use of force. Our only option is communication of a radically different sort. We're getting to the point now where no army is able to prevent terrorists from poisoning our streams or fouling the air. We are getting to a point where our best protection is to communicate with the people we're most afraid of. Nothing else will work.

APPENDIX 2

List of Feelings and Needs

Feelings When Needs Are Met

AFFECTIONATE
Compassionate
Friendly
Fond
Loving
Openhearted
Sympathetic
Tender
Warm

CONFIDENT
Empowered
Open
Proud
Safe
Secure

INSPIRED
Amazed
Awed
Wonder

ENGAGED
Absorbed
Alert
Curious
Engrossed
Enchanted
Fascinated
Interested
Intrigued
Involved
Spellbound
Stimulated

REFRESHED
Enlivened
Rejuvenated
Renewed
Rested
Restored
Revived

GRATEFUL
Appreciative
Moved
Thankful
Touched

EXCITED
Amazed
Animated
Ardent
Aroused
Dazzled
Eager
Energetic
Enthusiastic
Giddy
Invigorated
Lively
Passionate
Surprised
Vibrant

Feelings When Needs Are Not Met

AFRAID
Apprehensive
Panicked
Petrified
Scared
Suspicious
Terrified
Wary
Worried

DISQUIET
Agitated
Disturbed
Restless
Startled
Uneasy
Uncomfortable
Unsettled

CONFUSED
Ambivalent
Baffled
Hesitant
Lost
Out of it
Torn

ANGER
Angry
Enraged
Furious
Livid
Outraged
Resentful

EMBARRASSED
Ashamed
Humiliated
Mortified
Self-conscious

FATIGUE
Beat
Burned out
Depleted
Exhausted
Tired
Worn out

ANNOYED
Aggravated
Frustrated
Impatient
Irritated
Ticked off

AVERSION
Appalled
Disgusted
Dislike
Hate
Loathe
Repulsed

SAD
Depressed
Despair
Discouraged
Down
Heavy-hearted
Unhappy

VULNERABLE
Fragile
Insecure
Needy
Open
Sensitive

YEARNING
Aching
Envious
Longing
Nostalgic
Wishing

TENSE
Anxious
Cranky
Edgy
Irritable
Nervous
Overwhelmed
Stressed out

DISCONNECTED
Alienated
Apathetic
Bored
Detached
Distant
Indifferent
Numb

PAIN
Anguished
Devastated
Heartbroken
Hurt
Lonely
Miserable
Regretful

Needs

CONNECTION
Acceptance
Affection
Appreciation
Belonging
Closeness
Communication
Community
Companionship
Compassion
Consideration
Consistency
Cooperation
Empathy
Inclusion
Intimacy
Love
Mutuality
Nurturing
Reciprocity
Respect/self-respect
Safety
Security
Shared reality
Stability
Support
To know and be known
To see and be seen
To understand and
    be understood
Trust
Warmth

HONESTY
Authenticity
Integrity
Presence

PEACE
Beauty
Communion
Ease
Equality
Harmony
Inspiration
Order

PLAY
Joy
Humor
Adventure

**PHYSICAL
WELL-BEING**
Air
Food
Movement/exercise
Rest/sleep
Sexual expression
Safety (protection from
    life-threatening
    situations)
Shelter
Touch
Water

MEANING
Awareness
Celebration
Challenge
Clarity
Competence
Consciousness
Contribution
Creativity
Discovery
Effectiveness
Efficiency
Growth
Integration
Learning
Mourning
Movement
Participation
Purpose
Self-expression
Stimulation
Understanding

AUTONOMY
Choice
Dignity
Freedom
Independence
Space
Spontaneity

Notes

1. Wink, Walter. *The Powers That Be* (New York: Three Rivers, 1999), p. 44.
2. Ibid., 42.
3. Eisler, Rianne. *The Chalice and the Blade* (New York: HarperOne, 1988), p. 73.
4. Rifkin, Jeremy. *The Empathic Civilization* (New York: Tarcher, 2009), pp. 8–9.
5. Eisler, p. 192.
6. http://www.google.com/search?hl=en&defl=en&q=define:empathy&sa=X&ei=lOu9TLfQGYb0tgOc9dHIDA&sqi=2&ved=0CBUQkAE
7. Piatigorsky, Gregor. *Cellist* (New York: Doubleday, 1965). http://www.cello.org/heaven/cellist/index.htm.
8. Williamson, Marianne. *A Return to Love* (New York: Harper Paperbacks, 1992), p. 190.
9. Kashtan, Inbal. *Parenting From Your Heart* (Encinitas, CA: PuddleDancer Press, 2004), p. 40.

Bibliography

Bryson, Kelly B. *Don't Be Nice, Be Real: Balancing Passion for Self with Compassion for Others.* Santa Rosa, CA: Elite Books, 2004.

Carkhuff, Robert R. *The Art of Helping.* 7th ed. Amherst, MA: Human Resource Development Press, 1993.

Eisler, Riane. *The Chalice and the Blade: Our History, Our Future.* San Francisco: HarperSanFrancisco, 1988.

Foucault, Michel. *Discipline and Punish: The Birth of the Prison.* New York: Random House, 1975.

Frankl, Viktor. *Man's Search for Meaning: An Introduction to Logotherapy.* New York: Washington Square Press, 1969.

Gendlin, Eugene. *Focusing.* New York: Bantam Books, 1981.

Kohn, Alfie. *Punished by Rewards: The Trouble with Gold Stars, Incentive Plans, A's, Praise and Other Bribes.* New York: Houghton Mifflin Company, 1995.

Lerner, Michael. *Spirit Matters.* Charlottesville: Hampton Roads Publishing Company, 2002.

Leu, Lucy. *Nonviolent Communication Companion Workbook: A Practical Guide for Individual, Group or Classroom Study.* Encinitas, CA: PuddleDancer Press, 2003.

Maslow, Abraham. *Toward a Psychology of Being.* New York: John Wiley & Sons, 1999.

Wink, Walter. *The Powers That Be: Theology for a New Millennium.* New York: Random House, 1998.

Resources for Learning Nonviolent Communication

We hope you have enjoyed this book, applied the principles to your own life, and benefited in your relationship with yourself and others. If so, you may be wondering: what next? If possible, I would urge you to find experienced NVC trainers to support you in your further practice of NVC. As you may have discovered by now, NVC principles are intellectually easy to understand. You may also have learned that applying and practicing these principles in everyday life can be extremely challenging. By working with a skilled trainer, you will have the opportunity to experience NVC "live" in real time and see it modeled effectively. The Center for Nonviolent Communication (CNVC) website, www.cnvc.org, can assist you in finding certified CNVC trainers, supporters, and groups supporting the learning and practice of NVC.

You may also wish to start a practice group with others interested in making NVC part of their daily lives. Two companion books, one by Lucy Leu and the other by Marshall Rosenberg, referenced below, are invaluable for this purpose. Many NVC centers offer teleclasses, workshops, courses, and retreats as well as individual training, coaching, and empathy sessions by phone. In-person training can offer a high level of community and connection, while learning via phone—whether via teleclasses or individual coaching sessions— can also work surprisingly well. A number of Listservs provide information and support for learning, as well. Further, you may wish to search for NVC videos online on YouTube. Following is a partial list of resources.

Websites

Center for Nonviolent Communication: www.cnvc.org
> This website offers inspiring articles about applications of NVC, information about trainers and trainings offered around the world (including Marshall Rosenberg's schedule of trainings as well as those of CNVC Certified Trainers), and an online store selling books and audio and video materials.

NVC Academy: www.nvcacademy.com
> A rich resource of both free and subscription events and learning opportunities, including teleclasses, applying NVC in many aspects of life. Subscribers receive a number of videos each month that they can download and watch. There are several useful free tools (such as instruction on how to write "nonviolent emails") and a weekly ninety-minute teleconference every Thursday that is facilitated by a Certified Trainer.

PuddleDancer Press: www.nonviolentcommunication.com
> A major publisher of NVC materials; its site contains an overview of NVC and an archive of NVC-related articles that cover a variety of topics.

Work Collaboratively: www.workcollaboratively.com
> This website includes details about the impact of NVC training in an organizational setting, exercises, and another shorter interview conducted by Dian Killian with Marshall Rosenberg in addition to the one reproduced in this book. You can also learn about upcoming NVC trainings and events, including the annual East Coast NVC Women's Retreat.

NVC Trainers and Organizations

For information about NVC centers, supporters, and Certified Trainers around the world and in your area, visit www.CNVC.org.

Discussions and Listservs

NVC and Social Change Listserv
> http://www.cnvc.org/connect/e-forums.html

The Synergy Communication Group
> This group provides opportunities to practice the NVC model interactively, including observations, feelings, needs, and requests: http://groups.yahoo.com/group/ synergycommunication/

The Pondering NVC group
> A place to discuss your thoughts, ideas, and theories about NVC. Whereas the Synergy Communication group is about practicing speaking and listening using NVC (in written form, in this case), the Pondering NVC group is more for talking about general principles and ideas. http://groups. yahoo.com/group/PonderingNVC/

Parenting Group
> Resources for parents, including a Listserv where parents share challenges, ideas, and experiences with NVC parenting, are available at http://www.cnvc.org/parents.htm

Books

Most of the following may be ordered at www.cnvc.org or by calling 1-800-255-7696 (which supports the Center for Nonviolent Communication) or at http://www.collaborative-communication.org (supporting NVC in NYC).

Bryson, Kelly. *Don't Be Nice, Be Real: Balancing Passion for Self with Compassion for Others*. Santa Rosa, CA: Elite Books, 2004.
> This book draws from the author's many years working as a therapist with individuals and couples. He applies NVC to relationship challenges that adults experience, and his

way with words makes the reading enjoyable. Order at www.
languageofcompassion.com. Quite a few of the chapters are
available to read for free at this website.

Hart, Sura and Victoria Hodson Kindle. *The Compassionate
Classroom: Relationship Based Teaching and Learning*.
Encinitas, CA: PuddleDancer Press, 2004.

Hart, Sura and Victoria Kindle Hudson, *The No-Fault Classroom*.
Encinitas, CA: PuddleDancer Press, 2008.

These books provide an organized overview of NVC and a
large number of delightful activities and exercises for teaching
NVC to children in a group setting. Many of these could be
readily adapted for use with older children (i.e., adults).

Kashtan, Inbal. *Parenting From Your Heart*. Encinitas, CA:
PuddleDancer Press, 2003.

This forty-eight-page pamphlet was written by the
founder of the Center for Nonviolent Communication's
Parenting Project. She shows clearly what it means to be
compassionate both to yourself and the children you may
be caring for. It includes many examples of using NVC in
this challenging terrain.

Killian, Dian, with Mark Badger (illustrator). *Urban Empathy: True
Life Adventures of Compassion on the Streets of New York*.
New York: Hungry Duck Press, 2008.

This graphic novel, written by the founder and director
of the Center for Collaborative Communication in NYC,
gives verbatim examples of practicing NVC in challenging
situations with family members, children, and complete
strangers on the streets of New York. Topics include
"difficult" conversations around race, anti-Semitism, and
homophobia as well as stories illustrating the practice of self-
empathy, making clear observations, and empathy for others.

Leu, Lucy. *Nonviolent Communication Companion Workbook: A
Practical Guide for Individual, Group or Classroom Study*.
Encinitas, CA: PuddleDancer Press, 2003.

This book provides a structured series of exercises
and activities that are coordinated with Rosenberg's book

Nonviolent Communication: A Language of Life. The first part of the book describes how to set up and run a practice group and contains invaluable advice distilled from many years of experience.

Rosenberg, Marshall B. *Life-Enriching Education*. Encinitas, CA: PuddleDancer Press, 2003.

This book shows the application of NVC in the classroom. It includes both theory and examples of NVC in practice.

Rosenberg, Marshall B. *Nonviolent Communication: A Language of Life. 2nd ed.* Encinitas, CA: PuddleDancer Press, 2003.

This is the "bible" of NVC, written by its developer. Although most of the theory in this book can be found in other NVC resources, this book contains Rosenberg's own examples and his experiences of using NVC around the world, including in high-conflict and war-torn areas. If you want to start a practice group using the Leu workbook (above), it would be helpful to have this book, with which it is coordinated.

Haskvitz, Sylvia. *Eat by Choice, Not by Habit*. Encinitas, CA: PuddleDancer Press, 2005.

This book describes a compassionate approach to issues of eating, food, physical well-being, and choice.

d'Ansembourg, Tom. *Being Genuine*. Encinitas, CA: PuddleDancer Press, 2007.

Another introduction to NVC; additional perspectives and experiences can be helpful.

Hart, Sura and Victoria Kindle Hodson. *Resptectful Parents, Respectful Kids*. Encinitas, CA: PuddleDancer Press. 2006.

Exercises, activities, and ideas for parents wanting to apply NVC in their family.

Larsson, Liv. *A Helping Hand: Mediation with Nonviolent Communication*. Friare Liv2011. Can be purchased at www.lulu.com/spotlight/Friareliv/

Describes how to use NVC to mediate conflicts between two or more people, potentially including yourself, using NVC.

Audio CDs and Downloads

A wide range of downloadable recordings (MP3 files) on a variety of topics by leading NVC trainers throughout the world can be purchased at http://nvctraining.com/courses/recordings/index.html

Rosenberg, Marshall B. *Speaking Peace*. Louisville, CO: Sounds True, 2003.

This is my favorite of the MP3s or CDs of Rosenberg explaining NVC at an introductory level. I especially appreciate his captivating anecdotes, clear explanations, and inspiring songs. I also value his showing how applying the NVC model can lead to change in both individuals and institutions. Other introductory audios are also available.

Rosenberg, Marshall B. A series of intermediate-level CDs from an international intensive training, available through www.cnvc.org. I really enjoy listening to these CDs, which raise many provocative issues and alternatives for how we relate to others and ourselves:

Giraffe Fuel for Life. Gratitude exercises, reward and punishment, hearing feelings and needs rather than thoughts, what stops us from celebrating.

Needs and Empathy. How to give empathy; distinguishing needs from strategies to meet them, other questions.

Intimate Relationships. Making requests that meet our need for love, hearing the need behind the "No," the cost of hearing rejection, giraffe love, role-plays.

Creating a Life-Serving System Within Oneself. Empathy for the chooser and educator, mourning in giraffe, restorative justice.

Experiencing Needs as a Gift. Hearing the need behind the "No," the cost of giving from non-giraffe energy.

Love, Inessa, Miki Kashtan, and Robert Gonzales. *The Heart of Connection: Guided Meditations for Inner Peace and Harmonious Relationships* can be purchased at www.nvcmeditations.com or amazon.com

Video Testimonials

If you want to get a sense of how different people have felt the impact in their lives of learning NVC, check out the video testimonials at www.cnvc.org. Ordinarily, testimonials are considered a very low level of "proof" for the effectiveness of any intervention. What impressed me about these, which I viewed before going to my first intensive training in NVC, was the qualitative nature of the shift in people's experience of themselves and others as a result of incorporating NVC in their lives.

Articles

Articles about applications of NVC to prisons, education, conflict in the Middle East, and other situations can be found at www.cnvc.org. Another source for a wide range of articles on topics such as social change, business, conflict resolution, parenting, and personal change can be found in the freeresources area at www.nonviolentcommunication.com

Index

"168 Applications of Nonviolent
Force," Sharp, 364

A

"abandoned," as judgment-feeling
word, 35–36
abortion issue, listening
empathically, 100–01
accuracy, reflection requests for, 139
Adam and Eve, and Myth of
Redemptive Violence, 14
advertising agencies, and needs
awareness, 52–55
advice-giving, as nonempathic
listening response, 76–79
affirmations, to support values of
NVC, 311
"aggressive" self-empathy, 250
ahimsa, 2 (note)
aikido, to support self-connection
and NVC values, 311
"always," as judgment word, 113–14
analysis, 77–79, 356–57
anger
    floor map, 237–46
    and good/evil thinking, 233–36
    receiving, 226–33, 251
    taking responsibility for, 219–26,
    236–37, 247–50
Anglo-American culture, role of
    emotional expression, 19–20
appreciation. *See* gratitude
Appreciation You Would Love to
    Have Received Exercise, 295
approval, as judgment-based, 56–58
approval-seeking behavior, 230–33

Archbishop Simon, 360
Asking About Content Exercise, 86–88
Assailez, Nafez, 360
assistance, as nonempathic listening
    response, 77–79
Aurelius, Marcus, 228
authority-based paradigms, and
    demands, 132
autonomy about meeting needs,
    62–63, 132–33, 196–202
avoidance, as nonempathic listening
    response, 77–79

B

Babylonian creation mythology, 14
bad/good, as feelings, 19
bad/good thinking. *See* good/evil
    thinking
BaMbuti cultures, 16
behavior
    as attempt to fulfill needs, 58–59
    vs. intrinsic nature of humans,
    14–15
Being There Exercise, 82
beloved community, 311–12
"Beyond Good and Evil: Creating
    a Nonviolent World,"
    interview, 235, 267, 349–66
blame
    as nonempathic response, 184,
    202–03
    vs. personal responsibility, 37,
    59–60, 233–34
bodily sensations, and feelings,
    21–25, 161, 178–80, 185,
    237–39, 272

Borges, Jorge Luis, 15
Breaking Free of Self-Pity Exercise, 183
Broadening Our Horizons Exercise, 164
Bryson, Kelly, 263
Buber, Martin, 359
business motivation, and needs awareness, 51–55

C

capital punishment, 267, 362
Casals, Pablo, 284–85
Cause or Trigger? Exercise, 222–23
cause vs. stimulus of feelings and behavior, 59–65, 220–25, 233–34, 236
celebrating needs met, 189–90, 297, 300, 332
Celebration and Mourning Exercise, 289–97
Cellist, Piatigorsky, 284–85
Center for Nonviolent Communication, 351
The Chalice and the Blade: Our History and Our Future, Eisler, 16
Changing Pitch Exercise, 96–97
checking in with self, for NVC practice, 308–09, 312–13
checking-in requests, 136, 141–42
Chidvilasananda, Gurumayi, 175
childhood, lack of needs awareness in, 50
choices
    about meeting needs, 62–63, 196–201
    in responding to self and others, 201–07, 226–27, 338–39, 341–43
    and sacrifice, 153–54
"Choose," Sandburg, 342

the chooser, in Compassionate Communication model, 167–68, 170
the chooser and the educator, and conflict resolution, 186–89
civil disobedience and nonviolence, 265–66
clarity
    as quality of effective requests, 144–48, 171–73
    reflection requests for, 138–39, 161
coercion, underlying judgment-based compliments, 282
cognitive families of words, as clue to needs, 91–93
collaboration, 136, 162–64
collaborative communication, 2 (note)
colloquial use of NVC, 103, 321–30
communication, as effective strategy, 267, 366
comparison, as nonempathic listening response, 77–79
compassion, an innate human quality, 12, 16–17, 64, 130, 351
compassion, as innate human quality, 5–6
Compassionate Communication, 2, 168–71. *See also* Nonviolent Communication (NVC) model
compliments and praise
    as judgment, 269–71, 277–80, 357
    as strategy, 281–84
Composting Judgments Into Live Experience Exercise, 209
compromise, and unmet needs, 153
conflict about strategies, 44–45, 47
Connecting the Dots—Strategies and Needs Exercise, 47
Connecting the Energy of Feelings to Life-Enriching Needs Exercise, 46

Connecting With Connection
    Requests Exercise, 142
connection requests, 136–42, 161
The Connor Compassionate
    Communication Index,
    246–47
consequences, inherent in demands,
    131–32
contributing to others, as human
    need, 5–6, 64, 130
core beliefs, 12–15, 332–37
core needs, 97–98, 188
couples, demands in, 133
criticism, as expression of unmet
    needs, 357
ctc.learnnvc.com, 310

D

deep empathy, 334–35
"delight, not compromise" scale,
    156–59
demands, vs. requests, 131–36,
    159–60
Descartes, René, 19
deserve thinking, 234–35, 352
Developing Choice in Responding to
    Anger of Others Exercise,
    226–27
diagnosis, as nonempathic listening
    response, 77–79
dialogue, and protective use of force,
    259–60, 265
disagreement about strategies, 44–45,
    47
Distinguishing Observations From
    Evaluations Exercise,
    114–15
Do You Seek the Approval of Others?
    Exercise, 232–33
do-ability of requests, 144, 148–51,
    171–73, 240
dogging for your needs, 155, 161, 338
domination culture, 360–61

Don't Be Nice, Be Real, Bryson, 263
Dryden, John, 228
the duck criterion, 156–59

E

the educator and the chooser, and
    conflict resolution, 186–89
Einhorn, Lois, 176
Eisler, Riane, 16, 17
Elliot, Conal, 134
email, for practicing NVC skills, 310
embarrassment, as double judgment,
    193–96
emergency empathy, 309
emotional response habit patterns,
    60–62
emotions. *See* feelings
Emoto-Meters Exercise, 23–24
empathetic response to hearing "no,"
    151–52
empathic connection, feelings as core
    element, 18
empathic guesses, sentence frames
    for, 83–88, 90–91. *See also*
    listening empathically to
    feelings and needs of others
empathic predisposition of humans,
    5–6, 12, 16–17, 64, 130
empathic response vs. judgment,
    106–09
empathy, 267, 282–83. *See also*
    listening empathically to
    feelings and needs of others
empathy before education, 99–102,
    205–07, 248, 358
empathy buddy, 309, 315–16
empathy from hell, 313–16
Empathy in Action Exercise, 250
empathy journal, 308
ends justify the means, 265–66
Engaging the Powers, Wink, 361
entertainment, emotional response
    to, 25

evaluations. *See also* judgments
  vs. observations, 111–15,
    121–26, 358–59
  posing as feelings, 35–40
exercise, to support self-connection,
    311
external/internal aspects of NVC
    model, 129–30
extrinsic vs. intrinsic consequences
    of behavior, 262–63, 282.
    See also punishment; reward
    systems, as motivators

F

fake empathy, 313–16
families, demands in, 133
fear
  communication to address, 267,
    366
  of judgment, 193–96, 228–33
  manifesting as aggression,
    260–61
  of punishment, as motivator,
    261–63
feeling and sensation journal, 27
feeling sorry for ourselves, 180–83
feelings. *See also* listening
    empathically to feelings
    and needs of others; *specific
    feelings*
  cultural influences, 18–22,
    95–96
  denial of, as nonempathic
    listening response, 77–79
  as indicator of needs, 41,
    207–09, 356
  in NVC model, 123–24, 167–71,
    273–77
  and physical sensations, 21–25,
    161, 178–80, 185, 272
  range of intensity, 96–97, 328
  street expression of, 323–24,
    327–29

thinking as cause of, 28–32, 220
  vs. thoughts, 32–40
  value of, 22–23
  vocabulary of, 26, 367
  when needs are met/unmet, 44,
    46, 54–55, 169, 224–27
feelings log, 38
fist vs. open hand metaphor, 159–60
focusing and inner relationship
    focusing, 311
Force and Feeling Exercise, 17
Four Ways of Responding—
    Awareness and Choice
    Exercise, 203
The Four-Step Dance of Compassion
    Exercise, 204
Frankl, Viktor, 200
Freeing Ourselves From Shoulds
    Exercise, 185
fulfilled feelings, when needs are
    met, 44, 46

G

Gandhi, Mahatma, 259
Getting to the Root of Anger
    Exercise, 224–26
"gifting" yourself, 301–02
gifts, and authenticity, 286–88
Gill, Raj, 237
glass half-full approach to unmet
    needs, 162
Goebbels, Joseph, 68–69
Gonzalez, Robert, 179 (note)
good/bad, as feelings, 19
good/evil thinking. *See also* right/
    wrong thinking
  approval and self-esteem as,
    56–58
  as cultural norm, 12–16, 341,
    352
  "head listening" and, 74
  as judgment, 113–14, 118,
    255–56, 360

Grateful for Judgment? Exercise, 270–71
gratitude
    expressing empathic, 271–77, 300–02
    as judgment, 269–70
    politeness and, 286–88
    receiving, 289–96
    requesting from others, 298–300
    toward self, 296–97
gratitude journal, 308
GROK magnets and cards, 309
guessing, when listening
    empathically, 83–88, 90–96, 244–47

H
Hackett, Buddy, 357
Hafiz, 311
hand shaking, implications, 160
Haskins, Henry Stanley, 175
"have to," 131–32, 199–201
"head listening," 74
Hearing the Life in Anger Exercise, 244–46
heart-centered listening, 73–74
helping, 101–02
HERA, 358
hierarchical nature of power-over structures, 55
Hubbard, Elbert, 355
"hungry duck" index, 156–59

I
"I can top your story," as nonempathic listening response, 77–79
"I" statements, in reflection requests, 138
images, to expand awareness of feelings and needs, 211–12
imagining feelings and needs of another, 94

imperative demands, 132
indecision, self-empathy and, 175–76, 196–99
inherent innocence of humans, 13
inner relationship focusing, 311
insults, as expression of unmet needs, 357
intangible nature of needs, 49–50
integration, reflection requests for, 139
intensity of feeling words, continuum of, 96–97
intention, empathic, 103, 131
intention, underlying use of force, 257
internal/external aspects of NVC model, 129–30
interpretations vs. observations, 111–15, 124–26
intrinsic human nature vs. human behavior, 14–15
intrinsic nature of needs, 49–50
intrinsic vs. extrinsic consequences of behavior, 262–63, 282. *See also* punishment; reward systems, as motivators
inverted compliments, 280–81, 283

J
journaling, for NVC practice, 27, 38, 215–16, 299, 308
judgment journal, 308
"judgment show," 236
judgment-feeling words, 35–36
judgments
    as cause of feelings, 28–32, 222
    as clue to needs, 91–93, 236–39, 266
    vs. empathic response, 106–09
    as expression of unmet needs, 193–96, 357
    as nonempathic listening response, 76–79
    vs. observations, 111–15, 123–26

posing as feelings, 35–40
positive, 56–58, 269–70, 277–81
taking responsibility for, 1–2,
    116–22, 207–09, 220–26
"juicy request" questions, 133–35,
    262–63
justice, 234–35, 267, 352–55, 362–64

K

Kashtan, Inbal, 343
Kashtan, Miki, 119 (note)
King, Jr., Martin Luther, 311
Krishnamurti, Jiddu, 175
!Kung societies, 16

L

Language
    as clues to needs, 91–93
    confusing needs and strategies,
        48–49
    confusing thoughts and feelings,
        32–40
    implying judgment, 113–14
    of "street" NVC, 103, 321–30
    usage in this book, 8–9
Lasater, Ike, 19
Lasater, Judith, 156
"late," as judgment word, 113–14
"leaderful" groups, 310
Lerner, Michael, 13
Leu, Lucy, 237, 310
Life-Enriching Education, Rosenberg,
    351
life-serving judgments vs. moral
    judgments, 235
Like Oil and Water Exercise, 37
listening empathically to feelings and
    needs of others. See also
    self-empathy
    empathy before education,"
        99–102, 205–07, 248, 358
    guessing to facilitate, 83–91,
        92–99, 244–47

vs. judgments, 106–09
qualities of, 71–74
when receiving anger, 226–31,
    313–16
Listening to Your Chooser and
    Educator Exercise, 189
Listservs for NVC, 309, 373
Living Free of Demands Exercise,
    135–36
Living With Gratitude Exercise,
    295–96
Love, Inessa, 311

M

majority rule, and needs, 45
Making Needs-Meeting Choices
    Exercise, 197
Mandela, Nelson, 266
Man's Search for Meaning, Frankl, 200
marketing, and needs awareness,
    52–55
Maslow, Abraham, 51
mean people, 13
meditation, to support values of
    NVC, 311
men, and suppression of feelings, 19
metaphors, use in street NVC,
    329–30
minimization, as nonempathic
    listening response, 77–79
mistakes, self-empathy for, 183–92
moral judgments
    about needs, 45
    approval and self-esteem as,
        56–58
    as expression of unmet needs,
        357
    vs. needs-based judgments,
        58–59, 62–63, 235, 255–56,
        353
Morin, Judi, 237
mourning of unmet needs, 56,
    189–91, 297

movement, to expand awareness of
    feelings and needs, 211–12
The Movement of Emotions
    Exercise, 26–27
Moving From Hell to Heaven
    Exercise, 315–16
music, to expand awareness of
    feelings and needs, 211–12
must, 131–32
Myth of Redemptive Violence, 14

N
nature, connecting with, 311
needs. *See also* listening empathically
    to feelings and needs of
    others
    -based gratitude, 272–76
    -based judgment vs. moral
        judgment, 58–59, 62–63,
        235, 255–56, 353
    experiencing as met, 179–80,
        209–11
    inventory of, 302, 368
    -meter, 196–99
    met/unmet, and feelings, 169,
        182, 221, 224–27
    persistent attentiveness to, 155,
        161, 338
    vs. strategies, 4–5, 48–56, 67–69,
        131, 236, 355
    translating judgments into,
        224–29, 238–40, 244–46
    universality of, 3–4, 41–48,
        357–58
needs awareness, lacking in
    psychology courses, 51
"never," as judgment word, 113–14
newbie NVC, 313–21
"no," hearing with empathy, 151–52,
    161
"No, Thanks" as a Gift Exercise,
    288
nonempathic choices, 201–03

nonempathic listening strategies,
    74–81, 101–02
nonviolence and civil disobedience,
    265–66, 364–65
Nonviolent Communication (NVC),
    learning and practicing,
    7–8, 103–06, 306–13,
    315–16, 371–77
Nonviolent Communication (NVC)
    model
    colloquial expression of, 165–66,
        273–77, 321–27
    overview, 123–24, 167–71
    as a process, 129–30, 160–61
"NVC is simple—but not easy," 305
"NVC pushback," 314–15
NVC trainings, 309–10

O
observations. *See also* stimulus
    vs. cause of feelings and
        behavior
    vs. evaluations, 111–15, 121–26,
        258–59
    and requests, compared, 129
    taking responsibility for, 116–21,
        272–77
offered/requested reflection requests,
    138–40
Oliver, Mary, 311
open hand vs. fist metaphor, 159–60
opinions, ownership of, 120–21
opposites, as clue to needs, 92–94
Osler, William, 111
Other Than Empathy Exercise,
    78–79
"overworked," as judgment-feeling
    word, 36

P
pacing, reflection requests for, 139,
    161
Paleolithic era, 16

parental focus on strategies (vs. needs), 50–51
partnership-based culture, 17
passive resistance, demands and, 133
past situations, present tense framing, 83–85
pause/take a moment, 161
people-pleasing behavior, 230–33
Perle, Richard, 68–69
physical sensations, and feelings, 21–25, 161, 178–80, 185, 237–39, 272
Piatigorsky, Gregor, 284–85
pitch of feeling words, range of, 96–97
Planning to Practice Exercise, 312–13
PLATO, in observations, 117–20
politeness, 286–88
positive focus
    of empathic guesses, 88–89
    of expressions of gratitude, 275–77
    of requests, 146–48
positive judgments, approval and self-esteem as, 56–58
positive value of all needs, 44–45
possibilities, generating, 162–64
power-over paradigm, 55–56, 132, 361. *See also* punitive use of force
power-with paradigm, 55–56
practicing NVC, 8, 103–06, 306–13, 371
praise and compliments
    as judgment, 269–71, 277–83, 357
    as strategy, 281–84
present-oriented focus
    of empathic guessing, 83–85
    in practicing self-empathy, 178
    of requests, 144, 150–51, 240
protective use of force
    anecdotal examples, 263–64
    in nonviolence and civil disobedience, 265–66

vs. punitive use of force, 256–63, 266–67
public affairs, lack of needs awareness in, 50–51
punishment
    inherent in demands, 131–32
    as learning tool, 230, 255–56, 261–63
    strategies as, 50
punitive use of force
    beliefs underlying, 255–56, 261–63
    vs. protective use of force, 260–61, 266–67
punitive violence myths, 14

R
Rajendrum, Chris, 360
rape, restorative justice and, 353–55
Real Feeling Exercise, 34
reassurance, as nonempathic listening response, 75–79
recidivism in prisons, 363–64
recipe for requests, 134–35
Reflecting on Reflection Exercise, 140
reflection requests, 136–40
regret, self-empathy and, 175–76
religious groups, and compassion, 359–60
repeated experiences, and core beliefs, 335–37
requests
    for connection, 136–42
    as connection with outside world, 129–30, 143
    vs. demands, 131–36, 159–60
    hearing responses to, 151–59, 161
    in practicing self-empathy, 178, 192, 214–15
    qualities of effective, 144–51, 171–73, 240

resentment/retaliation, and unmet
    needs, 153–54
Responsibility, Action, and Response
    Exercise, 63
responsibility, for needs and feelings
    of others, 64–65, 230–33
responsibility, for our own
        experience. *See also*
        stimulus vs. cause of
        feelings and behavior
be the change you wish to see,
        331–32
    and "have to" thinking, 199–201
    vs. judgments, 1–3, 36–37,
        65–67, 116–22, 220–21
restorative justice vs. retribution,
        235, 267, 352–55, 362–64
retaliation/resentment, and unmet
    needs, 153–54
retribution vs. restorative justice,
        235, 267, 352–55, 362–64
reverse golden rule, 176–77
reward systems, as motivators, 230,
        263
right/wrong thinking. *See also* good/
        evil thinking as cultural
        norm, 12–17
    vs. needs-based thinking, 45,
        62–63, 220–21
Rogers, Carl, 350
Rokeach, Milton, 359–60
role-plays, for practicing NVC skills,
        310
root meanings of words, as clue to
        needs, 91–93
Rosenberg, Marshall
    on "deserve" thinking, 235
    development of NVC, 6–7
    dog and apple metaphor, 58
    hungry duck test, 156
    interview with, 235, 267, 342,
        349–66
    on requests, 134

Rumi, 12, 311
The Rush of Feeling Exercise, 25

S

sacrifice, and unmet needs, 153
salvationist thinking, 360
Sandburg, Carl, 342
Satir, Virginia, 230
scarcity, as core belief, 55, 153
Seeing Our Judgments, Creating
        Compassion Exercise, 180
self-acceptance, as universal need, 58
self-check-ins, 206–07
self-empathy
    for celebrating needs met, 212–13
    converting judgments into,
        183–92, 207–09, 247–50
    for core beliefs, 332–37
    NVC model for, 177–80, 214–17
    as response option, 201–07,
        228–29, 330
    vs. self-pity, 180–83
    silent, 204, 330
    through images, music,
        movement, 211–12
    value of, 175–77, 213–14
    when listening empathically, 99,
        101, 193–96, 313–15
    when making choices, 196–201
self-empathy journal, 308
self-esteem, as judgment-based, 56–58
self-judgment, 183–85, 191–92,
        228–33, 334–35
self-pity, 180–83
self-respect, as universal need, 58
sentiment/sentimental, 20
Separating the Bee From the Sting
        Exercise, 60–62
shaking hands, implications, 160
shame, as double judgment, 193–96
Sharp, Gene, 364
Shifting Self-Judgments to Self-
        Empathy Exercise, 191–92

"should" thinking, 131–32, 184–85, 220–24, 238–40

silent empathy, 96, 203–07, 330

social media, for practicing NVC skills, 310

social status, as strategy, 53

"sometimes," as judgment word, 113–14

Speaking Peace in a World of Conflict, Rosenberg, 351

specificity
    in observations, 117–20, 284
    of requests, 147–51, 171–73

spiritual practice, to support NVC consciousness, 311

sports, emotional response to, 25

static view of self and others, 184

Stimulation and Response Exercise, 28–32

stimulus vs. cause of feelings and behavior, 59–65, 220–23, 233–34, 236, 238–40

storytelling, as nonempathic listening response, 77–79

strategies for meeting needs
    discovering alternative, 157–59, 162–64, 172–73, 236, 249
    layering of, 67–68
    moving to prematurely, 142
    vs. needs, 4–5, 48–56, 67–69, 131
    overview, 42–47

strategies for responding when listening to others, 75–81

strategies in compliments, 280–83

"street" use of NVC, 103, 321–30

succinctness, in empathic listening, 89–90

sympathy, as nonempathic listening response, 76–79

T

tai chi, to support self-connection, 311

take a breath, 161

Taking Responsibility for Our Experience Exercise, 117

talking head show, 91–93

Taming Double Judgment Exercise, 195–96

Taylor, Gail, 162

thank you, 286–88

Thatcher, Margaret, 19–20

thoughts. *See also* judgments
    as cause of feelings, 28–32, 222
    vs. feelings, 32–40
    as stimuli for actions, 17

threatened consequences, inherent in demands, 131–32

To the Heart of the Matter Exercise, 90–91

Tracking Judgments Exercise, 115

triggers, and core beliefs, 334–35

Trying to Buy Love Exercise, 54–55

Tutu, Desmond, 266

U

"unappreciated," as judgment-feeling word, 36

Uncovering Choices Exercise, 201

Unearthing Needs in Roots and Oppositions Exercise, 93–94

"unfulfilled" feelings, when needs are unmet, 44

universal needs, overview, 3–4

unmet needs, 56, 180–83, 189–91

Unplugging Judgments in Stereo Exercise, 229

Urban Empathy, Killian, 311

"usually," as judgment word, 113–14

V

values-based judgments vs. moral judgments, 58–59
violence
    in communication, 11–12
    as cultural norm, 14–17, 261–63, 362
    as expression of unmet needs, 338–39
visceral listening, 73–74
visual images, to expand awareness of feelings and needs, 211–12

W

walking in another's shoes, 94
"walking on the sunny side," 88–89

wars, and right/wrong thinking, 262
When Students Love to Learn and Teachers Love to Teach, Rosenberg, 351
White, David, 311
Wink, Walter, 14, 352, 361
women, and emotional expression, 19–20
Working the Index Exercise, 247
workplace, demands in, 133
wrong/right thinking. *See* right/wrong thinking

Y

Yoda, 104
yoga, to support self-connection, 311
YouTube NVC videos, 308

The Four-Part Nonviolent Communication Process

Clearly expressing how **I am** without blaming or criticizing	Empathically receiving how **you are** without hearing blame or criticism

OBSERVATIONS

1. What I observe *(see, hear, remember, imagine, free from my evaluations)* that does or does not contribute to my well-being:

   "When I (see, hear) . . . "

1. What you observe *(see, hear, remember, imagine, free from your evaluations)* that does or does not contribute to your well-being:

   "When you see/hear . . . "

   (Sometimes unspoken when offering empathy)

FEELINGS

2. How I feel *(emotion or sensation rather than thought)* in relation to what I observe:

   "I feel . . . "

2. How you feel *(emotion or sensation rather than thought)* in relation to what you observe:

   "You feel . . ."

NEEDS

3. What I need or value *(rather than a preference, or a specific action)* that causes my feelings:

   " . . . because I need/value . . . "

3. What you need or value *(rather than a preference, or a specific action)* that causes your feelings:

   " . . . because you need/value . . ."

Clearly requesting that which would enrich **my** life without demanding	Empathically receiving that which would enrich **your** life without hearing any demand

REQUESTS

4. The concrete actions I would like taken:

   "Would you be willing to . . . ?"

4. The concrete actions you would like taken:

   "Would you like . . . ?"

   (Sometimes unspoken when offering empathy)

About Nonviolent Communication

Nonviolent Communication has flourished for more than four decades across thirty-five countries selling more than 1,000,000 books in over thirty languages for one simple reason: it works.

From the bedroom to the boardroom, from the classroom to the war zone, Nonviolent Communication (NVC) is changing lives every day. NVC provides an easy-to-grasp, effective method to get to the root of violence and pain peacefully. By examining the unmet needs behind what we do and say, NVC helps reduce hostility, heal pain, and strengthen professional and personal relationships. NVC is now being taught in corporations, classrooms, prisons, and mediation centers worldwide. And it is affecting cultural shifts as institutions, corporations, and governments integrate NVC consciousness into their organizational structures and their approach to leadership.

Most of us are hungry for skills that can improve the quality of our relationships, to deepen our sense of personal empowerment or simply help us communicate more effectively. Unfortunately, most of us have been educated from birth to compete, judge, demand, and diagnose; to think and communicate in terms of what is "right" and "wrong" with people. At best, the habitual ways we think and speak hinder communication and create misunderstanding or frustration. And still worse, they can cause anger and pain, and may lead to violence. Without wanting to, even people with the best of intentions generate needless conflict.

NVC helps us reach beneath the surface and discover what is alive and vital within us, and how all of our actions are based on human needs that we are seeking to meet. We learn to develop a vocabulary of feelings and needs that helps us more clearly express what is going on in us at any given moment. When we understand and acknowledge our needs, we develop a shared foundation for much more satisfying relationships. Join the thousands of people worldwide who have improved their relationships and their lives with this simple yet revolutionary process.

About PuddleDancer Press

PuddleDancer Press (PDP) is the premier publisher of Nonviolent Communication™ related works. Its mission is to provide high-quality materials to help people create a world in which all needs are met compassionately. By working in partnership with the Center for Nonviolent Communication and NVC trainers, teams, and local supporters, PDP has created a comprehensive promotion effort that has helped bring NVC to thousands of new people each year.

Since 2003 PDP has donated more than 60,000 NVC books to organizations, decision-makers, and individuals in need around the world.

Visit the PDP website at www.NonviolentCommunication.com to find the following resources:

- **Shop NVC**—Continue your learning. Purchase our NVC titles online safely, affordably, and conveniently. Find everyday discounts on individual titles, multiple-copies, and book packages. Learn more about our authors and read endorsements of NVC from world-renowned communication experts and peacemakers. www.NonviolentCommunication.com/store/

- **NVC Quick Connect e-Newsletter**—Sign up today to receive our monthly e-Newsletter, filled with expert articles, upcoming training opportunities with our authors, and exclusive specials on NVC learning materials. Archived e-Newsletters are also available

- **About NVC**—Learn more about these life-changing communication and conflict resolution skills including an overview of the NVC process, key facts about NVC, and more.

- **About Marshall Rosenberg**—Access press materials, biography, and more about this world-renowned peacemaker, educator, bestselling author, and founder of the Center for Nonviolent Communication.

- **Free Resources for Learning NVC**—Find free weekly tips series, NVC article archive, and other great resources to make learning these vital communication skills just a little easier.

 *PuddleDancer* P R E S S

For more information, please contact PuddleDancer Press at:

2240 Encinitas Blvd., Ste. D-911 • Encinitas, CA 92024
Phone: 760-652-5754 • Fax: 760-274-6400
Email: email@puddledancer.com • www.NonviolentCommunication.com

About the Center for Nonviolent Communication

The Center for Nonviolent Communication (CNVC) is an international nonprofit peacemaking organization whose vision is a world where everyone's needs are met peacefully. CNVC is devoted to supporting the spread of Nonviolent Communication (NVC) around the world.

Founded in 1984 by Dr. Marshall B. Rosenberg, CNVC has been contributing to a vast social transformation in thinking, speaking and acting—showing people how to connect in ways that inspire compassionate results. NVC is now being taught around the globe in communities, schools, prisons, mediation centers, churches, businesses, professional conferences, and more. Hundreds of certified trainers and hundreds more supporters teach NVC to tens of thousands of people each year in more than 35 countries.

CNVC believes that NVC training is a crucial step to continue building a compassionate, peaceful society. Your tax-deductible donation will help CNVC continue to provide training in some of the most impoverished, violent corners of the world. It will also support the development and continuation of organized projects aimed at bringing NVC training to high-need geographic regions and populations.

To make a tax-deductible donation or to learn more about the valuable resources described below, visit the CNVC website at www.CNVC.org:

- **Training and Certification**—Find local, national, and international training opportunities, access trainer certification information, connect to local NVC communities, trainers, and more.

- **CNVC Bookstore**—Find mail or phone order information for a complete selection of NVC books, booklets, audio, and video materials at the CNVC website.

- **CNVC Projects**—Participate in one of the several regional and theme-based projects that provide focus and leadership for teaching NVC in a particular application or geographic region.

- **E-Groups and List Servs**—Join one of several moderated, topic-based NVC e-groups and list servs developed to support individual learning and the continued growth of NVC worldwide.

For more information, please contact CNVC at:

5600 San Francisco Rd., NE, Suite A, Albuquerque, NM 87109
Ph: 505-244-4041 • Fax: 505-247-0414
Email: cnvc@CNVC.org • Website: www.CNVC.org

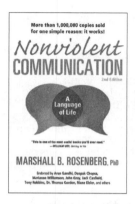

Nonviolent Communication:
A Language of Life, Second Edition
Life-Changing Tools for Healthy Relationships
Marshall B. Rosenberg, PhD
$19.95 — Trade Paper 6x9, 240pp
ISBN: 978-1-892005-03-8

In this internationally acclaimed text, Marshall Rosenberg offers insightful stories, anecdotes, practical exercises, and role-plays that will literally change your approach to communication for the better. Nonviolent Communication partners practical skills with a powerful consciousness to help us get what we want peacefully.

Nonviolent Communication has flourished for more than four decades across thirty-five countries selling more than 1,000,000 books for a simple reason: it works.

"Nonviolent Communication is a simple yet powerful methodology for communicating in a way that meets both parties' needs. This is one of the most useful books you will ever read."
—**William Ury**, coauthor of *Getting to Yes* and author of *The Third Side*

"I believe the principles and techniques in this book can literally change the world, but more importantly, they can change the quality of your life with your spouse, your children, your neighbors, your co-workers, and everyone else you interact with."
—**Jack Canfield**, author, *Chicken Soup for the Soul*

SAVE an extra 10% at NonviolentCommunication.com with code: **bookads**

Nonviolent Communication Companion Workbook
A Practical Guide for Individual, Group, or Classroom Study

by Lucy Leu

$21.95 — Trade Paper 7x10, 224pp
ISBN: 978-1-892005-04-5

Learning Nonviolent Communication has often been equated with learning a whole new language. The *NVC Companion Workbook* helps you put these powerful, effective skills into practice with chapter-by-chapter study of Marshall Rosenberg's cornerstone text, *NVC: A Language of Life*. Create a safe, supportive group learning or practice environment that nurtures the needs of each participant. Find a wealth of activities, exercises, and facilitator suggestions to refine and practice this powerful communication process.

Available from PuddleDancer Press, the Center for Nonviolent Communication, all major bookstores, and Amazon.com. Distributed by Independent Publisher's Group: 800-888-4741.

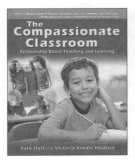

The Compassionate Classroom

Relationship Based Teaching and Learning

by Sura Hart and Victoria Kindle Hodson

$17.95 — Trade Paper 7.5x9.25, 208pp
ISBN: 978-1-892005-06-9

When Compassion Thrives, So Does Learning

Learn powerful skills to create an emotionally safe learning environment where academic excellence thrives. Build trust, reduce conflict, improve co-operation, and maximize the potential of each student as you create relationship-centered classrooms. This how-to guide offers customizable exercises, activities, charts, and cutouts that make it easy for educators to create lesson plans for a day, a week, or an entire school year. An exceptional resource for educators, homeschool parents, child-care providers, and mentors.

"Education is not simply about teachers covering a curriculum; it is a dance of relationships. *The Compassionate Classroom* presents both the case for teaching compassionately and a wide range of practical tools to maximize student potential."

—Tim Seldin, president, The Montessori Foundation

The No-Fault Classroom

Tools to Resolve Conflict & Foster Relationship Intelligence

by Sura Hart and Victoria Kindle Hodson

$17.95 — Trade Paper 8.5x11, 256pp
ISBN: 978-1-892005-18-2

Students Can Resolve Their Own Conflicts!

Offering far more than discipline techniques that move aggressive behavior out of the classroom to the playground or sidewalk, *The No-Fault Classroom* leads students ages 7–12 to develop skills in problem solving, empathic listening, and conflict resolution that will last a lifetime.

The book's 21 interactive and step-by-step lessons, construction materials, and adaptable scripts give educators the tools they need to return order and co-operation to the classroom and jumpstart engaged learning—from the rural school to the inner city, the charter school, to the home school classroom. *Curricular Tie-ins* guide teachers to use the conflict resolution tools they've developed to meet state learning requirements in social studies, language arts, history, reading, and science.

Available from PuddleDancer Press, the Center for Nonviolent Communication, all major bookstores, and Amazon.com. Distributed by Independent Publisher's Group: 800-888-4741.

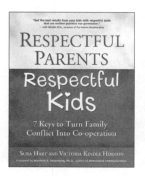

Respectful Parents, Respectful Kids

7 Keys to Turn Family Conflict Into Co-operation

by Sura Hart and Victoria Kindle Hodson

$17.95 — Trade Paper 7.5x9.25, 256pp
ISBN: 978-1-892005-22-9

Stop the Struggle—Find the Co-operation and Mutual Respect You Want!

Do more than simply correct bad behavior—finally unlock your parenting potential. Use this handbook to move beyond typical discipline techniques and begin creating an environment based on mutual respect, emotional safety, and positive, open communication. *Respectful Parents, Respectful Kids* offers *7 Simple Keys* to discover the mutual respect and nurturing relationships you've been looking for.

Use these 7 Keys to:

- Set firm limits without using demands or coercion
- Achieve mutual respect without being submissive
- Successfully prevent, reduce, and resolve conflicts
- Empower your kids to open up, co-operate, and realize their full potential
- Make your home a *No-Fault Zone* where trust thrives

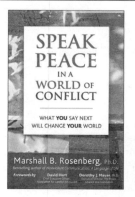

Speak Peace in a World of Conflict

What You Say Next Will Change Your World

by Marshall B. Rosenberg, PhD

$15.95 — Trade Paper 5-3/8x8-3/8, 208pp
ISBN: 978-1-892005-17-5

International peacemaker, mediator, and healer, Marshall Rosenberg shows you how the language you use is the key to enriching life. *Speak Peace* is filled with inspiring stories, lessons, and ideas drawn from more than forty years of mediating conflicts and healing relationships in some of the most war-torn, impoverished, and violent corners of the world. Find insight, practical skills, and powerful tools that will profoundly change your relationships and the course of your life for the better.

Discover how you can create an internal consciousness of peace as the first step toward effective personal, professional, and social change. Find complete chapters on the mechanics of Speaking Peace, conflict resolution, transforming business culture, transforming enemy images, addressing terrorism, transforming authoritarian structures, expressing and receiving gratitude, and social change.

Nonviolent Communication has flourished for more than four decades across thirty-five countries selling more than 1,000,000 books for a simple reason: it works.

Available from PuddleDancer Press, the Center for Nonviolent Communication, all major bookstores, and Amazon.com. Distributed by Independent Publisher's Group: 800-888-4741.

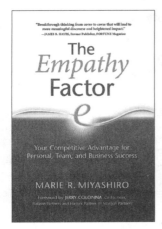

The Empathy Factor

Your Competitive Advantage for Personal, Team, and Business Success

by Marie R. Miyashiro, A.P.R.

$19.95 – Trade Paper 6x9, 256pp
ISBN: 978-1-892005-25-0

"Breakthrough thinking from cover to cover. *The Empathy Factor* will help thoughtful business people add substance and dimension to relationships within the workforce—colleagues and customers."

—JAMES B. HAYES, Former Publisher, FORTUNE Magazine

In this groundbreaking book, award-winning communication and organizational strategist Marie Miyashiro explores the missing element leaders must employ to build profits and productivity in the new economy—Empathy.

The Empathy Factor takes Dr. Marshall Rosenberg's work developing Compassionate Communication into the business community by introducing *Integrated Clarity®*—a powerful framework you can use to understand and effectively meet the critical needs of your organization without compromising those of your employees or customers.

SAVE an extra 10% at NonviolentCommunication.com with code: **bookads**

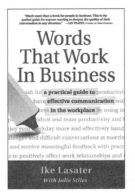

Words That Work In Business

A Practical Guide to Effective Communication in the Workplace

by Ike Lasater
with Julie Stiles

$12.95 – Trade Paper 5-3/8x8-3/8, 144pp
ISBN: 978-1-892005-01-4

Do You Want to Be Happier, More Effective, and Experience Less Stress at Work?

Do you wish for more respectful work relationships? To move beyond gossip and power struggles, to improved trust and productivity? If you've ever wondered if just one person can positively affect work relationships and company culture, regardless of your position, this book offers a resounding "yes." The key is shifting how we think and talk.

Former attorney-turned-mediator, Ike Lasater, offers practical communication skills matched with recognizable work scenarios to help anyone address the most common workplace relationship challenges. Learn proven communication skills to: Enjoy your workday more; effectively handle difficult conversations; reduce workplace conflict and stress; improve individual and team productivity; be more effective at meetings; and give and receive meaningful feedback.

Available from PuddleDancer Press, the Center for Nonviolent Communication, all major bookstores, and Amazon.com. Distributed by Independent Publisher's Group: 800–888–4741.

Peaceful Living

*Daily Meditations for Living With Love,
Healing, and Compassion*

by Mary Mackenzie

$19.95 — Trade Paper 5x7.5, 448pp
ISBN: 978-1-892005-19-9

In this gathering of wisdom, Mary Mackenzie empowers you with an intimate life map that will literally change the course of your life for the better. Each of the 366 meditations includes an inspirational quote and concrete, practical tips for integrating the daily message into your life. The learned behaviors of cynicism, resentment, and getting even are replaced with the skills of Nonviolent Communication, including recognizing one's needs and values and making choices in alignment with them.

Peaceful Living goes beyond daily affirmations, providing the skills and consciousness you need to transform relationships, heal pain, and discover the life-enriching meaning behind even the most trying situations. Begin each day centered and connected to yourself and your values. Direct the course of your life toward your deepest hopes and needs. Ground yourself in the power of compassionate, conscious living.

SAVE an extra 10% at NonviolentCommunication.com with code: **bookads**

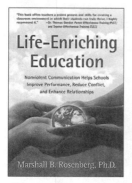

Life-Enriching Education

*Nonviolent Communication Helps Schools Improve
Performance, Reduce Conflict, and Enhance Relationships*

by Marshall B. Rosenberg, PhD

$15.95 — Trade Paper 6x9, 192pp
ISBN: 978-1-892005-05-2

Filled with insight, adaptable exercises, and role-plays, *Life-Enriching Education* gives educators practical skills to generate mutually respectful classroom relationships. Discover how our language and organizational structures directly impact student potential, trust, self-esteem, and student enjoyment in their learning. Rediscover the joy of teaching in a classroom where each person's needs are respected!

NVC Will Empower You to:
- Get to the heart of classroom conflicts quickly
- Listen so students are really heard
- Maximize the individual potential of all students
- Strengthen student interest, retention, and connection to their schoolwork
- Improve trust and connection in your classroom community
- Let go of unhealthy, coercive teaching styles
- Improve classroom teamwork, efficiency, and co-operation

Available from PuddleDancer Press, the Center for Nonviolent Communication, all major bookstores, and Amazon.com. Distributed by Independent Publisher's Group: 800-888-4741.

399

Being Me, Loving You: *A Practical Guide to Extraordinary Relationships* **by Marshall B. Rosenberg, PhD** • Watch your relationships strengthen as you learn to think of love as something you "do," something you give freely from the heart.
80pp, ISBN: 978-1-892005-16-8 • **$8.95**

Getting Past the Pain Between Us: *Healing and Reconciliation Without Compromise* **by Marshall B. Rosenberg, PhD** • Learn simple steps to create the heartfelt presence necessary for lasting healing to occur—great for mediators, counselors, families, and couples.
48pp, ISBN: 978-1-892005-07-6 • **$8.95**

Graduating From Guilt: *Six Steps to Overcome Guilt and Reclaim Your Life* **by Holly Michelle Eckert** • The burden of guilt leaves us stuck, stressed, and feeling like we can never measure up. Through a proven six-step process, this book helps liberate you from the toxic guilt, blame, and shame you carry.
96pp, ISBN: 978-1-892005-23-6 • **$9.95**

The Heart of Social Change: *How to Make a Difference in Your World* **by Marshall B. Rosenberg, PhD** • Learn how creating an internal consciousness of compassion can impact your social change efforts.
48pp, ISBN: 978-1-892005-10-6 • **$8.95**

Humanizing Health Care: *Creating Cultures of Compassion With Nonviolent Communication* **by Melanie Sears, RN, MBA** • Leveraging more than 25 years nursing experience, Melanie demonstrates the profound effectiveness of NVC to create lasting, positive improvements to patient care and the health care workplace.
112pp, ISBN: 978-1-892005-26-7 • **$9.95**

Parenting From Your Heart: *Sharing the Gifts of Compassion, Connection, and Choice* **by Inbal Kashtan** • Filled with insight and practical skills, this booklet will help you transform your parenting to address every day challenges.
48pp, ISBN: 978-1-892005-08-3 • **$8.95**

Practical Spirituality: *Reflections on the Spiritual Basis of Nonviolent Communication* **by Marshall B. Rosenberg, PhD** • Marshall's views on the spiritual origins and underpinnings of NVC, and how practicing the process helps him connect to the Divine.
48pp, ISBN: 978-1-892005-14-4 • **$8.95**

Raising Children Compassionately: *Parenting the Nonviolent Communication Way* **by Marshall B. Rosenberg, PhD** • Learn to create a mutually respectful, enriching family dynamic filled with heartfelt communication.
32pp, ISBN: 978-1-892005-09-0 • **$7.95**

The Surprising Purpose of Anger: *Beyond Anger Management: Finding the Gift* **by Marshall B. Rosenberg, PhD** • Marshall shows you how to use anger to discover what you need, and then how to meet your needs in more constructive, healthy ways.
48pp, ISBN: 978-1-892005-15-1 • **$8.95**

Teaching Children Compassionately: *How Students and Teachers Can Succeed With Mutual Understanding* **by Marshall B. Rosenberg, PhD** • In this national keynote address to Montessori educators, Marshall describes his progressive, radical approach to teaching that centers on compassionate connection.
48pp, ISBN: 978-1-892005-11-3 • **$8.95**

We Can Work It Out: *Resolving Conflicts Peacefully and Powerfully* **by Marshall B. Rosenberg, PhD** • Practical suggestions for fostering empathic connection, genuine co-operation, and satisfying resolutions in even the most difficult situations.
32pp, ISBN: 978-1-892005-12-0 • **$7.95**

What's Making You Angry? *10 Steps to Transforming Anger So Everyone Wins* **by Shari Klein and Neill Gibson** • A powerful, step-by-step approach to transform anger to find healthy, mutually satisfying outcomes.
32pp, ISBN: 978-1-892005-13-7 • **$7.95**

Available from PuddleDancer Press, the Center for Nonviolent Communication, all major bookstores, and Amazon.com. Distributed by IPG: 800–888–4741. For more information about these booklets or to order online, visit www.NonviolentCommunication.com

About the Authors

Teresa Castracane

Jane Marantz Connor, Ph.D., is a certified trainer with the international Center for Nonviolent Communication and founder of the New York Intensive Residential Training in Nonviolent Communication. She received her Ph.D. in psychology from the University of Wisconsin–Madison and is a graduate of the BayNVC North American Leadership Program. She taught psychology and human development for many years at the State University of New York at Binghamton, where she is currently associate professor emerita of human development. She taught courses in compassionate communication, multicultural psychology, and human services. The goal of her multicultural psychology course, for which Jane has had a special passion, is to help students from diverse backgrounds understand and connect with one another more effectively. Jane received the Chancellor's Award for Excellence in Teaching for teaching this course, which grew to serve more than 400 students a semester. Jane has enjoyed sharing NVC in the Middle East, Asia, Africa, South America, and Australia and now concentrates her teaching, training, and consulting in the Washington, D.C., area where she is also working as Coordinator of Restorative Practices at an inner city high school.

Eva Mueller

Dian Killian, Ph.D., is a Certified Trainer with the international Center for Nonviolent Communication, founder and former director of The Center for Collaborative Communication, and a certified life coach and faculty member with the distance learning Coaching for Transformation program. She has written a book of graphic vignettes (illustrated by Mark Badger), *Urban Empathy: True Life Adventures of Compassion on the Streets of New York*. Through her company, WorkCollaboratively. com, she designs and leads trainings with companies and organizations in the United States, Europe, and Asia. Clients have included Merck, Inc., the UN Development Program, HCL (India), Americorp, Haver Analytics, and Instrumentation Laboratories, among others. She offers programs at Kripalu, the 92nd St Y, the NY Open Center, and the Omega Institute, and is founder and director of the annual NVC East Coast NVC Women's Retreat. She also is a professional musician, and often integrates music in her retreats and is widely known for bringing humor, warmth, and a "down-to-earth" approach to her sharing of NVC. She can be reached at dian@workcollaboratively.com.